Knowing W...

Is ...
COOK...

Here are over 200 rec... page after page of sensible, specific advice for anyo... who's depressed, angry, lonely, bored, under stress, overweight, or in love—and would like to do something about it. For example:

THE HENRY VIII DINNER
Indulge yourself! Eat your way out of a depression with this delightful repast.

TIPSY TRIFLE
The crowning touch to the sexy supper—a seductive dessert combining two kinds of brandy, kirsch, and cointreau.

REVENGE COBBLER
Put your tension to work for you with this tasty pastry you can make in minutes.

DIET PIZZA AND DIET CHEESECAKE
Low-calorie ideas to appease that hungry feeling and make weight-control a pleasure.

"Lively, innovative . . .
This book is about discovery as much as it is about food."
—Psychology Today Book Club

COOKING
AS
THERAPY

LOUIS PARRISH, M.D.

 AVON
PUBLISHERS OF BARD, CAMELOT, DISCUS, EQUINOX AND FLARE BOOKS

AVON BOOKS
A division of
The Hearst Corporation
959 Eighth Avenue
New York, New York 10019

First Avon Printing, September, 1976

AVON TRADEMARK REG. U.S. PAT. OFF. AND IN
OTHER COUNTRIES, MARCA REGISTRADA,
HECHO EN U.S.A.

Printed in the U.S.A.

To my friend Arthur Demaris,
whose experiences with therapeutic cooking—
and results!—
stimulated my own thinking,
then this book.

Contents

Introduction

THERAPY, I've come firmly to believe, is one of the most frequently misused and misunderstood words of our time. It is equated too often by too many people with magic, a by-product, no doubt, of what has come to be known as "The Age Of Miracles" in medical science. We're ready to look everywhere from the analyst's couch to the consciousness-raising session to the latest pseudo-science for easy answers, forms of "therapy" that will somehow—hopefully with minimal effort— enable us to live problem-free lives in an increasingly problem-filled world.

As a practicing physician and psychiatrist, let me state at the outset that I do not have the "answer." Should someone, professional or layman, suddenly discover the key to perpetual happiness, I'll not only be the first to congratulate him, but will do my best to be the first person at his doorstep. Since this prospect, in realistic terms, seems about as likely as the discovery of the fountain of youth, I prefer to concentrate my efforts on getting along, coping with life on a day-to-day basis.

This one-day-at-a-time approach is one I preach as well as practice. My patients range from punctual lawyers whom I see once a year for their annual physical to eccentric performers with migraine headaches who appear thrice weekly, an hour before the curtain goes up. I even have one patient, a well-known novelist, who phones every week or so to report the latest symptoms of what he's convinced is "cancer of the hair"; my standard answer to him has become "I hope you do," since if so I'll go down in history as the discoverer and the disease will be named for me. But all my patients share one thing in common, in terms of treatment: total care, medical and—when indicated—psychiatric.

In my medical practice, I try to blur the distinctions between the two—not only because of my training—but because of my firm belief that there *are* few valid differences. What's wrong with the mind will almost invariably show symptoms in the body, and vice versa. So my response is to exercise *therapy* in the widest possible sense of the term. This therapy may include the standard items from the medical arsenal—illegible (except to the pharmacist) scribblings on a prescription pad or firm instructions to "stay in bed for a week"—or others, more unexpected: "Go to the movies every night for a week," "quit talking on the phone to your mother," even "have a drink now and again."

My only consistency is my approach to therapy. Therapy is what works; and what gets you through the night (and the day); and what, when you've made it through one day, is going to leave you with the strength —and, more important, the attitude—to get you through the next.

"Easier said than done," say at least six patients a day, and as familiar with human frailty as my practice keeps me, I admit they're right. But where they're wrong is to expect that because of my profession, I should have an easier time of it than most people. Doctors, the reasoning goes, are privy to inside information. New thoughts and ideas are constantly bombarding us via the professional journals.

The White Coat Complex, perpetuated by some

doctors it must be admitted, and enhanced by public image, is the cloak for a mythical figure of our time: the physician who is somehow above it all. From his lofty perch—perhaps atop Mt. Olympus General Hospital—he surveys human frailty and weakness and the gamut of emotions that play havoc with the lives of mere mortals. His expression is one of aloofness, tinged perhaps with a trace of disdain.

It sounds like nice work if you can get it, and maybe you can—I can't, and I know it!

Like everyone else made of flesh and blood, I'm one hundred percent human. The "white coat" I wear in my practice gives me a position of authority and perhaps assists me in helping my patients, but when I take that white coat off and stop by the dry cleaner's only to find that my "civilian" suits or jackets aren't ready on the promised day, I'm very much a mortal and my responses are as human as can be.

If I've had an easy day—when patients show up on time, emergencies are relatively few, and my general humor is good—I may slough it off. If I've had it rough, either at the office or in my personal life, I may put up an argument against life's assaults or, more likely, I may leave and direct my anger at myself for *not* arguing.

One thing, however, is almost certain: no matter what the crisis of the moment is at the end of the day, I'll retreat into my kitchen for solace, comfort, and gratification. Cooking is my personal form of therapy, therapy in the most practical sense of the word. It is a treatment, ongoing and adaptable, that helps me cope with life.

Almost all of us, out of either choice or necessity, spend some time in the kitchen. For some of us, me included, cooking is a hobby and therefore a labor of love. For others, it is an unavoidable and laborious chore, a function that must be performed for the sake of sheer physical survival.

I believe that since most of us have to cook, we

might as well make the most of it. And making the most of cooking means more than turning out something to eat. Cooking offers an obvious challenge to both the beginner and the experienced individual. In many ways, it parallels life: the more you work at it, the better you get. The better you get, the easier *it* gets. Though the kitchen is a workshop with specific tools, cooking is—or should be—a tool itself.

We can use it to vent our emotions, to express love and anger, hostility and happiness. Following a recipe, whether complex or simple, and producing a satisfying meal or dish enhances our vulnerable egos, rewarding us with a sense of achievement and pride in accomplishment. Inventive cookery, either elaborating on basic recipes or creating dishes from one's own ideas, is an excellent outlet for personal expression. Among challenging arts that take relatively little time, it is relatively inexpensive.

The man or woman who prepares a delicious meal to the delight of his or her own palate and the praise of friends and family feels a natural and well-deserved sense of pride. Yet meals and menus need not be elaborate. No guests need be invited, and no dinner party organized to make the time spent in the kitchen rewarding psychologically as well as nutritionally. Going into a restaurant and sitting at a table for one while surrounded by companionable couples and festive groups, can make even the chef's specialty taste bad. Cooking a good meal for yourself when you are eating alone and enjoying it at your own table can be a delicious form of privacy. In the same way, good food can be an intimacy for friends and lovers to share, a form of communication that is extremely personal.

The kitchen may not hold the "secret of happiness," but it is for me and can be for you "great escape." The pace and pressures of contemporary society make all of us—even the best adjusted—susceptible to the anxiety/depressive syndrome that may well be the chronic disease of our time. We are pressured further by the kind of lives that most of us live, lives that hinge to a large extent on our professional and personal relationships with others. In these relationships, we must often sublimate many healthy, natural instincts. "Coping" to too many of us means trying to attain some imaginary level of existence where we are unaffected by the strains and tensions of living, a most unrealistic goal.

The man or woman who has a problem on the job, as all of us do from time to time, cannot afford to risk a confrontation with a co-worker or superior. There may—and should—be a moment of pride in one's self-control at such times; but moments pass. When work is over, this same individual may take his suppressed feelings out on his wife (or husband, or children) or perhaps he will internalize it, depressing himself further and compounding the mood.

The kitchen, I've found, is an ideal place for expressing not only culinary talent, but basic gut feelings. And it can be, too, a place where we learn about ourselves, our problems, and potential solutions that will improve not only what's happening on the stove, but in our daily lives.

Naturally, cooking does not solve every problem in the world, and *Cooking as Therapy,* both book and concept, is not a substitute for professional help when it is needed. Yet the kitchen, ideally, should be a personalized landscape, and it should offer terrain for both learning about oneself and learning to live with oneself. This is true not only for my patients, many of whose experiences I've cited in the following chapters (with identities and circumstances rearranged) but for myself as well.

About a year and a half ago, I found myself in an uncomfortable personal position. I was going through a divorce and at the same time I was in the process of extricating myself from several less than pleasant financial situations. I believed that in time my problems would be worked out. But as is so often the case, that belief was no panacea for frequent moods of depression and anxiety.

For some reason—I'm still not positively sure of what triggered the association—I found myself thinking about some cornmeal fritters I'd eaten at a luncheonette near Nashville, Tennessee, when I was stationed in the Navy. Perhaps, in retrospect, my time in the service seemed relatively uncomplicated; maybe I just wanted a good fritter.

In any case, I began to work up a fritter batter. My early attempts were disasters. There was too much cornmeal, or not enough dough. Deep frying made the fritters too greasy and hard. Reducing the amount of stock, an essential ingredient, made them dry and grainy. My friends were aware of what came to be known as the "Fritter Project," and frankly, at that point in time, I much preferred conversing with them about my progress with the fritters to working out my personal problems.

The more time I spent on the fritters, the more important the recipe became. It wasn't an obsession—I'm much too disorganized to make a good obsessive–compulsive—but in a way, it became both an escape from and a focal point for the various crises I faced. If I could turn out a good fritter, maybe I could come up with workable solutions to my other problems. The sense of accomplishment and well-being I felt that first time I bit into a perfect fritter of my own devising was, to put it mildly, intense.

I was proud, happy and truly reassured. My ego had done a lot of suffering, and bolstered by that first batch of really good fritters, it came back to life. I was ready to meet my problems head on, and I was confident of my control over their outcome.

In my practice, I've used cooking as a form of therapy in various situations. Don't misunderstand me, please—I don't dispense chicken soup, or chili, or fritters, for that matter, good as they are. But I have tried to share with my patients my belief that cooking is an excellent form of physical and occupational therapy: since it's something one must do anyway, it can and should be done to maximum advantage.

This book is about discovery as much as it is about food. As is so often the case in working with patients, I've learned as much as I have taught. Just as I hope that my recipes will be pleasing, I hope my concepts will be beneficial. I've found that the kitchen can be more than just a place where one cooks: it can be a comfortable, personalized environment, something all of us need in an increasingly depersonalized world.

The activities that go into preparing food, the seemingly prosaic cutting and chopping and pounding, can be outlets for emotions that unexpressed can impair the health of both the mind and the body. Cooking can be a beginning way out of depression or slump and back into life. It can be an escape, a form of communication, a challenge and an outlet for creativity with virtually limitless horizons.

I have found, too, that cooking is excellent therapy for the overweight. The obese man or woman often munches his way through whatever is already at hand —the chronic over-eater is so busy eating that he often opts for "instant" or packaged foods, rather than foods he prepares himself. Cooking may be an unusual piece of advice for a physician to give an overweight patient, but I've found it valid.

Taking an *interest* in food rather than regarding it as a dull necessity is a positive step toward better health for all of us, at any weight. One can learn to live better, to eat food that is more nutritive. Vitamins, calories, cholesterol and other food substances are transformed from concepts into fact through practical use.

The man or woman whose life seems to be in perpetual chaos can often reorient himself toward better organization by starting in the kitchen. It's all too easy to be overwhelmed by a sense of total confusion: a focal point is necessary. If you can organize your kitchen, you can at least start to organize your life.

The compulsive organizer, on the other hand, is often tense and angry because it is impossible for him or her to compartmentalize every aspect of his life. In trying to adapt his professional and personal relationships to his personality type, he runs into trouble and frustration. The kitchen, for him, can be a psychological playground—all the toys and tools are in their perfect place within this private, personalized environment.

If it is possible to cook one's way out of a temporary depression (and I know it is because I've done it) it is also important to think of the kitchen as a testing place. We all need to test ourselves from time to time; any degree of success and satisfaction, once attained, can become dull and mundane. It is far from practical, often impossible, to change careers or marriages simply because we feel "in a rut"—but the kitchen offers challenges galore. And unlike the garage-built boat that may sink at a loss of hundreds of dollars and hours of time, producing new frustrations and aggravation, the popover that refuses to pop can be thrown out. One doesn't lose much money, the ego suffers only the most minimal damage, and as my experience with my fritters has shown me, the final perfect version tastes all the better for the effort that has gone into the attempt.

Knowing *what* to cook *when* is important—and it's an important part of this book. I've learned that timing isn't merely a matter of how long the stew simmers, but of mood. When you're having a difficult day or week, it's best to stick to proven winners—foolproof recipes that offer a guaranteed result without frustration. Experiments should be undertaken on days when you can afford—in emotional terms—to fail. Learning these concepts is as important as learning to cook itself.

One's life in the kitchen can be as public or as private as one chooses to make it, and in writing this book, I'm choosing to "go public" in the broadest sense with both my recipes and my ideas. My ideas about the therapeutic value of cooking will speak for themselves in the following chapters, but I must, for the record, speak about recipes.

There is a parallel between cooking and life, and it would be foolish to expect every moment spent in the kitchen to be golden. Part of the problem may be physical (though we'll be spending some time on how to make your kitchen as comfortable and practical a place as possible) and part of the trouble is the frustration that recipes can and do cause.

My recipes are intended as guidelines, and that is how they—and all recipes—should be used. If a recipe calls for an ingredient that you don't have on hand, common sense and ingenuity can dictate a suitable substitute. By the same token, personal taste is an important factor—if you don't like one of the ingredients included in a recipe, don't automatically discard the whole idea. Think of reworking it with something you do like in its place, or see if the recipe will work just as well without the "offensive" substance. A chicken stew, obviously, needs chicken; what else goes into it is a very individual matter of what's on hand and what appeals to your own taste buds.

Many of the recipes I've developed have been improvised from looking at a refrigerator full of leftovers. Your refrigerator can and should dictate to you as mine does to me. I cook not only to my own taste (meaning I adjust seasoning and ingredients to my own preference) but at the mercy of my own stove. Ovens, as we all know, are very independent instruments, and I've yet to see two that work the same way. Use common sense, and experience, to vary cooking time. In other words, if your oven tends to be very hot (hotter at 350 degrees than 350 should be, or is on someone else's oven) cook at 325 degrees or so.

I have a strong personal dislike for recipes that must be followed to the letter in order to turn out edible meals. As someone who knows what he's doing in the kitchen, I resent them. If *you* know what *you're* doing, feel free—*please*—to adapt, enhance and improvise.

As a man who enjoys cooking, I own a number of cookbooks, and I know only too well how confusing and irritating they can be. While *Cooking as Therapy* is much more than a collection of recipes, I've tried to make the recipes as easy to read as possible. The last thing I'm in the mood for after a day at my practice—which includes more than its share of fine print and attention to the most minute details—is trying to distinguish among assorted cooking abbreviations. You'll note here that "teaspoon" and "tablespoon," for example, are always fully written out. It means hitting a few more keys on the typewriter, but I hope it will make the recipes easier to read and follow.

You'll find, too, that there is a loose way with portions or number of servings. One man's appetizer is another's main dish, and anyone intelligent enough to read a recipe and follow instructions can judge about how much the recipe will yield. So recipes are handled in obvious quantities—easy to halve or double. The important thing I've tried to keep in mind in developing the recipes is simplicity of measurement and ease of direction. For more important than the recipes themselves is to get you into the kitchen and cooking.

Here is *Cooking as Therapy*. Read, enjoy, and feel better. Good cooking!

1

The Kitchen
as Environment

THERE was a time, not too long ago, when the kitchen wasn't just a room: it was a "living" room. Its status had something to do with what was on the stove, of course, but culinary masterpieces and *haute cuisine* were not the criteria. Instead, it was a matter of atmosphere—the atmosphere of a vital, buzzing place where something always seemed to be going into the oven or coming out of it, but where regardless of how much cooking was being done, there was always time and room for tears, laughter, and someone to share them with. It was the family meeting place.

The kitchens of the past, as many of us still remember, smelled of chicken soup, or tomato sauce, or cornbread, or some other ethnic specialty or family favorite. The aroma was a kind of fragrant security blanket. Most families ate in the kitchen. One member, a mother or grandmother or a particular aunt, seemed literally to live at the stove. There was a sense of "things coming out right" that was unrelated to what we ate. If we didn't feel well, the kitchen also served as the place where body ailments could be treated along with wounds to the psyche.

The Eat-This-It's-Good-For-You syndrome is still with us; though spinach ("it will make you strong like

Popeye") and oatmeal ("it sticks to your ribs") and some of the other foods with which children have traditionally been force-fed in the kitchens of the world may well be more healthful than the so-called "health" foods that people faddishly recommend to each other!

The biggest difference is that changes in our society have changed the way we feel about and use our kitchens. Many people, both those with families and the increasing number of single men and women, live in apartments: the high-rise buildings of the post-World War II housing boom didn't place an emphasis on the kitchen, which as many of us know only too well, can be a quarter the size of a country closet.

Our society is mobile. We go out more, and eat at restaurants more frequently than in the past. And, nowadays, food also *comes* to us—we can have everything from Chinese food to pizza delivered. When we cook at home, we prepare food easier and faster than ever before. Frozen and convenience foods save time (one of our society's primary preoccupations) and work, and we take them for granted, too often overlooking the fact that while they may be easier, some are not as nutritionally valuable and healthful as the "from scratch" originals.

The kitchen is no longer a center of family activity, even for eating. The average family is likely to eat from TV trays in the den. The value of the community meal (in or out of the kitchen) has decreased as a background for informal group therapy. More foods, in greater variety, are available today than ever before. Grabbing a bite has supplanted dining, and meals tend to be an individual experience rather than a family happening.

Oddly enough, the kitchen has become depersonalized not only in usage, but in style as well. Look through some home-decorating magazines, or look at any of the television commercials advertising kitchen supplies or equipment. The room, no matter what size, isn't just clean—it's sterile! It is as if we want our kitchens to look as though they are on display rather than rooms we live in.

Granted, some kitchens have more atmosphere than others. The man or woman who reads *Gourmet* magazine and enjoys *haute cuisine* may have a lot of fancy cooking equipment. The individual who dotes on "health food" may have assorted other paraphernalia. But the kitchen, for the most part, has lost a lot of its importance to society, and to us as individuals.

The loss may be much greater than we realize. As life becomes increasingly frenetic, as the world we live in becomes more and more depersonalized, as our own individuality seems harder to hold on to, the kitchen is the ideal place for us to be ourselves.

I believe that whether you live in a house or an apartment, whether you are a single person or a man or woman with a family, whether your kitchen is big and spacious or pullman size and style, it can and *should* be an important and highly personalized place in your life . . . not just a room, but an environment.

The kitchen isn't just a place where food is kept and cooked—it is a place to live in. Within its confines, we can create. There we can do constructive things for ourselves, such as preparing food that pleases our tastes and offers nutritional benefits. In the kitchen we can please others—friends and guests as well as family members. And perhaps most important of all, we can be masters of our private mini-universe, be totally in control. Tensions can be acted out and released at the sink or cutting board. Depressions can be worked through on the front burner. Life can be coped with in the kitchen.

Let me use my own experience to show you just what I mean. As a physician with a large practice, I have a good-sized office, and I try to keep my office and daily work routine as organized as possible. In my work, however, there is only so much organization that I can impose. Yes, my secretary can plan appointments so that each patient is allotted his needed time, and some days she even manages to schedule an hour or so for my professional reading and for the paperwork that is so much a part of a doctor's life.

But even the most carefully arranged schedule goes completely out of whack when an unscheduled emergency crops up, as it so often does, or when a patient's needs demand more time than originally designed. As a result, I'm often running late, trying to play a type of "Beat The Clock" for the benefit of patients who have taken time from work or their daily routines for an office visit, and at the same time seeing to it that each case gets the needed attention.

The pressure can be great, and I certainly can't take it out on the women and men who are coming to me with their physical and psychological problems. At the end of the day, though, I find a release: sheer escapism!

My New York apartment has an unusually large kitchen (one of the reasons why I took the place), and I've made it into a room in which I feel totally relaxed and comfortable. I enjoy cooking. I love to eat, and I love good food. But more than that, my big new kitchen is the ideal setting for do-it-myself therapy . . . a place to relax, create, and when the mood strikes me, shut myself away from outside pressures.

Admittedly, my attitude might be different if I had to be in the kitchen all the time. Today, the women's movement has influenced the way all of us—men as well as women—think. It's true that for too long a time the kitchen was thought of as "a woman's place." The clichés of being "chained to the stove" and "a slave to the kitchen" were often sad realities.

I have no intention of being enslaved by my kitchen, and the first step I took—and hope you'll take—was to make sure the kitchen has nothing of a prison atmosphere. One needn't spend a fortune on the services of an interior designer to create a comfortable, liveable kitchen environment: some of the most comfortable kitchens I've seen are those that have been "decorated" by those who live in them.

In my kitchen, I surround myself with things I like—and not all of them have to do with cooking. I've painted the room in vegetable colors: green, white, and yellow. The Tiffany lampshade I was lucky enough to get years ago, before the craze for Tiffany shades drove prices sky-high, is a prized possession of mine, and my kitchen is where I enjoy it. A collection of old advertising trays decorates my walls; and I have on my window sills an indoor garden of plants, with an emphasis on herbs that I use in my cooking.

I believe that one of the best ways to get the most out of your kitchen is to maximize space. There's never such a thing as "too much" counter space, and the butcher-block counter in front of my windows also functions as a desk and table. Though I have a formal dining room, I find that when I'm alone I'm very happy to eat in the kitchen.

Sitting at the head of a table that seats twelve is a nice experience when you have guests. When you're eating by yourself, it can make you feel lonely. Eating in the kitchen on the other hand, gives you a sense of continuity, a kind of "at oneness" with yourself.

The kitchen should not be a symbol of hostility, frustration or depression. How you decorate it is a big factor. Use colors that you like, colors that are soothing and at the same time conducive to the activity. Avoid the traditional—unless you truly like it. Personally, I find that while white kitchens can be attractive, they are impossible to keep clean in a city environment. If a kitchen is small, white makes it look larger, say some decorating manuals. Often, I feel, an all-white kitchen looks sterile, devoid of any personality.

If you have money to spend on making your kitchen a comfortable, personalized place, the only limits you face are your imagination and your budget. Yet creating an environment doesn't mean, necessarily, spending a lot of money. Cut out photographs, as a young lady I know did, of fruits and vegetables from magazines.

Mounted on cardboard or glued to cabinet doors and shellacked, they can brighten up a room.

Surround yourself with things *you* like. I have a small television set in my kitchen, and frequently have it on while I cook. A kitchen speaker (a temperamental speaker in my case—one of these days I'll get around to having it fixed!) is hooked up to my music system. An inexpensive chart of herbs and spices that I had framed hangs on the wall, as do some of my favorite photographs, right in the entrance way.

The most natural things to decorate with, and certainly the most practical in terms of the kitchen, are food and cooking equipment. A wire basket of onions, potatoes, and squash is a three-dimensional still life; a bowl of lemons and other fruit is practical, pretty and fragrant. I have never seen a kitchen that had enough cabinet space or too many drawers: peg boards are the answers, and hanging everything from pots and pans to garlic presses and vegetable peelers makes it easy to find and use the things you need. Some equipment, of course, just won't hang; use drawers for such items—but use a wide-mouthed crockery jar next to the stove for spoons and ladles, both wooden and metal.

If you've created an environment that you like, you'll want to spend more time in the kitchen. And if environment alone doesn't make cooking more of a total experience for you, the problem may not be the ambience but how you function in it. The kitchen is a good place to learn something about your own personality, and you can learn best by thinking about *how* you cook.

Some people find themselves constantly confronted by problems such as pots that boil over and casseroles that mess up the oven. The pot they select, or the casserole dish, never turns out quite up to the job. In the same way, when it comes to straightening up after a meal, the storage container holds most—but not quite all—of the leftover soup, stew or whatever.

These things are undeniably aggravating. They express, perhaps, some "tightness" of individual personality, some senseless gesture of frugality. Certainly they reflect poor organization and judgment. Conversely, some people cooking a small quantity of food, let's say a few green beans or peas, will use the largest saucepan they have. Such extravagance is ill-rewarded; the water in the pan evaporates before the vegetables are cooked, and the result is a sticky, inedible mess. Moreover, even if the vegetables cook properly, looking at such a small quantity of food in a big pot can be depressing—even to the "manic" types who picked the wrong pot to begin with.

The kitchen, therefore, can function as a learning environment, one in which we learn about ourselves. How to judge, predict, conceptualize—these are things that are important in cooking, and in life as well. Knowing which pan, pot or baking dish to use may not be the key to the mystery of a happy existence—but we all have to start somewhere. The kitchen is as good a place as any and better than most, and by examining how we cook, we can undertake an exercise in positive self-analysis. More important—or at least equally so—we don't have to settle for learning the proverbial lesson: we can put our new knowledge to use.

There are some personality types who are never satisfied: they don't cook because they don't have "all" the equipment they *think* they need. Learning to make do is an important part of maturity, particularly in these troubled times. It's true, none of us comes into the world with a fully-equipped kitchen, but not whipping egg whites because you don't have a cold copper bowl is ridiculous. This type of behavior is compulsiveness at its most self-destructive. Several meals prepared with the kitchen equipment you do have, instead of eating out at the nearest restaurant, can provide the extra money for a particular piece of equipment that you really *do* need.

The opposite extreme is a type of behavior that borders on the masochistic. All of us know someone who insists on holding on to a faulty peeler, a toaster that consistently burns the bread or a dull, worn-out knife, rather than replace it. Rarely is money the problem, particularly with smaller items. Yet these individuals repeatedly frustrate themselves needlessly, rather than taking the initiative to make their lives more comfortable. If they behave this way in the kitchen, they almost always act similarly in other rooms—and other areas of life.

I should point out that I have no objection to eating out. In fact, I think it's a wonderful experience, on many levels. I enjoy trying to duplicate a dish that I have liked at a restaurant, and letting someone else do the cooking is often a welcome change of pace. But I hate spending money on food that is poorly prepared and haphazardly served; and I know myself: if I'm feeling lonely, I'm much better off in my own kitchen, cooking and eating alone, than I am sitting at a table for one in a restaurant, watching other people, listening to their chatter, and having my mood of loneliness and self-pity reinforced.

I have no doubt that if I had to prepare several meals each day for a large family, my feelings might be very different. Cooking would be a monotonous, ungratifying chore; dining out would seem a great luxury—and perhaps dining out all the time would appear to be the greatest luxury of all. But organizing the family for going out, getting everyone to make up his mind what he wants to order, and supervising children during dinner could prove a much more harrowing experience, on a regular basis, than a simple meal at home.

The point is learning to budget—not only money, but time. The kitchen is the perfect place for the individual whose finances are never in good shape to start learning to organize himself and his money. But it is important, too, to know how to budget our leisure time, to learn when it's better to eat out (and when the experience will be the most enjoyable) and when not.

Meals at home need not be elaborate to be tasty and nutritious. Some of the best are the most simple. There is a time and a place for quick meals out of a can or out of the freezer, just as there is a time and place for elaborate meals with several courses. But seldom, at least to my way of thinking, is there a time for using foods that are "pre-prepared." Frozen pancake batter, vegetables such as green peas in butter sauce in boilable bags, and frozen, pre-breaded cutlets are, to my mind, rip-offs. The time they save, negligible at least, is completely out of proportion to their cost—unless you value your cooking time at fifteen dollars per hour or more!

Kitchen management leads to better life management. Learn what consumerism really means—how to spot the good buys and avoid the overpriced items that promise more than they deliver. Some canned and frozen foods are good. They do save time and may be better tasting than the same dishes prepared by yourself. But it doesn't take much expertise to flavor some rice, regular or quick-cooking, with herbs. Nor does it take a degree in home economics to learn how to take advantage of foods in season, or on sale. Storage space and a freezer help to take advantage of specials at the local market.

The answer that you have a small refrigerator with a smaller freezer compartment may be a cop out—I had an extra half-size freezer installed in my kitchen, and it saves me a fortune. Think about it.

Even if you don't want to or can't operate on a very large scale, you can learn better management by cooking in extra quantities and refrigerating or freezing portions of food against the day when you don't have the time to cook—and by learning to use leftovers to full advantage. Meats, poultry, and vegetables can all be used in new main dishes. The money you'll save can pay for vacations or other luxuries, or go into your savings—and there is no way to put a price on the sense of accomplishment you'll realize.

In the kitchen, and in terms of food, attitude is very important, so let's not think of what you do or don't do without thinking about *how you feel* about it.

A friend of mine, a very talented young lady who writes about medicine, recently called me in a panic: she'd impetuously invited several guests to dinner, and was terrified. "What am I going to do?" she wailed. "My kitchen is so tiny, and I'm not sure I'll be able to cook something decent. What if they don't like it?"

I let her cry the anxiety out of her system before telling her about my cousin Virginia, a wonderful woman whom I dearly love and who taught me a great deal about cooking. When Virginia came to New York, she had a small studio apartment, kitchen nonexistent. An inventive woman, Virginia managed to turn out some of the best dishes I ever ate from a hot plate—and after dinner, we all would pitch in and wash our dishes in her bathtub! Virginia always cooked with a sense of positive thinking, and those who were invited to a meal at her apartment were indeed fortunate.

Most anyone who has accepted the invitation to dinner in someone else's home is in a very positive and receptive mood, and why not? Someone else is doing the shopping, the cooking, and the cleanup. So my medical-writer friend had already won half the battle. In short, if you *think* you are going to fail, you probably will. If you think you'll succeed, you have excellent chances of doing so.

If the kitchen is a place to learn, one of the best lessons of all is how to accept failure. Nobody needs advice on making mistakes at the stove—they happen to even the most expert cook. But learning to accept a defeat, how to laugh at yourself, is very important—and experience is the best teacher.

I still laugh when I remember a dinner party that I gave several years ago: it has to go down in history as one of the all-time disasters. For some mysterious reason (I wish I could think of a good excuse!) everything was inedible. My guests were too polite to inform me of this fact, but my palate was only too truthful. I didn't get hysterical, nor did I have any intention of making my guests suffer through a wretched meal. Instead I called a halt to the dinner, moved the guests back to the living room where we'd had cocktails earlier, and sent out for fried chicken. With the fire blazing, it was a delightful evening.

I was more resourceful recently with a meal that fell to pieces before I could get it to the table. I was foolish enough to try to serve six people a brunch of Eggs Benedict—foolish because I can neither poach eggs nor make Hollandaise sauce. I had started the sauce and was just sliding the first egg into the whirling vinegared water; as I tried to wind the white of the egg around the yolk, I noticed that the Hollandaise was separating. I hurriedly added a little more butter to the sauce —and fetched the solitary yolk from the skillet. Whirling the water again, I managed to break the second egg before I had even slid it off the plate. I was terribly discouraged: none down, twelve to go! The Hollandaise was still separating, and just to make the disaster complete, my green peas, the side dish, were boiling over.

Suddenly I remembered a dish I'd had in Italy. That July lunch in the yellow-stoned piazza of Trastevere came back to me in all its glory. Spaghetti con Prosciutto e Piselli. *Allora! Facciamo!*

I diced the slices of Canadian bacon, beat up several of the eggs and added them to my still-separating Hollandaise in the double boiler. I added some olive oil, salt and pepper, and heated the mixture. Once it was hot, in went the green peas. I covered the pot and let it sit until I'd cooked up some spaghetti, then I mixed the two. It was a most remarkable spaghetti brunch. The taste still lingers on, not because of the failure, but because of the recovery. I've simplified the recipe. Try it on its own, or keep it in mind if you're *trying* to make Eggs Benedict!

SPAGHETTI CON PROSCIUTTO E PISELLI

Serves 4

1 pound cooked ham (prosciutto, preferably; smoked ham, smoked butt or Canadian bacon will do)	⅓ cup olive oil
	4 eggs
	1 tablespoon lemon juice
	1 pound spaghetti
	salt to taste
⅓ cup butter	2 cups cooked green peas, fresh or frozen

Cut the ham into small cubes and sauté them in a bit of the oil (if needed) in a skillet until brown. Drain on a paper towel, then put in the top of a double boiler with the butter and oil. Beat the eggs slowly, adding the lemon juice. Mix this with the ham, and warm over medium heat, stirring occasionally.

Cook the spaghetti in heavily salted boiling water. When this is almost done, add the peas to the egg and ham mixture. Drain the spaghetti. Combine the sauce and the spaghetti (use the spaghetti pot, empty now) and heat gently for a minute, tossing, over a very low flame.

Many disasters, the kitchen teaches us, can be salvaged. And cooking also teaches us how better to cope with tension—the same kind of tension that we face in every aspect of our daily lives. Last year a friend of mine mentioned my cooking to Craig Claiborne, a man whose column in *The New York Times* I read faithfully, and whose recipes I've always found to be excellent. Mr. Claiborne was kind enough to call, and I planned a dinner. I was pleased that my cooking had been brought to his attention—but the idea of having to cook for a master whose expertise I'd admired so much made me nervous. I planned menus and rejected them. I went through my recipes over and over. When Mr. Claiborne arrived, he made me feel completely at ease—and with his help and some excellent suggestions, the meal went off well.

As we cooked, and as we later ate, I encouraged criticism of the meal; good food, I've found, can always be made better, and criticism can be very constructive. If we can learn to accept suggestions about our soups and stews, we can open ourselves to improvement in other areas of life as well.

Often, however, we leave ourselves open to problems and frustration, rather than solutions. Realism should be an important guide. A closet-sized kitchen simply isn't able to turn out a seven-course meal for ten. Work with the space you have, and instead of concentrating on what you can't do, become a master of one-pot cookery. Space doesn't limit your culinary efforts so much as it challenges them.

And don't forget common sense. If you only have two burners, don't plan a meal where three things need to be boiled. In a small kitchen, try to use the oven for the main dish, the burners for the side dish and coffee, and the refrigerator for salad, dessert, and perhaps an appetizer that you can make ahead and serve cold. Don't try to bake two dishes requiring different temperatures if they have to be ready at the same time. That's asking for trouble: and you'll doubtless get it.

Management, once again, is the key word. When it comes to cooking for others, plan your meal so that most of the work is done before guests arrive. That way you can enjoy their company and they yours. Many people feel that having company for dinner demands expensive food and fancy dishes. It simply isn't true: just as less expensive cuts of meat can be turned into delicious meals, expensive cuts can be ruined through poor cooking. Most people I know would rather have a good hamburger than a burnt filet mignon. And most people you know would, too. Some guests, of course, are going to be snobbish. There are people who don't realize that making a good meatloaf takes a lot more effort chopping and mixing than simply broiling a steak. If you're on a meatloaf budget and entertaining steak-minded friends, why not wrap your meatloaf in pie dough, bake it in the oven, and, *voilà*, serve Meatloaf Wellington? An impressive but not diffi-cult dish.

The kitchen is your domain, and you should feel to-tally comfortable in it. Comfortable enough, in fact, to ask people to leave if they get in your way when you are trying to cook. A good-sized kitchen, of course, offers the advantage of space. Often when I'm trying a new recipe, I'll have a friend or two over for dinner, and I may serve cocktails very informally while I work at the stove. I find that they enjoy watching me cook, and often they offer valuable suggestions.

Some people, of course, insist that they "can't boil water." I'm prone to dislike this type of individual— perhaps because I was one of those people myself until I was twenty-four years old. I had eaten at home until I went off to school, and then eight years of cafeteria and hospital dining-room food had replaced home cooking. Even after I moved into my own apartment, the kitchen was part of the foyer—I passed through it going to and coming home from work.

Then one Saturday when I wasn't on duty at the hospital was the magic day. I was hungry, but I'd had my fill of hamburgers, which I usually went out for, and the guess-what-kind-of-meat in gravy and over-boiled vegetables that are so much a part of institu-tional cooking. I made several phone calls, all of which failed to produce a dinner invitation, and I sud-denly realized that I was on my own. My cupboard and refrigerator were empty, and I was angry and de-pressed.

I stormed out to the grocery store, which, surpris-ingly, turned out to be a fascinating place. I remember buying a steak, one potato, some lima beans, lettuce and one tomato, bananas, vanilla wafers, and some heavy cream. I hurried home, I cooked a meal—and I liked it. Out again I went, stocked up for the next day, and experienced a marvelous feeling of independence.

I began to feel comfortable in the kitchen, first growing accustomed to it, and then to looking forward to the time I spent there. The more I cooked, the more I began to personalize that first kitchen—and over the years, as I've moved around, I've always made the kitchen the first place I felt "at home."

An ongoing kitchen should be full of life and the life process. Onions that have sprouted have not become dead weight: clip off the sprouts, chop up, and add excitement to a dull salad. (The onions themselves are still fine to cook; and sprouted potatoes are still good for mashing!) Leftovers, too, can be recycled. Proper storage leaves them available for adding to dozens of recipes (see Chapter Ten for a few of them).

When it comes to the subject of life in the kitchen, I think first of growing herbs. An herb garden can be whatever you choose to make it—a few pots in the kitchen window or a formal garden. Suburban kitchens can extend themselves outdoors farther than just the patio barbeque pit; a full herb garden in the summer can be as attractive as a flower garden. Furthermore, the herbs offer you continued pleasure, not just a few days or weeks of pretty blossoms. Herbs gathered and hung to dry can be pleasant reminders of summer all winter long.

Commercial dried herbs, sold in any market, rarely have the special flavor of fresh, or those picked fresh and dried at home. Rosemary bushes planted along a driveway grow into small trees in mild climates; in a window box they may be less ambitious. But growing your own herbs is an instant formula for success in the kitchen. (If you are among the many gardeners with "brown thumbs," herbs offer at least one advantage over African violets: if your plant curls up and dies, you can throw what's left into a salad!)

Fortunately herbs are basically weeds and need only fair soil and a moderate amount of water. Plenty of direct sun—not just light—is, however, important. And you needn't worry about pilfering from your plants for kitchen use: herbs need the pruning to stimulate growth.

There are hundreds of different herbs, most of them available until recently only dried and bottled. I recently saw a list where 175 growing herbs were offered; naturally, I'd love to have them all. Realistically, though, a beginning herb gardener would want to start with basil, oregano, rosemary, sage, tarragon, and thyme. (I exclude parsley, though easily grown, since it's widely available fresh.) The basil is easily grown from seeds; the rest are easier to start from a small nursery plant. One or two plants each will probably be sufficient—but you'll soon find yourself loving and using your herbs so constantly (particularly the basil, I predict) that you'll expand.

Those not restricted to a window box might want to add chives, dill, chervil or fennel (theirs is a similar taste), mint, marjoram, savory, sorrel and of course parsley. The dill, chervil, basil and fennel usually must be started each year. The rest are perennials, though they should be replaced about every three years since they tend to lose their vigor and aroma, and hence taste.

Outside or in, herbs are generally pretty hardy, and most seem almost immune to standard garden pests. At the end of a growing season outdoors, clip the plants close to the base, tie the stems of herbs into bunches and hang upside down in your kitchen. Some herb growers advocate drying in the oven, but it's my experience that the essential oils are best retained when herbs are dried slowly—and upside down.

Starting an herb garden may seem like a painfully slow way to improve your kitchen environment, and I certainly don't advise waiting for summer to begin cooking creatively. But the message here—as with equipment and utensils—is start *somewhere*. And start *now,* so when your herb garden begins to yield (or when you've finally saved up enough pennies for that new blender), you'll be in a position to take full advantage.

Friends and patients who know of my interest in cooking—listening to much of my conversation makes it pretty obvious—often ask what are the truly essential kitchen utensils. I generally answer them, "Whatever you need." It's not a facetious answer, either; I firmly believe that your cooking should dictate your purchases, not the other way around.

Besides, "essential" is a pretty limited category. I suppose the only genuinely essential items in a kitchen are one knife, one spoon and one pot (preferably a big one). I know more than one cook who's managed fairly well on not much more.

Sometimes I answer these questions by simply listing what I have in my kitchen. It makes for quite a list, after two decades of pretty steady cooking, and one probably appropriate to no kitchen but my own. Still, for those who want guidance on this matter from a party more disinterested than the salesperson at the department store, I've come up with a fairly complete list of what would come in handy in almost any kitchen.

POTS: One-, two-, three-, and perhaps four-quart saucepans. (Get the heavy-bottomed kind, and—if you can—those fitted with an interior pan for use as a double boiler.) Size three, five and nine iron skillets (read the instructions carefully about seasoning them). One enameled skillet or "chafing dish." One iron Dutch oven. One deep pot (with lid) suitable for use as a stock pot (see Chapter Two). One "steamer" pot—or a wire steaming device that will fit one of your other pots. One whistling steam kettle (nothing like a pot that "talks") or teapot.

UTENSILS: One large "French cutting" knife. A small paring knife. A serrated-edge knife. A small and large wire whip. Wooden spoons (nothing scratches the daylights out of your pots and skillets more—particularly copper or enameled types—than metal spoons). A rubber spatula. A ladle. A peeler. A sifter. A colander. A slotted spoon.

OTHER PARAPHERNALIA: Set of mixing bowls (preferably oven-proof). Butcher's string. Mortar and pestle. Scissors. And lastly, of course, the American kitchen standbys: aluminum foil, waxed paper, clear stretching wrap (nothing better for fitting over bowls, of leftovers), and plastic storage bags (a new variety features a tracked locking system that, though hard to operate, seems to provide for complete airtightness).

APPLIANCES: I don't care what anyone says—or even what I have in my own kitchen—the only *necessary* appliance is the blender. Toasters, mixers (unless you are heavily involved in baking), and—especially—electric can openers are foolish convenience items. And the convenience they provide is rarely worth the money they cost, or the electricity they waste.

More important, of course, than what you *have* in the kitchen, is what you *bring* to the kitchen.

Cooking—even for a large family—does not have to be a chore or just an obligation. It involves two simple goals: furnishing nutrition and making it tasty. The accomplishment of these goals can be as easy or as complicated as you choose to make it—and you should choose according to your own feelings.

Remember that the kitchen is your tool; you are not its slave. Remember, too, that the kitchen can be a wonderful environment. It offers security, challenge, comfort and limitless possibilities for creativity. It affords both privacy and potential for sharing. In its own way, it's a microcosm of life.

No matter the size of the kitchen or the pocketbook;

no matter what is in season and what is out; no matter whether you are depressed or manic; whether you're simply cooking to get it over with or cooking creatively; whether you're in a hurry or have the whole day to occupy—cooking can always serve your purpose.

All you'll need—as you'll discover in the next chapter—is "good beginnings."

2

Good Beginnings

IF I stress the importance of a good kitchen environment to work in, it's because I'm writing out of my own experience. My first, futile attempt at cooking something began not in a room that was well equipped and conducive to creativity, but over an open fire.

I was a teenager at the time, and I wasn't really interested in preparing a meal. As a Boy Scout, my sights were set not on soufflés, but on merit badges—and I had to get a badge in cooking to move up the scouting ranks. Until that time, I'd never gone near a pot or pan. Our kitchen was the province of Clydie Mae, who cooked for us until the U.S. involvement in World War II, when defense work drew her from the stove to the assembly line.

But since I had to cook something to get that merit badge, I looked through the scout handbook. Something called "twists" seemed like the most simple recipe, a form of biscuit dough that was wrapped around a stick and roasted over an open fire. Clydie Mae and I conspired to make my cooking debut foolproof—or so we thought. Clydie carefully measured out the ingredients, wrapping them separately so that there'd be no problem when the Big Moment came.

Then came the moment of truth around the campfire. As my peers looked on, I carefully selected a tree, then a twig, which I cut with my official Boy Scout knife. I mixed the "twist" ingredients as Clydie Mae had taught me, anticipating both a culinary triumph and the merit badge that would enable me to become a Life Scout. The fire was blazing as I twisted the dough around the twig—and then came disaster.

Instead of merely cooking around the stick as the handbook had promised, the dough began to rise and lose shape (due, I've always suspected, to Clydie Mae's attempt to "better" the official recipe). I began to twist, turn, and shake the twig in a desperate attempt to keep the dough attached. Obviously I wasn't destined for a merit badge in contortions, either—my "twists" untwisted completely, falling into the fire.

The Boy Scouts and I parted company soon after, and I didn't try to cook another thing for at least fifteen years. The moral of the story, if indeed it has one, is this: one can make a good beginning at any time, sometimes later rather than sooner.

Most of us do our cooking in kitchens rather than over Boy Scout campfires—a fact of life which I am particularly thankful for. Having a kitchen set up in the best-functioning and most pleasant manner possible is very important. Good beginnings mean good results, and the smooth operation of a "constant kitchen" yields better food with less work.

For Lucille, a young patient of mine, beginning seemed a major problem. For her the kitchen was a source of insecurity. Having completed college and gotten her first job with a publishing company, Lucille had looked forward to her first apartment. But as she sat across the desk from me, it was clearly evident that she was suffering from a combination of anxiety and depression at being, finally and for the first time, on her own.

"There's something wrong with me," she told me, "and I just don't know what it is. Lately I've found myself going out with people I don't really like just so

I won't be home alone. And Dr. Parrish, when I was in college, living in a dormitory, I couldn't *wait* to be on my own. I used to dream about it—the luxury of privacy, the pleasure of living the way I wanted, decorating an apartment the way I wanted, and all the rest of it. Now I feel . . . I don't know . . . kind of like I want to start my own life but don't know how. Does that make sense?"

I assured Lucille that it did. Many of us have looked forward positively to a dramatic change in our lifestyles, only to find ourselves feeling confused and bewildered when that change occurs. Having just gone through a divorce, I not only sympathized with my patient, but empathized with her disorientation.

"Do you do any cooking for yourself?" I asked Lucille. "You might find that the kitchen is a good place to begin 'your own life.' After all, you have to eat—"

"And I *do,*" Lucille said, not hiding the anger she felt at her own behavior. "I'm going to be voted the Best Customer of the Year by the coffee-shop owners' association, if there's such a thing. Look at my face. I'm breaking out from eating junk food. I know better, but I just can't get started doing it for myself."

We began to talk about the expectations Lucille had held of life on her own. She became much more relaxed as she shared with me the decorating schemes she'd devised while daydreaming during her college years, complete to the color of the picture frames on the wall. She talked about the meals she'd planned on cooking—they, too, were planned down to the last course.

"And what do you think is stopping you from accomplishing what you want to do?" I prodded.

Lucille sighed. "Well, for starters, I never thought about money, but I'm learning that fast enough! And getting anything done is just so frustrating. But one of the real problems is the kitchen. Dr. Parrish, I know that it sounds silly, but it scares me to death! I look in the refrigerator, and there's nothing much in there. My shelves are empty. I know I should get started, but I just can't. . . ."

Lucille wasn't, I realized, so much afraid as she was frustrated. And the kitchen, in her case, had become the focal point of her frustration. Stocking up, organizing, and starting to cook for herself seemed to be an overwhelming challenge. The challenge wasn't merely a matter of selecting pots and pans, but rather a kind of physical and psychological admission that my patient was, after a long time of looking forward to it, "on her own," and that being on her own wasn't the problem-free existence she'd once imagined.

I suggested to Lucille that she begin trying to look at her situation not from the standpoint of what was going against her, but what she had going *for* her. Instead of thinking of herself as "lost" in the kitchen, and the general framework of her new lifestyle, I tried to help her see that she was in a position to be open-minded. Lucille was overcome by a lack of ideas of her own— but things would be a lot easier if she could be made to believe that this feeling meant she was open to *good* ideas from other sources.

"I've had my apartment for years," I told her, "and it hasn't been the way I want it—not once in all that time. As soon as I get one problem solved, something else goes wrong. Paint begins to peel on the ceiling, the refrigerator breaks down, and the pipes leak. But Lucille, 'real life' is like that."

"Dream" houses and apartments can often be plagued by nightmares, as many of us know! This applies as well to jobs, human relationships, and every area of life. Perfection, by definition, is an unobtainable goal; were it easy to grasp, it wouldn't be worth working toward. And were it easier to achieve, we'd have little if any motivation to work toward improving ourselves and changing various aspects of our lives. But Lucille needed practical help, a motivation to "get started" and a place to start. The kitchen, it seemed to me, was ideal.

"I sympathize with the problems of a new apartment," I told her, "and I know what it feels like to want it all to be done—organized and well-ordered—right away. But facing the fact that you have to take it a piece at a time, why not start with the kitchen?"

"The secret for making the most of the kitchen, in total terms," I said, "is to remember that it is a room that is built on compromise. Never have so little on hand that you are constantly forced to improvise and substitute in order to create a meal, but never have so much food that you are forced to eat, even when you aren't hungry, just to use it up." I urged Lucille to do some shopping, to prepare one meal for herself, no matter how simple.

"Even a peanut butter and jelly sandwich would be fine," I said, "though I think you can do better than that. But make something for yourself, and you'll feel as though you belong in your kitchen—and your apartment."

Lucille took my advice. The next day she called my office, proudly telling me that she'd made herself a hamburger and some boiled carrots.

"It's not exactly the image I had of myself," she confided. "I'm not sure when I'm going to get to all those recipes I cut out of the magazines. . . ."

"Give yourself time," I urged her. "At least you've made a start."

"You know," my patient said, "I feel that way, too."

All of us need to feel a sense of belonging. We look for it in our marriages, friendships and other personal relationships. We try to find it in our work—on the job, in the office. But our primary sense of security comes from the home, the real "constant" in our lives. This sense of security can, I believe, be best fostered in the kitchen.

Cooking, besides being practical, necessary to sheer survival, can offer a reassuring sense of the continuum of daily life. Creating meals is satisfying in itself, but learning to cook things that "keep on going," that is, things that can be used in a variety of dishes and meals, is a very positive step, not only in terms of the kitchen but in the broader terms of our general lives.

Cooking requires some ability to follow directions—but then, what doesn't? Most of us, given the chance, would much prefer to go our own merry way in everything we do. In the kitchen, we have to learn to measure out the required ingredients, to regulate the timing, to know what goes with what—and to temper other people's advice, whether it comes to us via a recipe or through general principles of cooking, with our own experience.

Not every recipe need be written down: some of the best cooks I know couldn't follow a recipe if they tried. But these fortunate cooks have a natural gift refined by experience. Unlike mathematics, cooking requires common sense more than it requires a set of rigid rules. Knowing how thick a liquid should be for the purpose it is to serve, knowing when a crust is beginning to burn rather than becoming flaky, when there is too much salt, too little spice, when everything on the plate looks too monochromatic and needs the glint of a red or green vegetable, when a crunchy texture is needed to complement a soft bite—these things come with experience, and experience means making mistakes.

Beware, for your own sake, of compulsiveness in the kitchen. Striving toward culinary perfection is natural, and healthy. But obsessive compulsiveness is deadly. Not being able to enjoy a steak and potato just because the Hollandaise for the asparagus you planned on serving with it didn't turn out right is self-destructive. Having to use the last drop of everything, insisting on everything perennially in perfect order—not for a minute being able to let anything fall loose or to let those last few wisps of whipped cream remain in the bowl—these forms of behavior limit the function of cooking, which is not only to produce an edible result, but should be to make you feel better for having done so.

Recipes, we must recognize from the start, involve

variables. Eggs are not always the same size—neither are turnips or breadcrumbs—nor is the strength of stock unvarying. There are some factors we simply cannot control, and instead of fretting about the realization, trying to scoop out the last minute milligram of baking powder to make a recipe "right," both our cooking and our nerves will be improved if we let ourselves feel free. Rights and wrongs mixed together have a way of turning out to be delectable. Freedom of self-expression, liberation from hang-ups and from authoritarianism— these are the secret values of cooking.

Common sense tells us that some recipes are more limiting than others, better suited to those times when we want to give up some of our own authority. *Haute cuisine,* foreign dishes and pastries usually require precise adherence to given instructions. They're well suited to those times when we're in the mood to take direction, to be submissive.

Other recipes, by their nature, afford us more freedom and latitude. The difference of one egg can make or break a cake; when you're cooking a stew, a few carrots more or less really don't alter its nature. Most foods can be left over low fires unattended for long periods of time, but there are exceptions. Sauces, if not watched every minute, can become disasters: soups, on the other hand, rarely "turn" or curdle just because they're not constantly supervised. Any food, it should be noted, can stick to a pot—and even a soup that can simmer by itself for hours needs an occasional stirring.

Many people are frustrated in their attempts at cooking because they don't make the important first step of admitting what they know and what they have to learn. Mincing, chopping, and cubing are different things: sautéing is not the same thing as frying, nor is beating the same as folding. Some ingredients blend well with others, and some tastes and textures clash disastrously. A "low flame" and a "hot oven" are vague terms that become specific only in terms of our stoves (the most individualized and temperamental instruments ever created). If you don't know what a specific term means, save yourself aggravation, frustration, and disappointment by finding out!

Nobody would think of driving a car without learning how, yet often people try to cook dishes that they are simply not qualified to turn out. Without broadening our horizons, we are doomed to monotonous repetition of a few recipes, and cooking becomes a dull, unrewarding chore. Learning—being willing to admit what you *don't* know—saves waste and prevents problems, and in the long run enables you to cook a wide range of dishes with very few failures.

Basic cookbooks can help, and *The Joy of Cooking* and *Fannie Farmer Boston Cooking School Cookbook* are excellent and reliable. Another reliable choice is *The New York Times Cookbook,* by Craig Claiborne, an authority who appreciates the fundamental practicalities as well as the sensual refinements. I consult cookbooks frequently, despite all the experience I've had in the kitchen, and my recipes are the better for it. Yours will be, too.

There's such a thing, however, as too slavishly following cookbook recipes—and I include my own!

Your good judgment should always be a guide when working with any recipe. Salt and pepper, however specifically they are measured in the recipe, should always be adjusted to your own taste; you're the one, after all, who has to eat the result—no Fannie Farmer. In my recipes, I have consciously tried to recommend only the minimum amount of salt. We Americans use entirely too much salt already, and if I would err, I wanted to err on the side of good physical health. But if you require more salt, and are willing to accept the long-term medical consequences, then, if you must, forget the carefully measured quarter-teaspoons.

"Yield" is another area where your own judgment is the best guide. When a recipe says "serves four," that's a very subjective guess. Obviously, what's a full portion for one person only whets the appetite of another. The basic rule of thumb I use—which you can adjust to your own situations—is simple: a half pound of meat serves one; a cup of vegetables represents a good-sized portion.

The basic message I'm trying to get across is equally simple: remember that the recipe is meant to work for you, not the other way around. If you like a thicker sauce or gravy than a recipe yields, don't hesitate to add that extra bit of flour or other thickening agent that will make a dish—for you—successful.

Of course, there is the personality type that insists on altering every recipe—for the very sake of change. Asserting yourself over a recipe may be important for your sense of self expression, but as with everything we do in life, we must then accept the consequences. If these consequences represent an evening meal you've waited all afternoon for, you may want to think twice about foolish meddling.

The "cure" for both extremes—intimidation and needless tinkering—can come only with kitchen experience. Like any art, cooking is a cumulative learning experience. The more you try, the more you learn; the more you know, the more you *are*.

Friends and patients alike are always complaining to me that their time in the kitchen seems to run in spurts. For weeks on end, they pay careful attention to running their kitchen, with excellent results. "Then it all falls apart," they tell me.

"I can tell my days are numbered," my friend Lorraine once said, "when the flour cannister turns up empty. Suddenly I'll start running out of everything—vegetable oil, spices, even salt. Then I won't even be able to find that egg I had tucked away on the bottom shelf—and I literally run away. Harold starts having his breakfast sent in to his office, and I make him take me to restaurants every evening."

Lorraine happens to be a wonderful, instinctive cook, and I've had some delicious meals in her home during those times when her kitchen is running smoothly. She admits that her escapes from the kitchen tend to take place after periods of heavy kitchen duty, such as when her children are visiting during holidays.

Many of us have similar situations in our own cooking experience. After a particularly overstuffed Thanksgiving-to-New-Year season, the last thing I want to see is a plate of food—from my own kitchen or anyone else's. But the problem remains: how to make yours a full-time kitchen. The answer, as usual, involves some effort.

What I like to think of as the "constant kitchen" is more than simply seeing to it that the flour supply is ample. It's a total approach to your kitchen life—reflecting the sort of cooking you plan to do, as well as the foods you'll want to eat.

For example, I use a great many herbs in my cooking, and I find a very basic element of my "constant kitchen" is the shelves of growing herbs I have in front of the kitchen window. Maybe you're dependent (or think you are) on the dried-and-bottled variety available in any market, but there are ways of adding a year-round fresh herb element to your cooking.

The first is through the use of herb butters. Using either home-grown or the fresh herbs you can buy in season, you can prepare herb butters ready for use in many recipes.

Their preparation is simple. Melt a half pound of salted butter and mix with 1½ cups of finely-chopped fresh herbs and ½ teaspoon salt (salt helps preserve the butter). No cooking necessary. If you wish to try herb butters using prepared dried herbs, use my basic equation for dried vs. fresh herbs: 1 teaspoon dried $=$ 3 teaspoons fresh. (This equation applies to all other herb uses as well, so it's good to keep in mind.)

Kept refrigerated or frozen, your herb butters are available for hundreds of appropriate uses. Obviously you can't use herbs in butter form for salads, but in any dish calling for butter or oil, they add a delightful touch. Just consider a tablespoon of herb butter equivalent to a teaspoon of the dried herbs called for in the recipe. But *remember* then to adjust the amount of oil or butter required by subtracting ½ tablespoon for each tablespoon of herb butter used.

If herb butters are available in your constant kitchen, you'll doubtless find many ways in which they fit into your cooking plans. And here are a few of my own suggestions: Rosemary butter is a delightful addition to carrots, and dill butter can be used in any fish recipe. Basil butter is the perfect thing for baked potatoes— add a scoop of sour cream, if you like. Sauté veal scallopini in thyme butter, and cook omelets in tarragon butter. Even canned tomato soup can be perked up with a tablespoon of oregano or marjoram butter.

And then there's my recipe for Sage Burgers, the best thing to happen to ground beef since the invention of the cow!

SAGE BURGERS

2 servings

1 pound ground round steak	½ teaspoon ground sage
	1 tablespoon sage butter
½ teaspoon salt	1 tablespoon flour
¼ teaspoon pepper	¾ cup stock

Mold ground round, spices and sage into two Salisbury steaks (hamburgers). Broil until slightly rarer than you like. Reserve steaks in warm oven.

Melt sage butter in a skillet; stir in flour and bubble over a low heat for one minute. Then add the stock and cook until thickened. Pour sauce over steaks and serve.

Herb vinegars are another way of preserving fresh herbs for future use. They add individuality to any dish that calls for vinegar. A watercress salad, for example, can be dressed with any vinegar—but a *rosemary* vinegar punches up even the limpest old watercress. Or that roast you're going to marinate will be much tastier if you substitute for the vinegar any of a number of herb vinegars.

The principle is simple: add eight to ten generous sprigs of an herb to a pint of vinegar (preferably wine or cider). You can buy bottles of ordinary vinegar, pour out just a tiny bit, then add the herbs and recap. Your herb vinegar generally needs several weeks to develop a full taste. After that, it will last almost indefinitely. In addition, once you've used up one bottle, you can fill it up with vinegar again, wait another week or so, and you're back in business. (Perhaps you're thinking that you can buy some herb vinegars, and of course you're right; only why not make your own?)

Our "constant kitchen" is not only a matter of advance preparation. To be sure, having things like herb butters and vinegars—or some of the home-made sauces for which I provide recipes at the end of this chapter—can give any cook a head start on kitchen readiness. There is also the leftovers question, answered more fully in the last chapter; for now I'll restrict my discussion to the stockpot.

More than anything else I do in the kitchen, the cultivation of a stockpot has been for me the most therapeutic. A natural miser (though an actual spendthrift!) I've always hated to throw away unused or uneaten food. So I don't; I put it in the stockpot. I'm not sure that it saves me money, but I know it saves me anxiety. Stock in cubes or in powders is not very expensive. But the prepared varieties don't salve my guilt over the immense waste that goes on in most kitchens. With the stockpot, I can joyously save everything—and receive in return a broth far superior to anything available in the supermarket.

Simmered in water, these rejected bits of food provide a foundation for the creation of many new delightful dishes. Innumerable recipes call for stock, and in many more, stock can replace water. Rice, for instance, cooked in stock rather than water is practically a whole different dish.

I usually keep three different stockpots going at once: meat, chicken, and fish. All leftovers go immediately into the appropriate pot; vegetables, or their peels, can go anywhere. Kept in the refrigerator, the stockpot can be removed whenever you've accumulated sufficient leftovers, and simmered for several hours.

When boiling your stock, make sure that there is always sufficient water to cover all the leftovers. You'll want to keep a close enough eye on the simmering pot that it doesn't get that "burnt" taste. As the stock reaches the strength you desire, strain through a colander, then allow to cool and refrigerate. This cooling will bring any excess fat to the top of the pot, where it can be easily skimmed.

If you're a little slow gathering leftovers, take care that your pot doesn't go sour on you in the refrigerator. Taking it out, covering with water and bringing to a boil at least twice a week will prevent this. Just return to the refrigerator, and think of it as your "ongoing" stockpot. Label and freeze your reduced and strained stock, unless you have immediate plans for it. Frozen hard, it should keep almost indefinitely.

A good variation for summertime with your leftovers is the *cold* stockpot. Simply keep a sealed bowl in your refrigerator, and fill it with leftover or extra salad makings and dressings. When you have gathered enough of your leftover rosebuds, you can run them through the blender, and have the basis for a delicious gazpacho soup.

Stock is a real *basic* of cooking—in more ways than one. It's a starting point for almost any soup or stew and, in addition, the genuine essence of food. A good stock is an encyclopedia of its food inputs, encompassing both their nutrition and their taste. And a good stockpot is a simple, basic way to getting your kitchen going, putting it to work for you.

I feel the same way about some of the homemade sauces I've developed. Not only are they a handy way to really dress up simple meals, they are bound to make you feel more at home in the kitchen.

Preparing a sauce to keep around your kitchen will give you a greater sense of kitchen mastery—you cannot have a disaster with an ongoing sauce, since it's not something you're planning to put on the table for guests within the hour. So here's an ideal opportunity to get into the kitchen without worrying about the results. As in other areas of life, the lack of anxiety over failures is likely to be the key to success.

Recipes for my basic meat and fish sauces are at the end of this chapter, along with a delicious peach chutney and other, more individualized sauces. But none is so simple—and so basic to all cooking—as my Salvation Sauce. You can make some up ahead of time, or whip it up when disaster must be averted at the last minute.

As both experience and my friend Arthur have taught me, when in trouble use butter, lemon juice, sour cream, and maybe cornstarch. Thus:

SALVATION SAUCE

For 1 dish

2 tablespoons butter	1 teaspoon lemon juice
½ cup sour cream	1 teaspoon cornstarch

Heat in a double boiler over boiling water until well blended.

The variations of this principle are innumerable. To hold a casserole together, add an egg. For low-calorie cooks, substitute imitation butter or margarine and sour-cream dressing. For use in any meat dish, add a teaspoon of Worchestershire sauce, some herbs and tomato sauce. For vegetables add some grated cheese. In a dessert add a dab of honey or a pinch of sugar or sweet liqueur.

People often refrain from taking a chance in their kitchen, thinking there are secrets to which only cooking pros are privy. I wouldn't know about the existence of such secrets—no one has taken the time to tell me any of them—but there *are* basic principles.

Nothing in cooking is quite so clear-cut as mathematical equations, but certain formulas ease the preparation of everything from soups to salad dressings. A few such formulas appear at the end of this chapter, and here I'll give the basic principle of purée soups.

PURÉE SOUPS

3 cups or so

2 cups stock	¼ teaspoon pepper
2 cups chopped vegetables	½ teaspoon salt

Simmer for 15 minutes, then run through the blender in small batches.

That's the principle, now here are refinements you might want to try. Stir in ½ cup half-and-half per cup of stock for a creamier soup; then serve hot or refrigerate and serve cold with a dollop of sour cream on top. Or 1 to 1½ teaspoons of instant mashed potatoes can be blended in for a heartier soup.

Some qualification on the principle might be in order, especially for beginners. For instance, if you're using a heavy-flavored vegetable—turnips, for instance—you'll want to adjust by using a stronger stock, beef rather than chicken. The reverse holds true: mildly flavored vegetables are better matched to a light stock.

Much of this basic material will seem awfully

simple-minded to the seasoned cook. I know dozens of good cooks who can put together delicious purée soups, but could not repeat a formula for preparation if their lives depended on it.

Of course there are the other cases: people who know the formula or recipe by heart, and still can't get good results. In all my years of cooking, nothing has intimidated (and irritated) me more than my inability to make a pie crust. Either it stuck to the board or rolling pin, fissured as I tried to flatten the pastry, or fell to pieces as I tried to transfer it into the pie plate. No matter how hard I tried, whose recipe I used or what trick I employed, all effort was for naught. Deep inside, I guess I was still trying for that merit badge I'd missed years before.

But there's a happy ending to this saga, encouragement for those who'll come after me. It's never too late for good beginnings—in the kitchen or elsewhere. So here it is:

FOOLPROOF PIE CRUST

For a 2-crust pie

2⅓ cups flour	1 teaspoon salt
⅔ cup vegetable oil	¼ cup ice water

Sift 2 cups of the flour and mix well with the oil and salt. Chill. When ready to roll out, remove from the refrigerator and let return to room temperature. Then add the ice water. Knead well.

Lay a piece of wax paper on a flat surface. Sprinkle it generously with part of the remaining flour. Work the pastry into a thick circle 6 to 8 inches in diameter, trying to keep the edges from fringing. Sprinkle with flour.

Cover with another sheet of wax paper. Then roll out with a pin. When at least an inch larger in diameter than your pie plate, strip off the outer wax paper. Set your pie plate beside your pastry and flip pastry onto it. Remove the wax paper before fitting the pastry down into the plate.

Trim off the extra pastry, flute the rim and prick the bottom. If you want a partially baked crust, put in a 450 degree oven for 10 to 20 minutes (depending on how well done you want it).

Continue with your pie recipe. (A lower-calorie crust is on page 202.)

Since there's no remedy for turning up short, I've designed the recipe above to be on the long side. But don't throw away the leftover pastry. As I've tried to indicate, nothing keeps your kitchen going like utilizing everything that is made in it. So take the extra pastry and put it to work with the recipe that follows.

CHEESE BITS

2 parts leftover pie pastry	crumbled red pepper and salt to taste
	1 part grated cheese

Mix and mold into finger-sized bits. Bake in a 350 degree oven for 15 minutes. Then, for extra browning, run under the broiler for another 3 minutes. Serve as appetizers.

Now here are the collected recipes for good beginnings that I've been promising.

WHEN-YOU'RE-READY ROUX FLOUR

A genuine secret of cooking lies in the preparation of a roux, a cooked mixture of flour and oil. Making a roux, or last minute thickening of sauces and gravies, can be simplified by precooking your flour.

4 cups all-purpose flour   2 teaspoons pepper
4 teaspoons salt

Mix all ingredients together and put in baking pan large enough that the mixture is no more than ¼ inch deep. Bake in a 425 degree oven for 1¼ hours until the flour is dark gold in color. Let cool, then seal in a jar. Keep refrigerated.

When ready for use, your flour mixture should be blended with an equivalent amount of oil or butter. This is your *roux*. Use a tablespoon of the *roux* for each cup of liquid—perfect sauce or gravy every time!

THE PRINCIPLE OF SALAD DRESSINGS

I'm always somewhat offended by advertisements on television for salad dressing "mixes." Watching the worst cook I ever knew—he didn't have a taste bud in his head—unfailingly turn out delicious salad dressings, I knew anyone could manage it. This is the bottom line of all my salad dressings:

6 tablespoons vinegar   ½ teaspoon ground
1 teaspoon salt   pepper
10 tablespoons olive oil

Adjust the recipe to your desired amount, and blend well.

Variations are almost endless, but I'll list a few you might otherwise be tempted to buy commercially.

HERB DRESSING: Substitute one or your own herb vinegars for a "name brand."

SEED DRESSING: Add
¼ teaspoon each mustard seed, celery seed, fennel seed, dill seed, caraway seed, ¼ cup mayonnaise

Grind seed in a mortar and pestle and add to basic recipe. Terrific, especially for fruit salads.

CHIFFON DRESSING: 1 raw egg to basic recipe and blend.

ITALIAN DRESSING:
2 cloves garlic, minced
1 teaspoon oregano

Blend with basic recipe.

RUSSIAN DRESSING:
1 hard-boiled egg, chopped
2 teaspoons ketchup
2 tablespoons pickle (or "hot dog") relish

Blend with basic recipe.

FRENCH DRESSING:
¼ teaspoon paprika
¼ teaspoon sugar
¼ teaspoon lemon juice

Blend with basic recipe.

CREAM DRESSING:
¼ cup heavy cream
¼ teaspoon chervil

Blend with basic recipe.

CHEESE DRESSING: Add ½ cup crumbled cheese to basic recipe.

HOUSE SPECIALTY: Add any or all of the ingredients below to the basic recipe for your own "house dressing":
¼ cup bacon, chopped
¼ cup olives
2 tablespoons anchovies
1 pimiento
¼ cup sour cream
¼ cup diet mayonnaise (for a dieting "house")
1 tablespoon dried herbs
1 tablespoon raisins, chopped
1 tablespoon capers
1 tablespoon horseradish
1 tablespoon pickled onions

DILL BUTTER SCROD

Here's a terrific use for that dill butter you prepared; substitute any fish for scrod, if you prefer.

2 teaspoons dill butter	2 pinches pepper
3 teaspoons butter	1 pound scrod filets
¼ teaspoon salt	4 teaspoons lemon juice

Melt butters, salt and pepper in a skillet over a low heat. Coat the filets with lemon juice and sauté for 4 minutes on each side.

TOMATO SOUP

2 or 3 servings

Dress up a can of tomato soup with one of your herb butters—marjoram or oregano is best.

A 10-ounce can of	1 teaspoon oregano or
tomato soup	marjoram butter
1 cup milk	1 teaspoon butter

Warm tomato soup and milk. Mix herb and regular butter. Then put a dab into each cup of soup.

MEAT SAUCE

A quart

This meat sauce is invaluable as a base for seasoning and basting all kinds of meat. Substitute fish for meat stock, and you have an equally hearty fish sauce.

4 cups strained, skimmed	2½ tablespoons
meat stock	cornstarch
	4 tablespoons soy sauce

The stock should taste very strong, but not over-powering. If too strong, correct with water. Dissolve the cornstarch in the soy sauce in a saucepan. Stir in the stock, and simmer until it thickens, then 10 minutes more. Pour into a bottle and cork. Keep in refrigerator.

SORREL SAUCE

About 2 cups

Sorrel, or sour grass, is the first herb up in the spring; and no matter how much you cut it, will serve you until the fall. This sauce is good for fish—shad roe and salmon steaks, for instance—and can serve as a base to be diluted with more broth and cream for a hot or cold soup.

1 cup sorrel leaves	¼ teaspoon pepper
2 tablespoons butter	2 tablespoons flour
1 tablespoon minced shallots	1 cup chicken stock
½ teaspoon salt	(¼ cup light cream)

Wash, stem, dry and chop the sorrel leaves before measuring. Over moderate heat melt the butter in an enamel pan. Add shallots, salt, pepper and sorrel. Stir and cook for 5 minutes. Add 2 tablespoons stock. Sprinkle with the flour, mix well and cook for a few minutes. Gradually stir in the rest of the stock until smooth. Simmer slowly until thick, about 10 minutes. (Add the cream) Warm when ready to serve.

MARINADE

Per ½ pound of meat

To tenderize cheaper cuts of meat—or to add a new flavor to expensive cuts—let them sit for a few hours or overnight in the following:

4 tablespoons dry red wine	1 teaspoon lemon juice
	2 teaspoons soy sauce

Multiply recipe as necessary.

PEACH-PINEAPPLE CHUTNEY

About 1 quart jar

1 pound peaches, peeled and chopped
¼ pound sweet green pepper, chopped

½ pound fresh pineapple, peeled and chopped

Make a syrup by boiling the following ingredients:

1½ teaspoons ginger, peeled and finely minced
1 teaspoon peppercorns
½ ounce mustard seed

½ clove garlic, finely minced
1 cup cider vinegar
6 ounces brown sugar

Mix and simmer very slowly in an uncovered saucepan until most of the liquid has evaporated, maybe about 2 hours.

GREEN RICE

4 servings

Nothing is more basic to meal preparation than the old standby, rice. Here's an easy variation to keep your interest up and your tastebuds titillated.

2 cups water
1 teaspoon cracked pepper
4 teaspoons salt

1½ cups stock or canned broth
1½ cups rice
½ cup chopped fresh herbs

Bring water and stock to rapid boil in a medium casserole. Add pepper and salt. Slowly add the rice without breaking the boil. Stir in the fresh herbs. Cover. Boil for 10–12 minutes. Drain. Place in a low oven (250 degrees) till ready to serve.

PÂTÉ

About 3 pounds

A *pâté* is always handy to have around, either as an appetizer or for a late supper. Besides, if you want to impress guests with your kitchen expertise, nothing seems quite so "fancy" as a pâté. Go ahead, show off!

½ pound ground sausage	2½ ounces bottled capers
1 pound ground beef	
1 cup chopped vegetables	2 tablespoons meat sauce
¼ pound ground lamb	2 tablespoons herb potpourri
1 pound chicken livers	
½ cup salted peanuts	3 tablespoons port

Simmer the sausage (frozen sausage can be substituted for fresh) in a large skillet with ¼ inch water until almost brown. Add the ground round (or an equal amount of leftover meat loaf) and chopped vegetables and sauté until vegetables start to soften. Add ground lamb and chicken livers and continue to sauté until mixture is almost dry. Put in a large bowl. Chop the peanuts and add. Drain off the liquid then add the capers. Stir in the meat sauce, the herb potpourri and the port. Mix until soft and well blended. Put in a well-greased dish or terrine. Keep covered in the refrigerator until ready to serve.

PICKLED OKRA

15 pint jars

Somehow the culinary cross-fertilization after the Civil War failed to introduce to the Northern states the delicacy of this simple relish.

8 cups vinegar	dill seed
8 cups water	garlic
1 cup salt	small hot peppers
12 pounds fresh okra	pickling spices

Sterilize the jars. (The dishwasher is an easy way to do this.)

Boil vinegar, water and salt for 10 minutes. Wash and stem okra and pack into jars. In each jar place 1 teaspoon dill seed, 2 cloves garlic, 2 hot peppers, 1 teaspoon pickling spice. Fill each jar with the hot vinegar mixture. Seal. Let pickle for at least 1 month. Chill before serving.

APPLE-PINEAPPLE CONSERVE

About 2 quart jars

In the fall when apples are everywhere, and you do not feel like making apple butter, try this conserve. Add it on some winter's night to an uninspired meat dish.

1 cup butter or margarine	4 cups pineapple, crushed
1 teaspoon ground cloves	6 cups apples, chopped
1 tablespoon salt	

Melt the butter and add the cloves, salt, pineapple and apple. Sauté this over a hot flame for 10 minutes, stirring frequently. Seal in sterilized jars and store.

GREEN BEANS AND GREEN BEAN SALAD

1 pound green beans, stemmed	½ teaspoon pepper
	½ cup clear stock
1 tablespoon butter	1 package dried
1 teaspoon salt	vegetable broth

Place beans in boiling salted water and cook until almost tender, about 10 minutes. Drain and rinse with cold water to stop cooking.

Make a sauce of butter, salt, pepper and stock. Add beans to saucepan and simmer for 3 or 4 minutes. This is a "good beginning" for a bean salad. Mix it with sliced red onions, chopped celery, green peppers and cooked peas and beans; even cauliflower buds. Make a lot of vinaigrette dressing and pour over the beans. You can keep the salad going all week and vary it from night to night with sliced cheese, slivers of cold meat, hard-boiled eggs or tuna fish. It is tasty and filling, and you don't tend to overeat it.

GLAZED PORK ROAST

Serves 4 to 6

Your homemade meat sauce is invaluable as a starter for glazes and bastes. This glaze combines the meat sauce with chopped orange.

½ orange (or 1 small one)	1 teaspoon pepper
	¼ cup meat sauce
3 tablespoons coriander seeds	(See p. 52)
	4 to 5 pounds roast pork
2 teaspoons salt	

Peel the orange and clean out as much pulp and white as possible. Chop then grate the peel with the dry ingredients in a blender. Add the meat sauce and blend.

Trim the fat from the pork. Rub this marinade all over the roast. Place the roast fat-side-up on a rack in a shallow roasting pan. Bake at 200 degrees for 45 minutes to an hour per pound, depending on your feelings about pork* and how well-done it must be.

After the roast has been in for about 2 hours, turn and baste. For the last 15 minutes of cooking, turn the temperature up to 350 degrees.

---

* MEDICAL WARNING: All pork products must be cooked at no less than 325 degrees, 45 minutes per pound or to 170 degrees internal temperature.

BITTER BEEF

3 to 4 servings

There are two points of interest in this recipe. First the rue, an herb known more for its medicinal than culinary value. Recommended as a preventive against snakebite, for the preservation of good vision and in the treatment of nervous disorders, it was also used in the Catholic rite of exorcism. The Italians still use it in their salads.

Second, the *beurre manié* is another time-saver, essentially a cold roux as described on page 48. Equal parts of butter and flour are cooked over a low flame for 20 minutes, then kept in a jar in the refrigerator.

1 cup rice	½ teaspoon salt
2 cups water	¼ teaspoon pepper
1 teaspoon rue leaves, chopped	1 tablespoon grated grapefruit peel
1 pound London broil, cut into thin slices 1 inch long	½ cup tomato sauce
	½ cup stock
	¼ cup beurre manié
2 tablespoons olive oil	1 head chicory

In a covered saucepan, boil the rice in salted water with the rue for 10 minutes. Uncover and let dry.

Sauté the beef in the oil with the salt, pepper and grapefruit peel until brown. Add the tomato sauce and stock; mix. Then add the beurre manié (or in this instance 2 tablespoons of butter with 2 tablespoons of flour simmered for 20 minutes). Cook the mixture for 10 minutes more.

Chop the chicory and cover the bottom half of a large, well-greased casserole dish with it. Layer on the rice, then the meat and then the sauce. Bake in a preheated oven at 325 degrees for 15 minutes.

3

Anti-Tension Cookery

"TENSE?" the advertisements ask.

"Is tension getting to you?"

"Are the effects of everyday tension making life difficult?"

Answering on behalf of myself, and most of the people I talk to, the overwhelming response is "Yes!" Life *is* difficult, and tension—a by-product of the hectic pace at which we function—doesn't make it any easier. Non-specific, free-floating anxiety is decidedly a disease of our time, and nobody, including myself, is immune.

There are days when the combination of seeing patients, running an office, and the ever-increasing number of health reports and insurance forms to be filled out really get to me. Sitting behind my desk and trying to help other people with their problems isn't a release for my own anxieties. I get tense, too.

I've learned, however, to make tension work for me when I get home and into my kitchen. It's the principal ingredient in some of my favorite recipes. The hostility and anger that I've repressed to such a degree that I can actually feel the tightening (or tensing) of my muscles goes into pounding, chopping and cutting. More than once I have approached my chopping block or cutting board with a stack of paperwork in mind.

Call it vengeance through vegetables; or tension relief through tough beef!

All of us—from the beginner with a limited repertoire to part-time chef capable of turning out intricate *haute cuisine* dishes—select the foods we eat on the basis of personal taste. The availability of foodstuffs and ingredients, what is or is not available at the butcher shop or in season at the grocer's, influences our choices. The nutritive values of foods should definitely be a factor in our decision making.

Choice in shopping and in cooking is something we take for granted, but in a world where jobs and to a lesser degree relationships demand that we spend a good deal of time doing things that we *have* to do, choosing what we eat and how it will be prepared is more than a matter of preference; it is a basic act of self-assertion.

The large, impersonal supermarket is hardly an atmosphere conducive to relaxation (one reason, in addition to the factor of freshness, why I prefer to do my shopping at the butcher shop and greengrocer's). However, no matter where we shop, buying what we want and exerting our own decision-making processes, can soothe the psyche as well as please the palate.

Granted, ever-increasing prices can temper the potential pleasures of shopping for food, and crowded, less-than-immaculate markets can also help to negate the experience. Surly cashiers, check-out help and store managers (in my more paranoid moments, I'm convinced they have to take and pass a rudeness test) who scowl and mutter an unintelligible response when a customer asks where the flour is, also contribute more to tension than they do toward its release. And that's a shame; there's a surplus of that in our lives already.

What makes us tense is as personal a matter as how well-done we like our steaks, or whether or not we like steak at all. As a doctor, tension is one of the most frequent complaints I hear from my patients.

Tension frightens us, which in turn creates more

tension. Not long ago a patient of mine, a successful advertising executive in his early thirties who had made great strides up the corporate ladder, sat across the desk from me. His nails were bitten to the quick, and he was fidgeting with his cigarette lighter. Jack, a man who had no problem being in control at meetings and who was well-liked by clients and co-workers, was obviously having a problem, and he was smart enough to recognize it.

"I'm drinking too much," he told me, "and, doc, the thing of it is I really don't like drinking. It started, I think, when I really had to sell the clients. I'd take them to lunch. Sometimes we'd do so much drinking that we never got around to ordering food."

Now his job no longer demanded frequent lunches with clients, but Jack found himself in the three-martini syndrome that is both a cliché and a fact of the Madison Avenue world. He would head for a local bar during his lunch hour in an attempt to wash his anxieties away with alcohol.

"I don't like what I'm doing," Jack said, "but I can't help it. That damn job of mine makes me so tense that I need something to help me. Could you prescribe a tranquilizer or something? God, why do I feel so tense?"

My first response was to congratulate Jack for recognizing his problem and resolving to do something about it, then I tried to help him.

"God could give us all some answers," I said, "but I'll do the best I can. One reason you're so tense is because you're alive. Tension is a fact of life. In your kind of very competitive, high-pressured work, tension is everywhere, all the time. As far as tranquilizers go, I don't think we'd be accomplishing too much if we exchange a dependency on drink for a dependency on pills. Let's look for some long range answers. Tell me— do you like to eat?"

Jack looked at me, surprised by my question. "Come

on now. You're not going to tell me that health foods are going to change my life, are you?"

I promptly answered that I didn't know what health foods were. To my way of thinking, foods that have nutrients for the body are health foods, though some foods are more healthful than others. Once Jack realized that I wasn't about to send him out for a bottle of kelp tablets, we began to communicate. He did, in fact, like to cook, though his wife had taken over the kitchen when Jack married and moved from a New York apartment to a house in Connecticut. Usually, he told me, his wife put the finishing touches on dinner while Jack told her the day's problems, sipping yet another martini.

"There's nothing wrong with having a drink when you come home from work," I assured him. "If it helps you relax and if you can control your drinking, then fine. It's your lunch-hour drinking that worries me. Tell me, Jack—since you like to eat and you like to prepare food, why not try some shopping on your lunch hour?"

"But there isn't a supermarket for blocks—"

"Good," I said. "Walking is the best exercise, and exercise and physical activity are natural ways for the body to release tension. Head over to Ninth Avenue. There are open-air fruit and vegetable stands where everything is marvelously fresh. Pick up the ingredients for a salad, and when you get home at night, tear the greens with your hands. It's a great way to release some of that tension. And while you're shopping, pick up some celery to keep in your desk. Try munching celery stalks instead of your fingernails."

My advice wasn't aimed at changing Jack's whole life. There is no prescription that can alleviate and eliminate tension and anxiety. Yet often in this age of "wonder" drugs and treatments, we look for a panacea at the expense of trying to find simple but effective ways to help us cope with the realities of existence.

One needn't be an executive to spend a lunch hour

shopping for dinner, though obviously an executive's time is more flexible than that of an office worker who has to punch a time clock. Nor, like Jack, does one have to have a drinking problem to need an excuse for a constructive break in the day.

Instead of spending the lunch hour at the local coffee shop, fighting the crowds and rehashing the problems of the job with co-workers, it's possible—in virtually every city or town—to find an open market section. The aroma of fresh food invigorates and stimulates the senses. The act of buying greens and vegetables reaffirms the fact that bad as the day may be—long and nerve-wracking as it seems—it will eventually end. You'll be able to go home and relax. Instead of concentrating on immediate problems, we put our minds forward a few hours. Ultimately, within an hour or so, we'll be back at our desks, and the tension-producing problems will *have* to be faced.

The change of environment, though brief, can relax us and reorient our thinking. It's not something to do every day, but on difficult, trying days it can work well. A stroll through an interesting food shop during one's lunch hour can also provide a welcome break in terms of diet. Instead of the standard coffee shop BLT or grilled cheese sandwich, enjoy a perfect pear and some cheese; new tastes can stimulate new thoughts, and new approaches to problems.

When I travel—something I enjoy almost as much as cooking—I try to have dinner at a good restaurant. Lunch, I've found, is a wonderful discover-it-yourself project. In Paris, I've enjoyed bread and cheese lunches sitting on the bank of the Seine. On the job, or after a morning of work in the house, a light lunch out-of-doors can be an equally relaxing break in routine. Walk to a local park, or drive to a nearby spot with a pleasant view. No matter what you eat, good relaxed surroundings can make it taste better.

Some people find that keeping busy during lunch hour is relaxing. If you've spent the morning hunched over a desk, or at home in the laundry room, get out and discover something. Search the specialty shops for the best of everything. Find out where the best cheese in town is, sampling of course to make your decision.

Where is the greatest assortment of teas and coffee? Find it and spend a pleasant half hour or so discovering and enlarging your own tastes. Specialty shops, in addition to offering good, interesting food, offer a relaxing ambience. I find that when the pressure mounts in my work or my personal life, I get a wonderful feeling from discovering the first fresh raspberries of the season, the very first fresh asparagus. Seek, as they say, and you'll be the first to find—and be stimulated by your discovery.

The searching can be done at lunchtime, or the idea works equally well after work hours, providing you are fortunate enough to find some shops that stay open till seven or so. It's better to clean your desk than to rush to the market right after work on a tense day—a throng of harried shoppers is anything but soothing to the nerves. The housewife can also find that a change in shopping habits helps alleviate anxiety. Children—we often need to remind ourselves—are people, too. The standard supermarket can be boring to them, particularly since they are constantly reminded of parental authority. Told to behave and not touch things on the shelf, they often seem to go out of their way to misbehave. In the open air or farmers' market, there are sights, sounds, and aromas for children to delight in.

They will still, of course, require a watchful eye, but may well need less constant supervision. And many a mother has found that a fussy eater who shuns canned peas will be far more receptive to vegetables he "discovered" himself.

Buying food, or rather *how* we buy food, can affect how we feel. But preparing food and relieving tension are natural soulmates. The hectic pace of our lives has been the subject of numerous books and articles. The pace may be frenetic, but the style for too many of us is sedentary. We sit behind the wheels of our cars, on buses and trains, and at our desks. Physical fitness has become an obsession for some of us, it's true—but for most people, exercise is a planned activity rather than a natural part of life.

The match between tension-relief and cooking takes place right in the kitchen. The hostility, anxiety, and repressed emotions that may be making you tense can be "taken out" on the ingredients of the recipes you prepare and put into delicious meals. If you've been sitting at a desk all day, the physical activity that goes into a recipe can be an ideal outlet for excess energy—especially if you select activity-involving recipes such as those at the end of this chapter.

If we are active, we are less susceptible to tension, or at least to the problems it can cause. It is important to remember that life can't be problem free. Living, working, interacting with other human beings and one's own environment are bound to produce anxieties. A certain amount of tension is good for us. Nervous energy is an input source we use to accomplish things. The problem is what to do with the overload, how to release the excess.

One of the best ways I've found is through cooking. Since using cooking to help fight tension and anxiety starts with shopping, we should use it not only as an immediate relief, but in terms of planning. I know, for example, that in my professional practice, Mondays are very busy. In addition to my normal schedule of appointments, there are always several patients who either suffered a slight accident over the weekend, or who tried to wait out a cold or some other problem on Saturday and Sunday. As a result, Monday means running late, handling an overload of patients—and an overload of tension.

The last thing I want to do after a long and trying Monday in the office (remember that doctors don't get a lunch hour—at least not this doctor) is to face the problem of playing "Beat the Clock" in trying to get to the stores before they close. I stock up on Saturday. If you know you're going to have a tough meeting or a long hard day of housework with no respite for a shopping break, do yourself a favor and shop the day before.

When you step into your kitchen, you should be in another world—at the very least another atmosphere. The kind of food that's best to prepare on a day when you're feeling tense is, quite simply, the kind you like best. Doing something you like is never more relaxing than when it comes after a day of doing things you *had* to do.

Most of us, of course, like many different things. How do we go about selecting a recipe that will accomplish the dual purpose of helping us fight tension and provide a good meal? The best guideline is an on-the-spot assessment of your mood, and the type of tension that's troubling you.

A common cause for tension is unexpressed emotions. Anger, hostility and irritation can mount when we don't give vent to them, and for all the talk there is these days about honesty and openness in relationships, I know of very few relationships that allow people to tell their boss or spouse just what they think of him or her!

Some emotions can't be expressed; others are self-contained because we are unsure of just how to express them, or because we don't want to hurt another person. The kitchen is the place where emotions can be given free reign and tension, as a result, minimized.

I remember a patient of mine who spent an hour discussing the hostility she felt for one of the clients she handled in her public-relations business. The man, an actor who was starring on Broadway in a hit play, was impossible, and my patient was forced to grin (at least in front of her client) and bear his impossible mood swings. She felt tense and hostile, frustrated at being unable to release her emotions. My patient was a bright and basically well-adjusted woman; and at the end of our session she summed up the crisis in practical terms: "I feel like killing that man, but Dr. Parrish, I can't afford to lose the account. So I guess I'll just go home and have a good cry."

A good cry, I agreed, might help unleash some of her pent-up hostility, but I offered an alternative, one that I myself resort to from time to time. "If you're going to cry anyway, why not do it over an onion?"

My patient looked at me as though I were on the wrong side of the desk, and in need of intensive therapy myself.

"I haven't lost my mind," I assured her, "and I'm not joking. Very often I find myself feeling the same way. What I do is go home, and before I as much as change clothes, I start to cook. When I feel the way you do now, I make something that calls for a lot of activity —lots of chopping and cutting. I chop away at my cutting board, thinking of whoever or whatever is making me angry. You'd be amazed at how much hostility it gets out of the system, and you end up with a good dinner, too."

My patient said that she was more than willing to give my suggestion a try, but confessed that her repertory in the kitchen was very limited. Reaching for a piece of paper, I hurriedly wrote down a simple recipe for chili—certainly the most unusual prescription I've ever written.

The next day when I went into my office, there was a covered dish of chili, along with a note.

Dr. Parrish, the note read. *I hope this tastes as good to you as it does to me. You were right—making it made me feel a lot better, and I managed to "chop out" some of my feelings about that actor. Now tell me— what can I cook when I start thinking about how much I hate my ex-husband?*

The recipe I gave her makes two generous servings of chili that makes sweat pop out on the forehead.

CHILI

About 2 servings

2 tablespoons bacon fat
2 teaspoons chili powder
1 teaspoon salt
1 teaspoon hot red
  pepper, crumbled
1 cup onion, chopped
1 pound ground round
  steak

¼ cup ketchup
1 cup precooked red
  beans (or drain a can
  of beans, reserving
  the juice)
2 cups liquid (bean juice
  from above, stock or
  water)

In a Dutch oven, heat the fat, add the chili powder, salt, and pepper. Stir for a few minutes and add the onions. When the onions turn transparent, add the meat. Break up the meat with your spoon, until it's beginning to brown. Then add the ketchup and beans. Once this mixture has come to a bubble, add the liquid. Boil covered for 15 minutes.

It isn't possible to chop all of one's troubles away by any means—nor by any stretch of the imagination. But the physical activity demanded in certain recipes can channel your expression of emotions, and these recipes are the ones to choose when you have a case of bottled-up feelings.

Stews and casseroles are perfect choices, since they involve a variety of ingredients and a lot of cutting and chopping. Just about any recipe that calls for chopped onions is a good bet when you want to "let it all out" but aren't sure of just how to go about it—the tearing effect that chopping an onion produces can be the ideal catalyst for a good, much-needed cry.

In addition to chopping, pounding is a wonderful way to work out one's anger. Often, if a recipe calls for beef, whether it's for a stew or a steak *au poivre,* I'll buy an inexpensive piece of chuck, not only to save money but for the physical pleasure of beating it until it's tender.

When we're angry, we instinctively want to pound, cut and tear. In addition to do-it-yourself tenderizing with a wooden or steel mallet, you can economize on recipes that call for boned meat, fish, or poultry and add greater emotional satisfaction if you do the boning yourself. A very sharp (and very carefully used) boning knife is all you need. If you've never boned your own meat before, start with a chuck steak that can be turned into stroganoff. Mistakes won't show in your finished result, and you can work your way through other dishes as you develop your technique.

Cutting a whole chicken into parts is more a hacking job than a boning exercise, and it's a very good way to get rid of hostility as more energy than expertise is needed. Chicken breasts, on the other hand, require a bit of mastery with the knife, but it's easy to come by.

At least that's what they say! I don't know whether it's my medical school training or just the way my mind works (a bit of both, I expect) but for me, boning is one of the most frustrating, aggravating, and tension-making activities in cooking. I'm not content to just separate the meat from the bone. Instead, I become compulsive about it. I cannot leave even a fragment of meat on the bone.

I've learned, therefore, that boning doesn't relax me. I avoid it at all costs on days when I'm irritated and tense, and indulge in it only when I'm in excellent spirits and can enjoy my own idiosyncrasy. All of us have our special dislikes when it comes to jobs in the kitchen. Tense days are not the time to do them. Rather, they are the days on which to avoid any unpleasant task—and any recipe that calls for it.

Much as boning upsets me, grinding delights me. My mortar and pestle come in handy when I want to grind the aggravation out of my system (or at least try!), and in the process I make marinades and salad dressings. The full flavor of herbs and spices can be pulverized into a deliciously fresh dressing that adds the flavor of summer to winter greens. Grinding with a mortar and pestle is also a good way to deal with ground cloves, or pepper when they're called for.

The next time you come home feeling that you want to smash someone or something, you can put your urge to constructive use dealing with garlic. It's easier than chopping, and a lot more fun. Take a clove of garlic, pinch the end, and peel away the skin. Then place the garlic on your chopping block. Take a large chopping knife and place it perpendicular to the block, with the garlic under the widest part of the blade and the blade edge of the knife facing away from you. The handle of the knife should hang over the edge of the counter so that the blade rests on the garlic.

Bring your fist down in one swift, smashing motion, with the force of the anger inside yourself. The first few times you try this technique you should be very careful; you'll quickly get the knack, though. Should you want to practice with no particular recipe in mind, feel free—the garlic can always be placed with some corn oil in a bottle. The result, after a few weeks, will be a garlic-flavored cooking oil that can be used for sautéing.

Beating is still another outlet for the emotions. Using a wire whisk or a wooden spoon, knock some sense into egg whites for a meringue. Or attack a bowl of corn-meal combined with boiling water. You'll end up with a mush that I use as a crust for my Hot Tamale Pie, and one that can easily be adapted to other casserole dishes.

HOT TAMALE PIE

Serves 2 to 3

Just how hot your tamale pie is depends on how much red pepper you use; personally, I vary the amount to match my temper! My favorite part of the recipe is the satisfaction I get at watching the instant reaction between the cornmeal and the boiling water.

1 pound ground chuck steak	2 cloves crushed garlic
1½ tablespoons vegetable oil	½ cup chopped celery
1 teaspoon salt	1 cup chopped onion
1 teaspoon crumbled hot red pepper	1 cup chopped green pepper
2 packages (individual servings) instant beef broth	¼ cup tomato purée
	1 cup grated cheddar cheese

Crust:

1½ cups yellow cornmeal	¾ teaspoon baking powder
1¼ teaspoons salt	2¼ cups boiling water

Place the ground meat in an iron skillet, and place in an oven preheated to 200 degrees for 10 minutes. Remove and set aside. Pour the vegetable oil into a Dutch oven, and sprinkle the salt, red pepper, beef broth powder, and garlic. Over a medium heat, sauté the vegetables and tomato purée for ten minutes, stirring occasionally with a wooden spoon. Pour the fat off the ground meat, and add it to the vegetables, sautéing for another ten minutes. Turn off flame. Stir in the grated cheese. Raise oven temperature to 400.

As the oven heats, combine the cornmeal, salt, and baking powder with the boiling water. Mix vigorously (with a wooden spoon) and pour the cornmeal mixture over the meat and vegetables. Place in oven, baking uncovered at 400 for fifteen minutes. Decorate with strips of green pepper and/or sprinkled paprika or chili powder if you wish.

NOTE: This recipe is very economical, and a little meat goes a long way. For further budget stretching, it's possible to stir in a cup of corn chips just before the cornmeal topping is added.

For me, a lot of tension and aggravation is caused by machines. The kitchen is the place where I strike back at the vending machines that always seem to break just when I've put my quarter in, the appliances that fail me when I need them most, and most of all my dreaded enemy the telephone. Mere words can't express my loathing for that particular instrument, which always seems to ring at the most inappropriate times.

With kitchen machinery, man is decidedly—or should be—the master. Using my blender never fails to put the "machine problem" in the proper perspective for me; when I see a variety of ingredients combined into a blended mass with a smooth, even texture, I realize that while things may not always come together in one's life, they can be forced into cohesiveness in the kitchen.

In addition to offering the cook a chance to get some emotionally inspired activity out of his system, stews help combat tension in another way. Like Southern cooking of the slow-simmer variety—my Sausage, Green Beans and Potatoes, for example—they encourage relaxation. No pressure is involved in terms of cooking time. After the initial work has been done, the dish literally prepares itself over a very low heat. An occasional stir, at the very most, is all that's needed, and even that isn't obligatory.

SAUSAGE/GREEN BEANS/POTATOES

2 servings

Good solid food. A meat-and-potatoes main dish that's more than meat and potatoes. And a good solid recipe: no frills or flowers, but a couple of simple procedures that yield a foolproof one-pot entree. After a day of depending on other people's time—early patients, late deliveries—I like being the master of my own meal. This dish allows me to pay as much or as little attention to the preparation as I like, and without fear that something is burning if I become interested in the television news. A diet-conscious option too: The sliced sausage can be simmered in boiling water and the fat drained off before mixing with the beans.

½ pound sausage, sliced   2 cups vegetable stock
1 pound green beans   or water
                                        6 to 8 new potatoes

Boil the sausage or not, depending on your whim or cholesterol count. Stir together sausage, beans and stock, and bring to a boil. Let it simmer as long as you like, until you are ready to add the potatoes. Simply place the scrubbed potatoes on top of the rest and cover the pot. The potatoes will be beautifully steamed in approximately 30 minutes.

In so many areas of life, time is a dictator. It's a welcome change, particularly in the kitchen where the clock, in many cases, must be watched, to make something that can sit, simmer and wait until we're damn good and ready to eat it!

Since tension is a physical and mental response to pressure, there is no point in making matters worse for yourself on a day when you're already aggravated by selecting a recipe that will imprison you in the kitchen. On a day when I'm feeling tense, you won't catch me timing as much as a three-minute egg.

Tense days are also a good time to use proven recipes so that the possibility of failure (and resulting aggravation and increased tension) is eliminated. If you want to experiment, feeling that you need the psychological benefits of creating something new, read your recipe over carefully to be sure that there are no tasks or steps which you personally dislike.

A friend of mine will do just about anything in the kitchen except paring. It's a less than inspiring task, to be sure, and for some reason she hates it. Certain dishes demand the paring of ingredients, but I'd never recommend one of these to her on a day when she didn't feel like performing yet another despised chore.

Actually, for some people those recipes that involve paring, peeling and similar forms of busywork are often an excellent way to relax. I put these unchallenging tasks under the general heading of "blueberry picking." When patients come to me complaining that they "can't stand" the tension in their lives, I find that they need some form of practical occupational therapy that presents little or no challenge, but is diverting. Jigsaw puzzles, filling in a children's coloring book and similar activities can help us forget our troubles long enough to learn the art of relaxation.

"Did you ever pick blueberries?" I ask my patients. "You go out to a blueberry patch and just pick away. Your hands are busy, and at first the physical activity becomes a point of concentration for your mind. After a while, you don't think about what you're doing. Your mind can unwind, and you can find yourself thinking about nothing at all."

Out-of-doors there are loads of "blueberry picking" activities that relate to food and help take tense minds off their problems. I have a friend, a prominent plastic surgeon, who leaves Manhattan each Friday for his house in Connecticut, and who spends hours in the garden.

Weeding, watering, and picking vegetables you've grown yourself is constructive, mind-occupying, busywork, and personally I wish that I had a garden to do it in! In the city, an assortment of potted herbs can help. Picking, pruning, and generally tending to my basil and oregano all relax me. The kitchen abounds with "blueberry picking" activities that seem dull and boring when one is in the mood for adventure and creative challenge, but which can be relaxing when we're feeling tense.

I find that the monotonous job of shelling peas is a welcome task when my mind is reeling with tensions I've brought home from the office, and I don't throw the shells away. I use them in my pea-picking recipe for Green Peas Perfection. I don't say that *I'm* perfect, but I do say that the boiled shells provide the perfect essence of the pea taste. And the recipe is ideal for days when you want a project to take your mind off everything.

GREEN PEAS PERFECTION

3 or 4 servings

2 pounds unshelled peas	1 teaspoon sugar
2 quarts water	2 tablespoons butter
2 teaspoons salt	

Shell the peas, saving the shells and savoring the busywork experience. Then, in a large pan, boil the shells in the water, adding 1 teaspoon of salt. Boil for an hour or so—as long as it takes to reduce the liquid to 1 cup. Discard the shells and boil the shelled peas in the cup of liquid, adding the remaining teaspoon of salt, the sugar, and the butter. Boil for 4 minutes—the peas should "pop" when bitten into. Serve the peas with the liquid.

There's lots of other "busywork" that you can find in the kitchen. Paring vegetables demands more effort than expected. Grating lemon peel, which can then be stored for future use, is another good activity. So, for that matter, is squeezing your own fruit juices, for both cooking and drinking.

Though I have a dishwasher, and will readily agree with those who say that cleaning up a mess is the worst part of cooking, there are times when the tedious tasks of washing and drying dishes are actually welcome. I will often wash dishes as I go along in the kitchen; it makes me feel virtuous, organized, in control. In addition this activity is of great value toward keeping the hands busy while giving the mind a chance to wander.

Medical science has established a number of factors that are linked to heart attacks, and we know that tension is one of them. Tension is a part of daily life, and to a large extent, it is unavoidable. But we can try to cope with it, possibly eliminating some of the factors that make us tense, and better manage our response to tension.

In the kitchen we can at least put our old enemy to work for us instead of against us, and in the process create meals and menus that help us to live longer and healthier lives.

CATHARSIS SOUP

Here's the moment to reduce the clutter of your life and kitchen without having to look at a single instruction to "light boil for ten seconds." And no half-teaspoon of this and two tablespoons of that, either. Just take the largest boiler you own and fill it up.

Open the refrigerator door. Take out that half package of wrinkled old bacon and bowls of left-over sauces and dressings. Also those tired vegetables and salad greens—and don't bother to cut off roots or leaves, unless bitter. Scrape out the remainders at the bottom of relish jars. Half a juice orange or a worked-over lemon —don't throw them out, throw them in.

Then take a look in the freezer. Liberate the Siberian wastes—everything that's been sitting in there for more than a month. Into the pot . . .

And the shelves? The cans at the back that haven't seen the light of day since Coronation Year aren't getting any better. Get out the can opener and remember to check the can for signs of botulism. Onions or garlic cloves that have sprouted; a spice bottle with only a few leaves hugging the bottom; anything and everything. (Some discretion is necessary. On my last attempt, I decided against some salmon juice, the can of crème de marrons I found on the top shelf, and a black banana.)

Cooking directions: Cover with a lot of water and simmer as slowly as possible for hours and hours. Strain and reduce the remaining liquid to desired taste. Then drink it as a broth right out of a cup, or for a hearty meal-sized soup add noodles, instant hash browns, or presoaked dried beans, and cook until tender.

Your satisfaction is doubled: a unique and nourishing taste, and the relief provided by dealing constructively with aggravating clutter.

SAUTÉ VEGETABLES OREGANO

8 to 10 servings

There's a lot of chopping and cutting in this recipe, and you can stir it whenever you please for good measure! What I like best of all is the fabulous aroma of this dish as it cooks—it forces you to take your mind from whatever is annoying you and concentrate on what you're about to eat.

2 tablespoons vegetable oil	2 cups coarsely chopped bean sprouts
⅓ cup chopped celery	3 cups cubed eggplant
1½ cups chopped zucchini	1½ cups wedged tomatoes
1 cup chopped mushrooms	½ teaspoon salt
1 cup chopped green pepper	¼ teaspoon pepper
	3 teaspoons oregano
	½ teaspoon lemon juice
	¼ cup tomato purée

Heat the vegetable oil in a Dutch oven, then add the vegetables, seasonings, lemon juice and tomato purée. Sauté, stirring occasionally, over a low heat for half an hour. This is an excellent one-pot meatless meal: economical and delicious when reheated.

STEAK AU POIVRE VERT

Serves 2 or 3

Poivre vert—green peppercorns—are not, I admit, the easiest thing in the world to find, but looking for them can take your mind off tension-making problems, and they're well worth the search. A chuck steak, even beaten tender, won't taste like filet mignon—but then you wouldn't knock filet mignon around!

2 pounds chuck steak	⅓ cup chopped shallots
2 teaspoons lemon juice	1 teaspoon salt
4 tablespoons green peppercorns	

Trim the excess fat from the meat. Combine the other ingredients in a mortar and grind with a pestle until combined—or until your arm gets tired! Beat the chuck steak with a mallet, doing a thorough job (on both sides) so that fibres will be broken down and the meat made more tender. Set the meat in a glass dish and pour the marinade over it. Let sit for 20 minutes, then spoon marinade over meat again, and leave for another 20 minutes. Broil the steak 8 minutes on each side.

LAZY MAN'S ROAST

You don't have to be lazy to cook a roast this way—
just in the mood for something that cooks itself without
constant supervision. Make sure that the oven is clean
to avoid a smoke-filled kitchen, and be sure your meat
is top-quality tender.

A 3½- to 8-pound eye   Salt and pepper to taste
   round of beef roast

Preheat your oven to 500, or the highest possible
setting. While oven is heating, sprinkle the roast
with salt and pepper. Place roast on a rack in a
shallow roasting pan, then bake in the oven for
exactly 4 minutes per pound. At the end of that
time, turn the oven off. *Don't* open the door. Leave
the roast in the oven for 1½ (for a small roast) to
2 hours (for a larger roast). The meat will be
browned on the outside, rare and juicy within—
and it will slice easily. A roast that has cooled (some
ovens don't hold heat as well as they should) can
be quickly reheated in a medium oven.

SEAFOOD GUMBO

4 to 6 servings

I learned to love the taste of this traditional meal when
I was growing up in Louisiana. It wasn't until I moved
to New York that I discovered how much better the
chopping, peeling and cutting made me feel on tense
days!

⅓ cup plus 1 tablespoon vegetable oil
10 tablespoons flour
1 cup chopped celery
1 10-ounce package frozen sliced okra
Salt and pepper to taste
3½ cups boiling chicken stock
½ cup diced ham
¼ cup water

½ cup chopped onion
1 cup chopped green pepper
1 hot red pepper, crushed
2½ cups cooked and peeled shrimp, coarsely chopped
½ cup shredded canned crab meat
Gumbo-filé powder

In a Dutch oven, mix the ⅓ cup oil and the flour. Stir constantly (and vigorously) over low heat until the flour is uniformly brown. The flour should be caramel colored, but be careful not to burn it! Add the onion and cook about 2 minutes, then add the green pepper and celery. Cook for 15 minutes, stirring occasionally. Meanwhile, in a saucepan, heat the tablespoon of oil and the okra. Cook, stirring, for 15 minutes. Sprinkle with salt and pepper, and add to Dutch oven, along with the chicken stock. Add the remaining ingredients, stirring. Simmer the gumbo for 15 minutes.

Serve hot, either in gumbo bowls with rice on the top, or over rice. Sprinkle 1 tablespoon of gumbo-filé over each serving.

REVENGE COBBLER

They say revenge is sweet, and "they" are right if they are referring to the classic Southern deep-dish pie.

I've spent an adult lifetime trying to recreate the favorite fruit dessert of my childhood—with little success. The critical problem is the two consistencies of pastry required. First, a regular pie crust—difficult enough for most of us—into which the peach or apple or whatever filling is poured. Then strips of pastry are dropped into the hot filling, much like dumplings.

My triumph over this obstacle: 1) buy a frozen fruit pie and let it thaw; 2) empty the contents into a lightly buttered casserole and hack it into large hunks; 3) bake as directed on the package.

An unconventional cookbook recipe, I'll grant you, but the results have been sufficient (especially smothered under first-class ice cream) to crown many a Southern dinner party in my home. Except for the time I tried to hurry the process up and found revenge not sweet, but cold in the center.

CHOKES AND PEAS WITH MUSTARD SAUCE

3 or 4 servings

1 8-ounce can artichoke hearts
2 tablespoons butter
1 8-ounce can sweet peas

2 teaspoons dry mustard
½ teaspoon salt
¼ teaspoon pepper
1 teaspoon flour

Drain liquid from cans and reserve. Cut artichoke hearts in half and sauté for 5 minutes in the butter. Remove them with a slotted spoon to the top of a large double boiler. Sauté peas for 1 minute, shaking the skillet to keep them rolling. Transfer to top of double boiler.

With some of the reserved liquid make a paste of the mustard, salt, pepper and flour. Slowly add the remaining liquid. Pour into the skillet and simmer until it has thickened. Then pour over the vegetables. Heat when ready to serve.

No stress, a little effort, and not bad coming from cans.

VEAL SHANK CHOPS

2 servings

2 veal shanks (cut in
    half), floured
3 tablespoons butter
1 carrot, minced
2 small stalks celery,
    minced
½ cup dry vermouth
½ teaspoon salt

⅓ cup parsley, minced
3 whole scallions,
    minced
1 cup chicken stock
juice from 2 pressed
    cloves of garlic
½ teaspoon pepper

Brown the shanks in the butter. Remove and reserve. Sauté the vegetables until soft, then add the
stock, garlic juice, vermouth, salt and pepper. Then
add the chops and simmer uncovered for ¾ hour.
Turn the chops two or three times. Cover and
simmer 15 minutes before serving.

The mincing in this recipe is a good outlet for the
finer anxieties. But remember you are still uptight and
make sure to keep the tips of your fingers out from
under the quick strokes of the knife. If you are particularly anxious, use one of those curved food chop-
pers with a handle.

SHREDDED SALAD

3 or 4 servings

⅓ cup mayonnaise
2 tablespoons herb
    vinegar
1½ teaspoons honey
1½ teaspoons salt
½ teaspoon pepper
1 teaspoon paprika

1½ cups shredded
    cabbage
1½ cups shredded
    carrots
⅓ cup raisins
½ cup apples, shredded

Make a dressing of the first 6 ingredients and pour over the cabbage, carrots, raisins and apples.

LAMB STEW

For yourself plus 1 or 2 guests

Hungry?
Anxious?
Cook this and get it over.

1½ pounds stewing lamb, cubed
1 bay leaf
1 teaspoon salt
½ teaspoon cracked pepper
2 beets, quartered

2 potatoes, quartered
½ cup sherry
2 cups stock
1 turnip, quartered
2 onions, halved
2 tablespoons cornstarch

Throw it all in a pot and simmer until you are ready to eat it.

LEMON-GARLIC CHICKEN

Serves 4 to 6

3 pounds chicken parts
5 garlic cloves
2 teaspoons salt

½ teaspoon pepper
½ cup lemon juice
¾ cup oil

Wash and dry chicken, then hack it up into bite-sized pieces. Mash and mince the garlic. Mix it with the salt, pepper and lemon juice. Pour over the chicken and roll.

In a large skillet, get the oil fairly hot. Drop in the pieces of chicken. Fry for 5 to 10 minutes on each side, depending upon the size of the pieces. Drain briefly on a paper towel before serving.

MASHED BRUSSEL SPROUTS

2 or 3 servings

If you don't like things mashed and you don't like Brussel sprouts, you won't like to eat this recipe. But you can enjoy making it.

1 10-ounce container sprouts	2 teaspoons salt
	1 teaspoon pepper
1 cup heavy stock	2 teaspoons lemon juice
1 tablespoon butter	

Boil the sprouts in the stock for 30 minutes. Drain. Mash the sprouts with the butter, salt, pepper, and lemon juice.

MARMALADE DUCK

Serves 2 or 3

⅓ cup oil	1 4- to 5-pound (Long
⅓ cup soy sauce	Island) duckling
2 cloves of garlic	1 bunch scallions, green
2 limes, juice of	tops only, chopped
2 teaspoons cracked pepper	½ cup marmalade, (ginger and/or lime)

In a blender make a marinade of the oil, soy sauce, garlic, lemon juice and pepper. Prick the duck well.

Generously rub the outside and cavity with the marinade. Fill the carcass with the scallion tops. Run a skewer through the center of the duck. Truss tightly with butcher cord, making sure to bind the wings.

Roast in a hooded rotisserie in front of a bank of hot, but not flaming, coals. Keep under the duck a pan with water for the fat to drip into. Also, have handy a bowl of water and a basting syringe to douse any flames. The skin should not be burnt (neither yours nor the duck's)!

Prick duck frequently to cook out all fat in the skin. Baste every 20 minutes with remaining marinade. During the last 15 minutes of cooking, coat with the marmalade. Duck is done when skin is crisp and dry, in 2 to 2½ hours.

There is no better treatment for a hard week in the office than charcoaling a duck on Friday night. Experience the relief as the blender decimates problems as well as ingredients. Invert reality as *you* do the skewering and trussing. Then with the out-of-doors as your kitchen, control the flaming coals. Relax as tensions unwind with each turn of the rotisserie. And finally, enjoy the marmalade duck; its glorious taste is your just reward.

JOE'S HEAD CHEESE

My patient M.P. promised me this recipe, which was her favorite home remedy in late autumn—hog-killing time when Joe was too busy to take her to the city for the openings. She never gave me the exact recipe, and I couldn't get a whole hog's head. So I came up with this, learning along the way that it takes care of a lot of time and a lot of hostility.

FIRST STAGE:

1 hog jaw	1 teaspoon thyme
8 pigs feet	1 strip cinnamon bark
3-pound pork roast	1 teaspoon fennel seed
2 onions, quartered	3 bay leaves
2 stalks celery, quartered	4 star anise seeds
4 cloves garlic	2 hot red peppers

Combine all these ingredients, cover with water and boil until the meat begins to fall off the bones. Drain and reserve the liquid in the refrigerator. Discard the vegetables and seasonings. Cool and pick the hog pieces, throwing away the fat and bones, but saving the skin and meat. Mince the skin and tear the meat into shreds. Combine this with the liquid, from which the fat has been skimmed.

SECOND STAGE:

2 bunches scallions, finely chopped	2 tablespoons vinegar
3 garlic cloves, juice of	¼ cup Worcestershire sauce
2 carrots, grated	1 teaspoon salt
1 teaspoon cayenne pepper	

Combine these ingredients with the meat and liquid from the first stage. Boil until very little liquid is left. (If you suspect that Joe's head is not going to stick together, dissolve a package of gelatin in ¼ cup cold water and add.) Spoon into several containers and refrigerate. When ready to serve, place containers briefly in hot water and unmold.

At least one container should be frozen to be served on New Year's Day with "Hoppin' John," a combination of rice and black-eyed peas. Down South, if you eat Black-Eyed Peas on New Year's Day, you'll have good luck the rest of the year. Possibly this will work in other parts of the country too.

BLACK-EYED PEAS

2 servings

Since outside of the South Black-Eyed Peas is considered a quaint dish of questionable edibility, I think it only fair to cook it Southern style—well-done. Other cooks may object to this preference, but they won't object to the variety of peas—purple-hull, field, cow, butter, and speckled—that are available south of the Mason-Dixon Line to relieve the boredom of the common green pea.

These special peas are best when fresh, but better dried or canned than never. They taste so good it is easy to forget they were originally grown as pasturage for swine. But so were peanuts.

1½ cups black-eyed peas	½ cup chopped onions
4 cups water or stock	½ teaspoon salt
¼ pound salted pork (fat back or streak o' lean)	½ teaspoon pepper (black or white)

Put all the ingredients in a generous saucepan and simmer until the peas are tender; how long depends on the type of pea you use. They are done when their skins are about to pop. Some additional liquid may be necessary.

OMELET OF CHOICE

Omelets are fancy scrambled eggs. As a rule things fancy taste and look better, and are also more trouble to prepare. An omelet is an exception—once you have gotten the knack. Not only does it have a special taste and texture, it is quick to make and can easily be suited to individual tastes.

Furthermore, the skill is something to be proud of. I am still putting in hours in the kitchen, trying to make the classic rolled omelet described so well in *Mastering the Art of French Cooking*. But meanwhile I, like you, can serve individual breakfasts, lunches or suppers with the following recipe and have more time to spend in the yard.

Per person, depending on his/her appetite

2 to 3 eggs	⅛ teaspoon salt
1 tablespoon butter	1 pinch pepper

Herbs, cheese, meat, vegetables or mixtures thereof (1½ teaspoons dried herbs to 1 tablespoon fresh herbs, to ¼ cup cheeses or meat, to ½ cup minced vegetables).

Approximate how many eggs you are going to need and beat them with proportionate amounts of salt and pepper in a big bowl.

Chop the herbs, grate the cheese, crumble the meat, chop the vegetables and put them in separate bowls near the stove. Let each guest choose the type of omelet he wants. Then cook it and slide it onto a warm plate. But cooking it, that's the sticky part.

Melt the butter in a specially seasoned pan, re-served for omelets. If you do not have this, try any big skillet. Don't worry; it is going to *taste* fine.

Let him who criticizes make a better one—and you be happy to take a lesson. Get the butter very hot and coat the bottom and sides of the pan. When the butter is about ready to brown, take a kitchen ladle full of beaten eggs and pour into the pan. Immediately start shaking the pan with one hand and scattering the eggs over the bottom of the pan with the other. Inside of mere seconds, they are cooking.

Lay down your fork; tilt the skillet backwards so that only part of the skillet, near the handle, rests on the burner. Use your other hand to sprinkle at this end the chosen ingredients. Lower the pan so that it is flat on the burner. Pick up your fork and start to roll the egg and extra ingredients toward the far side of the pan. As you roll, lift the handle part of the pan off the heat. By the time you have scrambled, or better yet rolled, all the omelet to the other side it is done and ready to be turned out onto a warm plate.

THE TRIBAL POT

The unglazed clay pot, an ancient instrument of cookery, has recently enjoyed a revival, and rightfully. Our ancestors could regulate their lives better than their fires, which the pot miraculously adjusted to. Today we can regulate our fire but we can't regulate our lives. The clay pot somehow adjusts to this modern chaos; we can stuff it hectically, then neglect it for an hour or so and it obligingly presents us with sausage and chicken, salad greens and carrots, potatoes and rice —all done to a turn.

If you can't wrap it all up and bake it in the glowing embers of a tribal fire, try the following recipe in an unglazed terra cotta pot.

⅔ cup rice
⅓ pound sausage, sliced
2 celery stalks, quartered
4 carrots, quartered
2 green peppers, sliced
1 potato, quartered
1 pound chicken parts
8 shallots, peeled

2 cups chopped salad
  greens
½ teaspoon thyme
1 teaspoon cumin
½ teaspoon pepper
1 teaspoon salt
1¼ cups stock

Line a clay pot with oiled paper. Spread the rice over the bottom, then add in order, the sausage, celery, carrots, shallots, green pepper, potato and chicken parts.

Mix the herbs and spices in the stock and pour over the other ingredients. Cover and bake in a 350 degree oven for 1 hour.

STRAWBERRY ICE

For 2 or 3

You've been infuriated for the last time by the basket of strawberries with the green and/or soft ones hidden underneath. This delicious dessert is an exercise in selection, with the good strawberries lightly chopped and the bad ones given the full zap by the vicious blender.

1 pint of strawberries
½ cup orange juice

1 cup sour cream
⅓ cup sugar

Reward your friends and confound your enemies: the bad half of the strawberries go right into a saucepan with the orange juice. Cover pan and simmer for five minutes. Add mixture to the sour cream and liquify both in the blender. Add the sugar and the better strawberries. Blend on lowest speed for just a few seconds. Freeze. (Stirring the mixture occasionally as it's freezing will prevent icing.)

4

On Top of the World— and How Not to Fall Off

A GARDEN, or a look at the greengrocer's stock, or the contents of the produce section of the supermarket all serve to illustrate a simple fact: nothing lasts forever. Summer squash doesn't grow in the winter. Asparagus, raspberries and many of the other foods we eat have their time—and that time passes.

We've mentioned depressions, which come and go, but we must face the fact that good moods are the same way: they come and they go, often without our knowing why. Just as the biocycle presents us with periods when we feel sad or anxious with no apparent reason, it also gives us times when we feel on top of the world. Depressions may be caused by specific factors—so can periods of elation. A promotion, a "good break," good news in the family or something pleasant happening to a friend or loved one can add to our own sense of well-being.

If depressions are to be minimized and worked through, then it stands to reason that good moods should be maximized and worked for. Most of us, however, seem to take them for granted. We like to think that elation is a natural state of being, something we're entitled to by the sheer fact of our existence.

Every doctor faces this type of behavior in his practice more frequently than he would like to admit. Patients who are feeling well don't come in for checkups. If they do show up at the office, they often balk at the suggestion of tests or preventative approaches to health management.

"Come on, doc," the standard response goes. "I don't need to worry about my cholesterol. You just told me that I'm healthy, and besides, I feel great!"

It's good to hear, of course, that my services aren't required, at least for the moment, but my reaction is always tempered by a kind of indignation. The times when we're feeling our best *shouldn't* be taken for granted. Instead, these are the precise times when we should use that elusive feeling of well-being to help ourselves feel better longer!

The pens I use at my office (the pens I am happy to have my patients "borrow") all carry the same imprinted message: Preventive Medicine Is The Best Medicine. But I think I'd be happier about losing so many pens if more of my patients would read them as well as write with them!

I admit that the temptation to just enjoy is very strong. So much of life is filled with problems and tensions that when we have a respite from them, we welcome the escape. When we feel well, we don't want to think about being sick. When we're happy, we don't want to think about being sad. But being an adult means viewing life on a long-term, rather than a day-to-day basis, recognizing that we are all subject to swings of mood, to periods of good health and periods of sickness.

Putting that knowledge to use—thinking ahead when we're feeling our best and recognizing that we won't always be feeling as well as we do at that moment— may seem at first like a sacrifice. We're healthy and we're happy, we reason. Why sacrifice even a fraction of happiness, of pleasure and enjoyment of the moment, to thinking about the future. The answer is simple and practical: because it pays off!

To get the most out of a good mood, we have to be willing to give a little, and to temper our natural reactions with good sense and reasoning. A feeling of elation is often accompanied by a kind of hedonism, and as a doctor, I know that it is not only self-indulgent, but downright dangerous.

Ross, a textile salesman, was a case in point. He came to me with a variety of complaints, and his symptoms seemed to suggest a condition of diabetes. I ordered some tests, and told him to phone me in a day or so, so that I could give him his results. One day passed, and then another, and then a third. I asked my secretary to get Ross on the phone for me, but she reported that she couldn't reach him. His office had told her that he was out of town on a vacation!

When two weeks later Ross casually showed up for an appointment, I was furious. I asked him why he hadn't followed my instructions, and added that I was particularly disturbed since all he had to do was pick up the phone.

"Well," he said, "I really started to feel good the next day. I must have had a bug or something, Dr. Parrish. I guess it just went away. I figured that I wasn't sick, and I guess I didn't want to find out that I had something wrong with me. So I went to Florida."

I had to really struggle to control myself. I was upset that my patient hadn't listened to me—but more so that he'd risked his own health. "As it turns out," I said, "you don't have diabetes. But suppose you had. Wouldn't it have been better for you to discover it when you were feeling well, and to learn about it through a doctor who could have helped you manage it, than to find yourself in some hospital in a diabetic coma?"

Ross was shaken. "I never thought of it that way," he confessed.

He isn't alone. Most of us don't think of "it"—whatever it happens to be—until it's too late. And when we're feeling our best, we forget that there are times when we don't feel well. We disregard our health, our home responsibilities, and our futures in the abandon of the moment. Perhaps if we could change our thinking, the moments of feeling our best wouldn't be so rare!

I believe that the times when we're on top of the world should be times of investment. We should invest some of our time in tomorrow, making plans for those periods when we won't be in such good physical and psychological shape. This can be done without sacrificing pleasure, and in fact it can make us feel even better: we're doing something for ourselves.

Instead of opting for the obvious pleasure activities on days when we feel terrific, we should learn to spend at least a few moments on the future. Rather than lying back and just indulging that good feeling, as we seem naturally inclined to do, we should get up, get out and get some exercise—a prescription that all of us, regardless of age, can benefit from.

When I'm edgy and irritable, the idea of shopping is the farthest thing from my mind. I'm not prepared to fight crowds and clerks, and I'm certain that the store must be out of whatever it is I want to buy anyway. But when I feel good, really good, I make it a point to walk across New York, going from my east-side apartment to Ninth Avenue on the west side, where meats and produce are sold in an open market atmosphere.

It isn't just that fresh food is available (though the taste of fresh fruits and vegetables is, in itself, worth the trip). I know that I need exercise, as we all do, to keep my heart and muscles healthy. Like most of us, I don't always get the exercise I need. So on days when I feel healthy and happy, I realize how important good health is to general well-being, and do something about it; you should do the same, and walking rather than riding—to the market or wherever—is a splendid idea.

Like most people, I'm very easily tempted to self-indulgence. But as a doctor, I know better. That doesn't mean I don't have exactly the same instincts as everyone else. If most things are going my way, I'm very tempted to keep everything going my way: listen to my favorite music, see my favorite friends, and above all, eat my favorite foods without thought to cholesterol, calories or nutrition. But I try to fight that temptation —and you can do the same.

When you're feeling your best is the ideal time to take a look at your general health. It's the perfect time for a complete physical checkup, something that most of us neglect. Chances are very good that if you're feeling that well, nothing is wrong with you—but why not let your doctor tell you? You'll feel even better getting the word officially. And in case there should be some health problem, it's easier to learn about it when you are in good spirits. You'll be less likely to panic, and better able to view the problem, and the treatment, realistically.

Just as I recommend using a recipe card to write down factors contributing to depression, I believe that a similar card can be useful when we're feeling well. Try to list factors that have contributed to your sense of well-being, the positive things that are "going right" in your life. Don't be surprised if there are few that you can actually specify.

Then, on the reverse side of the card, try to list the things that contribute to your positive feeling because of their absence: Is the boss away on vacation? Is that pain in your chest that you've been worried about gone?

If you find that one or more contributions to your feeling of well-being is the temporary absence of some problem—let's say those chest pains, which are gone for the time being, or perhaps a problem in a relationship that you don't have to worry about because the other person involved is out of town—why not try to utilize your positive mental attitude and apply it to these very problems?

It's tempting to settle for "leaving well enough alone," but what is left alone will probably have to be resolved sooner or later . . . and the resolution will be more difficult if you have to undertake it when you are anxious or upset. *Now,* when you're feeling your best, is the time to tackle troubles. So do have the checkup you've been putting off, and settle differences that will have to be settled anyway. You'll find yourself more open-minded, better able to understand someone else's point of view. You may, for the moment, be on top of the world, but why not look ahead to where you are going? Look over your finances, and see how your money management can be improved. Look at your professional interests or career. Try to map out a plan for the future.

The best-laid plans, as we all know, can't always be followed to the letter, as often factors outside our control influence them. But a plan made in a positive frame of mind is more likely to be followed than one arrived at in desperation. In other words, use your self-confidence to further your own interests.

In looking over various areas of your life, look long and hard at your diet. For many of us, the words "diet" and "reducing" go hand in hand. Since a positive attitude helps you to be receptive to new ideas, take advantage of your frame of mind to realize that it isn't that simple. "Diet" means a pattern of eating. There are diets that are designed to help you lose weight, diets that help you gain weight (some people, don't forget, are underweight!), diets that are part of the treatment needed for specific diseases and conditions.

The individual who is in good health should look at his diet in terms of general nutrition and what I call Preventive Eating. This means concentrating on foods that are healthy and avoiding those that we know or suspect are linked to health problems we don't want to have to worry about. I've discussed this concept with many patients, and the reactions have varied. Ben, a forty-three-year-old stockbroker who prided himself on staying in shape gave me a very good and succinct argument.

"You know," he told me, "I used to really worry about what I ate. But nowadays it's impossible to know what's good for you. One day you hear that something is supposed to be good, high in vitamins and all that. The next week somebody's on television talking about some study that proves that whatever it was that was good for you last week causes cancer or heart disease or God knows what!"

Ben had a point. In our constant search for instant answers, we tend to exaggerate both the claims made for specific foods and the dangers of others—often in the same breath. Food faddism, once the province of little old ladies in tennis shoes, has become a national pastime. Frankly, I'm amazed at some of my patients. Seeing intelligent people risk the invaluable asset of good health in order to follow the dictum of some supposed guru disgusts me. The key to good, healthy eating is simple:

EVERYTHING IN MODERATION.

I'll never forget the woman who, at fifty-three, had been coming to me for several years. She'd gone through the climacteric, several colds and flus, and a variety of other ailments. "By the way," she asked me one day, as casual as could be, "I was wondering if there were any particular kind of food I should be eating, or avoiding."

"Well, you certainly waited to ask that one, didn't you?" I replied.

My patient grinned. "I was afraid of the answer."

The answers aren't really all that frightening, nor are they that restricting. To start off, if you're feeling so open to new ideas, write down everything you remember eating during the past few days. Don't try to fool yourself—just remember that apple or orange and include the cheesecake, the French fries, and *everything*. You'll probably find that your diet consists of a little bit of everything. And if you're feeling of well-being is strong enough, you'll want to work at improving your diet so that you can live to enjoy similar feelings longer.

How much fat is in your diet? We know that too much fat—particularly saturated fat—is a factor in many diseases of the cardiovascular system. The effect is cumulative, and as we get older and metabolism begins to slow down and general body systems begin to function sluggishly, deposits of fat can clog the arteries, causing circulatory problems and arteriosclerosis.

Learn to curb the excess fat in your diet. The saturated fats found in meat, eggs, and some dairy products can be reduced through Preventive Cookery—a form of practical preventive medicine. Learn to trim the fat from meat (roasts, steaks, stew meats, etc.) before it is cooked. Some butchers will do an excellent job of this if you ask them, but it's less expensive and more satisfying to do your own trimming at home.

Ground or chopped meat, too, can be healthier if some of the fat is removed. In making Chili, Hot Tamale Pie (see previous chapter) or other dishes that call for ground beef, I follow a very simple procedure for this purpose. Simply place the quantity of beef to be used in an iron skillet of suitable size. Then place the skillet in an oven that has been preheated to "warm." Leave the meat in the oven for 10 minutes. This won't cook the meat—but it will melt some of the fat. After the 10 minutes are up, remove the skillet and leave it on top of the stove or on a counter. Another 10 minutes will add to the collected fat in the pan, which can be poured off.

This process allows you to use the less expensive varieties of ground meat—chuck instead of sirloin—in your recipes while still keeping the meat you use lean. With steaks, you can do yourself a healthful favor when you shop. The top-quality beef, as we know, is well-marbled with fat, bred by beef growers to our taste. Tasty and tender as well-marbled steaks may be, they are also high in cholesterol. Lean beef, round steak, for example, is less tender than a marbleized cut of choice sirloin, but it can be easily tenderized through a good pounding, or with the help of a marinade.

And when you select what you're cooking, think about how it can be cooked most healthfully. Broiling hamburgers, for example, instead of frying them, helps to cook out some of the animal fat rather than soaking it in. The same applies to steaks and chops.

Remember, too, that in following a recipe, there is no ingredient as important as common sense. Your favorite cookbook or Aunt Tillie's treasured meatball recipe may have been written before we were ever aware of the potential problems that cholesterol contributes to. As a result, bacon drippings or some other form of animal fat may be called for when it's time to fry or sauté. Make a healthful change by substituting corn or some other vegetable oil—it's much better for you.

Use common sense to get as much animal fat out of your food as possible. If you are cooking something that calls for sausage, parboiling is the perfect way to get the grease out. Slice your sausage or pierce it thoroughly with a fork, depending on what the recipe requires. Throw the sausage into a pan of boiling water for a few minutes, and drain. You'll have that delicious sausage, still tasty, in your recipe, but you won't have so much of the unneeded fat.

In the case of stews, soups and sauces, there are a number of ways in which fat can be removed. The simple and easy process of refrigerating what you've cooked in a narrow container is perfect for things that are cooked a day or so ahead. As your sauce or soup cools, fat rises to the top of the container and can be easily removed before reheating. For on-the-spot fat removal, you can use a skimmer, but I've found that a baster, the bulb and syringe type, works even better.

Fowl has less fatty content than meat, so include chicken and turkey (the white meat is particularly low in fat content) in your diet. Removing the skin with a knife and kitchen shears before cooking chicken is a good idea, since most of the fat is contained in and under it. If the idea of chicken with the skin removed sounds unappealing, you should try the following recipe. It's full of flavor, low in fat, and an excellent way of getting acquainted with clay-pot cookery.

CLAY-POT CHICKEN

Serves 3 to 4

1 chicken (approximately 3 pounds)	1 stalk celery
	1 teaspoon lemon juice
	1 teaspoon soy sauce
1 tablespoon vegetable oil	1 teaspoon salt
	3 parsnips
1 teaspoon pepper	3 onions
3 carrots	3 turnips

Skin the chicken. Make a paste of the oil, salt, pepper, lemon juice and soy sauce; rub the chicken with it, inside and out. Stuff the cavity of the chicken with some of the vegetables—don't pack too tightly—and place the chicken in the clay pot. Surround it with the rest of the vegetables. Bake for 1½ hours at 350 degrees.

NOTE: Most unglazed clay pots require the use of oil paper wrapped around the chicken and vegetables. Check your instructions.

A bird that's going to be roasted can get the same skinning treatment, be rubbed with pepper, salt and some lemon juice and roasted to a tempting golden brown in the oven—and the fat in and under the skin will have been cooked away rather than cooked in.

Fish is low in fat, and rich in minerals and nutrients. Almost all of us could and should eat a lot more of it, and learning how to cook fish well is a challenge. Almost any variety of fish can be broiled, poached, or baked—but don't ignore departures from the ordinary, such as my version of the classic fish soup, Bouilla-baisse.

BOUILLABAISSE

6 to 8 servings

4 pounds fish parts (trimmings, heads, bones, shells, etc.)
4 quarts water
1 cup onion, minced
¾ cup leek, minced
½ cup olive oil
4 cloves garlic, minced
2 teaspoons basil
1 bay leaf, crumbled
1 pinch saffron
½ teaspoon cracked pepper
1 teaspoon salt

2 pounds tomatoes, chopped
1 tablespoon grated lemon rind
½ cup parsley, chopped
½ teaspoon thyme
1 teaspoon ground fennel
2 pounds firm fish (calamari, clams, lobster tail, shrimp, etc.)
2 pounds tender fish (sole, cod, flounder, bluefish, etc.)

Boil the fish parts in the water, uncovered, over a moderate flame until the total volume is reduced to about 2½ quarts. This should take from 45 to 55 minutes. Allow this to cool sufficiently to pick out the hard shells and large bones (the small bones will be taken care of later, by the blender) and discard them.

Sauté the onions and leeks in the oil for about 5 minutes. Add the garlic, tomatoes, herbs and spices, and cook slowly for another 5 minutes.

Add the sautéed mixture to the stock and simmer for another 45 minutes to an hour. You should have roughly 2 quarts of soup by this point. Put the entire mixture (small portions at a time, please!) through the blender to liquify. (This should take care of any small bones that were neglected earlier.)

The soup should now taste fairly strong, with some body but not too thick. If you feel the broth is too weak—use your own judgment—you might want to pep it up with some bottled clam broth.

With the broth back on the burner, add the lemon rind. Then cut your fish into good-sized filets and add to the simmering pot: first the firm fish for 10 minutes, then add the tender fish for another 10. Scoop the filets of fish out and place on a platter, then pour the broth into a tureen. Serve with Garlic Mayonnaise.

GARLIC MAYONNAISE

¼ cup chopped green pepper
4 cloves garlic
½ teaspoon hot red pepper

¼ cup mayonnaise (the "diet" brand you prefer)
1 teaspoon lemon juice

Run all the ingredients through the blender for a minute or two.

Looking back at my own eating habits, I suppose that my childhood "finickiness" paid surprising dividends. I never was particularly fond of eggs, which we now know are high in cholesterol, nor was I very interested in milk. When I started to drink milk, I began to drink skim milk, and frankly I prefer milk in a low-fat form to whole milk.

If you've been a life-long milk drinker, it may take some effort to acquire this slightly different taste. Make the effort—and start when you're feeling your best, when you'll be much more receptive to change. Besides drinking low-fat milk, learn to use it in your recipes that call for milk. You'll find, with very few exceptions, that it works equally well, and that the dishes taste the same.

Learn, too, to use the cholesterol-free egg substitutes for cooking, and for scrambling. It may take a little bit of doing to adjust some of your recipes, but the effort is worth it. If you *have* to have whole eggs, try to limit them to 2 per week.

Butter, needless to say, is very high in saturated fats, and we all tend to use too much of it. Corn-oil margarine has less fat, and works well in many recipes. The imitation or "diet" vegetable fats are also a step in the right direction. Unfortunately, many people refuse to use these substitutes because they lack that "buttery" taste. For these people, I recommend a do-it-yourself "diet butter." Simply melt a cup of diet margarine and add 2 teaspoons of the imitation butter extract sold everywhere in small bottles. Combine in a blender and refrigerate. Then use as you would butter or margarine —without the worry.

There are other ways of cutting down on the amount of butter or margarine you use in cooking. First of all, of course, are the "scrub-free" coated pans, marketed under a variety of brand names, that require little if any oil or fat to cook foods. Next are the low-fat cooking sprays that have a similar effect.

The idea is not to cut out all fats entirely—we probably require *some* polyunsaturated fats in our diets—but to cut down on the saturated fats. When you do fry, whenever possible use an unsaturated medium, such as corn oil, and use just enough to do the job and no more. Be sure, too, that you drain fried foods well, no matter what they're fried in. There's no point in having your food greasy, and certainly not in having it greasier than need be.

Next to fat, another enemy of good health that's found in the average diet is too much salt. Some people find themselves in health situations where salt is totally forbidden in their diets. *All* of us would do better to minimize our salt intake. The reasons are many, but simply stated, salt causes the body to retain water and creates an additional strain for the heart.

Never salt your food before tasting it, and when you cook, don't add the extra pinch for the pot!

Once again, the time to start learning to do without so much salt is when you're feeling your best. You'll be most receptive then to new tastes, and don't be surprised if you find that by not using so much salt, you'll actually experience the flavor of the food you eat. Who knows? You may even like it!

Speaking of tastes, we live in an age when convenience foods are steadily available. Use your positive outlook to see just how convenient some foods are . . . and aren't. The vitamin content of fresh vegetables is reduced when they devolve to the tinned or frozen forms. Use vegetables in new ways. Zucchini-Tomato Soup is an excellent example: flavorful, marvelously fresh tasting, and easy to prepare.

ZUCCHINI-TOMATO SOUP

About 3 cups

2 cups beef stock	1 cup chopped zucchini
1 cup chopped tomatoes	1 teaspoon oregano
2 cloves garlic, chopped	

Simmer all the ingredients except the oregano in a saucepan for 15 minutes, then run everything through the blender for a minute. Sprinkle each bowl with a pinch of oregano before serving. (For a cream soup, add ½ cup baked or boiled potato, crumbled, and ½ cup sour-cream dressing to the blender mixture.)

This basic soup is a good springboard to elaborate

on when you are feeling inventive. Hearten it up with instant bacon bits, garnish it with chopped green pepper, or dream up something different to suit the type of cook you are.

When we're feeling on top of the world, we're secure enough to risk a fall. A good mood invites experimentation in the kitchen, just as depression is a signal to avoid it. The man or woman whose emotions are shaky doesn't want to risk a failure in the kitchen. His happier, more "up" counterpart, on the other hand, can afford to try something that doesn't quite work out.

In my kitchen, new recipes are usually reserved for weekends. After a tense day in my office, I don't want any additional frustration or disappointment. But when my professional week is over, I'm willing to take my chances. If a recipe doesn't work out, it's not a catastrophe—I can afford to laugh at my mistake and go on to something else.

Use a good mood to try that recipe you've been thinking about but weren't quite sure you were capable of undertaking. A good frame of mind will help you to read the instructions more carefully, without problems and pressures to cloud your thinking. Besides trying someone else's recipes, be creative and put your own ideas to work.

I did, and finally managed to master the art of the soufflé. Probably most people have tried, and failed, with this most delicate of cooking experiments. I know my own cooking history is littered with elaborate efforts at soufflés that turned into puffy pancakes before my eyes. My Herb Soufflé is (thus far, anyway) an everytime success. Try it yourself some evening when you're prepared for failure but ready for success.

HERB SOUFFLÉ

Feeds 3 or 4

4 tablespoons butter
3 tablespoons flour
½ teaspoon salt
¼ teaspoon pepper
1 cup milk
½ teaspoon cream of
   tartar

1 tablespoon Parmesan
   cheese
1 heaping cup chopped
   fresh herbs (see note)
5 eggs, separated

Note: If fresh herbs are not available, try:

⅓ cup minced parsley
⅓ cup minced scallions
2 teaspoons dry tarragon
2 tablespoons dry dill
   weed

2 teaspoons dry thyme
2 teaspoons dry
   marjoram
2 tablespoons dry basil

Melt 3 tablespoons of the butter and stir in the flour carefully. Bubble for 1 minute. Add the salt, pepper, ½ cup of the herbs, and the other tablespoon of butter. Bubble for another minute.

In another saucepan, bring milk up to a boil, then stir into the flour mixture. Place over a medium heat, stirring vigorously with a small wire whisk, until the mixture begins to thicken. Add the egg yolks, one by one, while continuing to stir. Whip the egg whites with cream of tartar and an additional pinch of salt until they are stiff.

Grease soufflé dish with butter and coat as lightly as possible with grated cheese. (Set aside any excess cheese—don't try to use it all.)

Stir into the soufflé dish a small portion (about ⅛) of the egg whites, then add the remaining ½ cup of herbs. Gently fold in the rest of the egg whites. Put into a 400 degree oven, then immediately reduce to 375°. Bake about 25 minutes.

Serve with my Soufflé Sauce.

SOUFFLÉ SAUCE

For 1 soufflé

⅓ cup sour cream
½ pound tomatoes,
  chopped

1 teaspoon lemon juice
¾ teaspoon cornstarch

Mix all the ingredients for a moment or two in the blender, then warm over low heat until thick.

NOTE: This also makes an excellent sauce for spaghetti.

Since a positive feeling goes hand in hand with a spurt of energy, use that energy constructively. Find recipes that freeze well, and cook in quantity, thinking in terms of one for the freezer instead of one for the pot. Casseroles, stews and a number of other dishes are suitable, and though it may mean a little bit of extra time at the stove, that precooked frozen dish will be appreciated when you find yourself having to cope with the problem of a meal on a day when you are too tense or tired to cook.

Along these lines, try to prepare your freeze-ahead meals with fresh, in-season foods. Eggplant, for example, may be in abundant supply when you're at a peak of positive feeling. A few weeks or months later, when you're feeling depressed, a ratatouille or some other freezable dish that contains eggplant may help lift your spirits, as well as save you time.

While you're doing that extra cooking and waiting for your casserole or whatever to come out of the oven, why not use a few minutes to learn more about yourself? I'm not talking about some form of on-the-spot analysis, but about reading something that will help you feel better.

Many of my friends in various fields share a common habit: they clip and save articles about health from newspapers and magazines, but somehow they never get around to reading them. In part, it's human nature, a throwback to a basic fear of the unknown. What we don't know, we reason, won't hurt us; besides, if there's a health problem, the doctor will tell us, won't he?

No doubt the doctor will (as this doctor does), but a well-informed patient is a good patient, and generally a healthier individual. The more you learn and understand about how your body works, the better you'll be able to help yourself feel good.

The feeling of being on top of the world is, without qualification, terrific. I wish that I had that recipe for cooking it up at will, and for keeping it indefinitely. But like so many of the delicacies of the world, it is transitory, an experience to be savored—and used to maximum advantage.

POULAY AUDRAY

Serves 12 to 16

Feeling good? Have a party. A patient, well-known as a hostess, confided that this recipe, which for several reasons she subtitles Social Security Chicken, removed her fears of entertaining large groups. I have seen her produce this dish in what it would be flattering to call a step-in kitchen. The following recipe can be easily multiplied. It can be prepared ahead of time and heated when ready to serve.

20 broiler chicken legs	4 green peppers
20 broiler chicken thighs	1 16-ounce can sliced
⅓ cup garlic salt	peaches
2 cups whole blanched	½ cup strong chicken
almonds	stock
1 pound button	1½ pounds brown,
mushrooms	granulated sugar
2 tablespoons black	
pepper	

Wash and dry chicken. Place in one layer in large baking pans. Season on both sides with the garlic salt and pepper. Next, core then cut the peppers into rings and arrange on chicken. Scatter on the almonds and button mushrooms. Arrange the slices of peaches on top.

Combine the syrup from the peaches and the stock with the sugar in a saucepan and stir over a low flame. When smooth, pour over the chicken. Bake uncovered in 375 degree oven for 1 hour, basting occasionally. For the last 15 minutes, increase oven temperature to 450 to brown the chicken and crust the sauce.

Serve with green rice.

INTERNATIONAL BEEF

3 to 4 servings

Meat and Marinade:

2 pounds chuck steak (Argentina)

¾ cup red wine (Austria)

2 tablespoons soy sauce (Japan)

2 teaspoons lemon juice (Israel)

¼ cup coconut milk (Africa)

2 teaspoons vinegar (Germany)

1 tablespoon pineapple juice (Central America)

Seasonings:

⅛ teaspoon chili powder (Mexico)

⅛ teaspoon paprika (Hungary)

⅛ teaspoon cumin (Morocco)

⅛ teaspoon turmeric (East Indies)

⅛ teaspoon allspice (Jamaica)

⅛ teaspoon poppy seed (Turkey)

1 clove garlic (Italy)

½ teaspoon salt (Russia)

COOKING AND SERVING:

2 tablespoons cracker crumbs (Canada)

1 tablespoon ketchup (United States)

1 tablespoon sour cream (Poland)

1 egg (Scandinavia)

2 tablespoons olive oil (Greece)

2 bell peppers (Near East)

Prepare it as your fellow world citizen would. The English would let the meat get "high" before they cubed it. The French would marinate the cubes in a mixture of the liquid ingredients. The Indians would grind the spices into a powder. The Austrians would bread it with a mixture of the powdered spice, the cracker crumbs, ketchup, sour cream, and a beaten egg. The Chinese would stir fry it in the oil with thin strips of the pepper. The Spanish would serve it with saffron rice, and the Irish would garnish it with chopped parsley.

An excellent recipe for when you have nothing to do, your fancy is free and you are feeling ecumenical.

GRILLED CALVES' LIVER

For yourself

Your best times are good times to experiment with overcoming a childhood prejudice.

½-to-¾-pound slice of calves' liver

1 tablespoon chopped fresh basil leaves

½ teaspoon chopped fresh sage leaves

½ teaspoon sugar

¼ teaspoon salt

½ teaspoon pepper

Blend ingredients and spread over slice of liver. Grill for 4 to 5 minutes on each side.

COMPULSIVE VEGETABLES

2 or 3 servings

Play beat-the-clock with this vegetable dish—and enjoy playing compulsive when you don't have to.

2 tablespoons olive oil
½ teaspoon salt
¼ teaspoon pepper
1 pound tomatoes, wedged
½ pound okra pods, halved

¼ pound mushrooms, quartered
⅔ pound spinach leaves
2 tablespoons fresh herbs (rosemary, basil, and oregano or marjoram are an interesting combination)

Place the oil over a low heat with the seasonings and stir. Add tomatoes for 5 minutes. Add okra pods for another 4 minutes. Add mushrooms for an additional 3 minutes. Add spinach for the last 2 minutes. Serve in 1 minute. Flat.

DEEP-FAT-FRIED ZUCCHINI

2 or 3 servings

Using polyunsaturated oil makes this a good recipe for a heart patient—or you, if you don't want to be one.

½ cup flour
¼ teaspoon crushed red pepper
½ teaspoon baking powder

¼ cup egg substitute
⅓ cup skimmed milk
1 pound zucchini
corn oil for frying

Blend the ingredients together, with the exception of the vegetable, and prepare your batter.

Dip your sliced zucchini into batter and remove; place in deep-fat fryer on moderately hot temperature till a golden brown. Drain on paper towels and keep warm. Serve with salt, or salt substitute, and pepper to taste. Or as the English sometimes eat their chips: sprinkle them with vinegar.

STEAMED CLAMS

For 6 to 10

Sometimes I have been able to blend the imitation butter flavoring and margarine, or vegetable oil, so well that it tasted better than butter. If it is not well-blended it crackles and pops. So keep covered whenever heating.

⅔ cup diet margarine
2 teaspoons imitation
   butter flavoring
3 dashes hot pepper
   sauce

3 teaspoons lemon juice
5 dozen clams
2 cups water

Mix thoroughly in a blender the diet margarine, butter flavoring, hot pepper sauce and lemon juice. Transfer to a saucepan. Cover and heat. Steam the clams with the water until they open, about 15 minutes. Serve the clams in a large bowl with the clam broth and sauce on the side. Dip the clams in the broth and then the butter.

PHILIPPINE STEW

4 servings

Really a painless, flexible dish to feed a lot of people. This will serve four, but it can be multiplied to serve as many as you want. Cost will depend primarily on the quality of the chicken parts and pork chops you buy.

I have served it buffet style from the top of the stove in the kitchen, keeping it over a warm flame, with the rice steaming in a colander over simmering water. Guests can help themselves as they please. A large vegetable and greenery salad can be the table's centerpiece and accompany the stew.

1½ pounds chicken parts	4 tablespoons pickling
1½ pounds pork chops	spices
1 cup stock	⅓ cup vinegar
1 cup water	4 tablespoons cornstarch
4 cloves garlic	½ teaspoon salt

Combine all the ingredients and simmer over very low heat until tender. You may want to tie the spices in cheesecloth, suspend in the stew by a string, and remove when ready to serve. You also want to skim off most of the fat.

5

Cooking Your Way
out of Depression

DEPRESSIONS and recipes have a lot in common. Both involve a number of separate ingredients or components; it's not just the onions that make an onion soup, and while one major or minor event may set off a depression, a number of factors are usually involved, "flavoring" the mood. Taste ultimately dictates what we like or dislike. No matter how nicely a trout is prepared, if we don't care for fish, we won't like the finished dish. Depression, too, is a highly personalized thing. What one person may find easy to take in stride and cope with, another may find completely overwhelming.

Fortunately, we can choose what we're going to eat most of the time, thereby avoiding the things we don't like. With depression, and the emotions in general, it isn't that easy. Blue moods and deep funks have a way of turning up in our lives at their own chosen time, and so far, I've never known one to arrive when I could afford to indulge it.

A certain amount of depression is not without value in the general makeup of one's life. Like the combination of sweet and bitter ingredients in my Conflict Cake, dark moods accentuate the sweeter (and we hope larger) part of existence. The thought may be of small comfort when your spirits are sagging, but if it weren't for the days when you felt depressed, how would you really know—and appreciate—the times when you are happy?

Just as our society is obsessed with youth, we're manic in our obsession with non-stop happiness. Many of us so persistently seek out and expect a trouble-free existence that depression, when it occurs as it undoubtedly does in every life, makes us feel guilty.

"There's something wrong with me," patients actually tell me, "I feel depressed."

What, I ask them, is wrong with feeling a universal emotion, a mood that is as much a part of life as joy?

Just as cooks don't always agree on what a dish should be called (it's possible to find the same recipe in three different cookbooks with three different names), the psychiatric community has, over the years, changed its names for various types of depression. One thing is certain: a bad mood by any other name feels just as rotten.

We should, however, remember that certain amounts and kinds of unhappiness are healthy—natural parts of a life. It would be unrealistic to expect every moment to be joyful. In the normal course of daily events, losses and disappointments are bound to occur. As feeling beings, we will react to them, and our moods will reflect our feelings.

Reactive depression—feeling bad because something happened—is a natural response. Some doctors call this grief, and try to distinguish it from depression. The death of a friend or loved one, a serious illness in the family, an unhappy love affair, the disappointments we confront in our personal and professional lives . . . these things in varying degrees make us feel depressed. The basically well-adjusted man or woman may cry and feel saddened in a reactive situation, but he can function and cope with life.

When we over-react to a sad event, when our ability to function on a day-to-day basis is impaired, we are then in a neurotic depression. The obsessive-compulsive personality can be prone to depressions of this type. Supportive therapy is needed and should be sought when normally sad events overwhelm us and make us too depressed to function.

Therapy is needed, too, when we are unable to cope with endogenous depressions. These are caused by a number of factors, some of which—e.g., the realization that we are getting older, illness—we can trace, and others, cyclic. These cyclic depressions, caused by biochemical changes in the brain, are often compounded by our search for a single causative factor, when in fact that cause is as complex as our own body machinery and chemistry. We take for granted the misconception that we are "supposed" to wake up every morning feeling on top of the world. It's a nice idea, but things just don't work that way.

Just as the body has its physical cycles, the mind is subject to cyclic changes. Levels of chemicals in the brain can and do affect our moods. Infections and medicines can sometimes play a role in changing the level of these components of our moods, but often the changes are unrelated to anything we do. The best we can *try* to do is roll with the punches. If we can accept the fact that some days are going to be "up" and others "down," we can go to work and live our lives without serious impairment. It is a self-management situation. It is also possible for cyclic depressions to make us incapable of normal function; when this occurs, help should be sought.

Professional support and therapy are needed, too, in cases of involutional depression. This form can be characterized as a state of withdrawal from life, and is frequently seen among older men and women. They lose interest in living; life holds no joys, and there is no motivation to do anything.

As a psychiatrist, I am often asked when a depression should be treated professionally. The answer is simple: when we can no longer treat it ourselves. While

there are various types of depression, we must also remember that there are degrees of feeling depressed. If
we can cope with daily life in spite of feeling unhappy,
so much the better. If we can't, the problem should be
brought to a physician or psychiatrist.

In this chapter, we are not speaking of severe depressions requiring intensive professional treatment, but
rather the "blue moods" and just plain "downs" that all
of us are subject to. It is essential to remember that
depression responds to time. We can intensify our depressions by spending all of our time sitting around
feeling depressed, or we can wait for time to pass with
the knowledge that we *will* feel better. And as we wait,
we can try to keep busy and involved with life. Cooking is excellent occupational therapy for depression.

And when it comes to analyzing moods, the little
index cards you use for recipes can be very useful tools,
particularly when you aren't quite sure what exactly is
making you so miserable. On the right side of one of
these cards, try writing down the things that are wrong,
no matter how foolish they may sound to you as you
record them. Be honest with yourself and don't try to
think out reasons that sound logical; depression doesn't
work that way.

It's very possible that you'll discover you're upset
about a number of things, some of them major and
some minor. Perhaps little Susie leaves her bicycle in
the driveway. Maybe the next door neighbor's dog
makes a continual racket. Depression is highly personalized, and any reason you have—anything that makes
you depressed—is worth noting, no matter how unim-
portant it might seem to somebody else.

Then, on the left side of the card, note the things that
are going right for you—things you're happy about.
Maybe you'll find that there's more going against you
than for you at the moment, but study and look at the
whole of your life, rather than just the parts. Just as a
number of ingredients go into a recipe, a number of
factors go into making up a life. What "ingredients" in

your life can you change or exert control over? When you look at the pluses and minuses, rather than just the minuses alone, you get a better perspective.

The point of this little exercise is to show you that while it is normal and natural to think about what's bothering you and, in a broader sense, normal to be depressed, you shouldn't lose your perspective on the positive things in life. Something has to be going right —think about it. And think, too, about the times when you've felt on top of the world. Depression, in the basically well-adjusted individual, is a phase. Like all phases, it will pass.

I've been very disturbed of late at the proliferation in popular magazines of self-help articles that try to deny depression completely. If you're feeling blue and blah, their message is, get out and mix with people. Don't sit home and sulk. This point of view is undoubtedly well-intentioned, but it's very unrealistic. All of us are subject to blue moods. They are uncomfortable enough for us to go through alone: there is no reason why we should feel compelled to rush out and inflict them on somebody else.

If you want company, by all means have it. Maybe a close friend, someone you can really talk to and whom you won't feel you have to hide your emotions from, can help you. Or maybe, like me, you need time alone to think about your problems and solutions to them. There is nothing wrong with wanting to be alone from time to time. Grieving, feeling sad, and being unhappy are part of life. We need to acknowledge them, often, and flow with them if we are to pass through them. To deny them—or try to deny them—is to deny a part of ourselves.

Recently I was feeling depressed and, against my better judgment, let myself be dragged to a party by a friend who was determined to "get me out of it." Watching everyone else have a good time when I felt miserable only made me feel worse. I didn't socialize much but spent a lot of time eating, not really tasting the food

I stuffed into my mouth, but looking, I think, for a good excuse not to have to make conversation.

Overeating when depressed isn't a foible of mine, at least not exclusively. The depressed individual often goes to extremes of one sort or another. Some patients of mine have no trouble sleeping when they are unhappy. For many, sleep becomes a refuge from reality, and I've known depressed patients who slept twelve, fourteen, and even sixteen hours a day. Others tell me that they *can't* sleep when they are depressed. In the same way, some patients react to depression by eating too much. Those with a tendency toward weight problems are likely to find some spiritual link between sadness and sandwiches. Other people do just the opposite: when they feel miserable, they don't eat at all.

If you know that depression sends you to the refrigerator, stock it with slimming foods. Lean meats, vegetables that can be used for salads or soups, and fresh fruit should be on hand if you are the type of man or woman who tries to eat his troubles away. There's nothing worse than coming out of a depression to find that you've gained ten extra, unwanted pounds. It's reason enough to get depressed all over again.

Should you be the type who refrains from eating during depression, force yourself. You don't have to have a whole meal, but concentrate on foods that are high in protein. One-pot dishes, such as Steak and Liver Pie, are good bets, since you can reheat them easily for on-and-off nibbling. We now know that there is a close link between biochemistry and moods. Imbalances and deficiencies in body chemistry can cause mood swings, and it works the other way around too—the body also reacts to the way we feel. If you're depressed and don't eat, you'll make yourself feel worse.

The thing to do is try to avoid thinking of a sudden reversal of moods. Instead we should direct our efforts to coping with our depressed feelings and letting ourselves feel better when we can. Troubles and depression cannot be cooked away like the excess liquid in a soup or sauce, but cooking can help us cope. The kitchen is a good place to spend a bad day. It was once—and in some societies still is—the center of family life. Many of us grew up in families for whom the kitchen was a communication center as well as the place where food was prepared. Many a piece of good advice (and plenty of poor advice as well) has been passed over the kitchen table. Mollie Goldberg—and her spiritual sisters of every ethnic background—did some of her best meddling and "fixing" through the open kitchen window.

If you've made the kitchen a pleasant room—a place that you *want* to be in—it's a good place to retreat to when your spirits are sagging. One of the main things that attracted me to my New York apartment was the big, sunny kitchen—a rarity in any city. I loved that room, and best of all I loved the fact that on the days when I was able to get home from the office early, there was a splash of sunlight coming through my window. My herbs flourished in the sunlight, and so did I —until the property next to my building was sold and the small building that had stood next to mine gave way to a brick high-rise that cut off my view.

This unwelcomed change occurred just around the time my marriage broke up. Coming home day after day, getting into the kitchen just in time to see the last work crew knock off, I'd measure their progress and feel terrible. What right did those people have to block *my* sunlight and kill *my* plants?

I've lost the view. The building was completed in record time. But, rather than face a brick wall and the constant reminder of what *was,* I managed to change my thinking to what *could be.* I had some special lighting installed over the plants and acquired more plants than ever—enough to block out the offensive sight completely. It doesn't bring back the sunlight, but it made my kitchen a happy place for me again.

Too often in our lives, all of us must confront the sad reality that there is an end to all things. Once something is gone, it won't *be* again. The friend or family member who has died, the husband, wife, or lover with whom we've broken up, the promotion or professional opportunity that we didn't get—what is gone is usually gone for good.

Grief is a natural reaction, and it takes some of us longer to grieve than others. There's no set time limit, nor should there be; the reaction, like the event, is extremely personal. Often, too, we mourn not so much for what was, but for what might have been.

I remember Carl, a graduate student and a new patient of mine at the time, who came into my office looking drawn and haggard. His father, he said, had just died. I told him that I was sorry, and his response was direct and honest.

"I'm not," Carl said. "I don't want to sound cold-blooded, but he was never a real father to me. He was a drunk, and until he got sick he ran around on my mother. I used to actually wish that he was dead. I don't feel much of anything."

That was what Carl said, but his face told me that he obviously felt something. I began gently to ask questions, and he admitted that he hadn't been able to sleep since he got the news about his father, nor had he had any appetite. Carl didn't know it, but he was in a reactive depression over the death of his father. Perhaps he didn't miss the man, but he certainly was hit hard by the finality of death and by the realization that the father-son relationship he'd never had would never be. His youthful wish for his father to die was probably a factor, too: the little boy inside Carl probably felt guilty over wishing his father dead.

Depression often has a root in our past, and our past is a good place to retreat from the pressure of immediate crises and concerns. There is a good escape path—and it leads to the kitchen. I find that at troubling times, I can be distracted from my problems long enough to cook a meal, something that has to be done anyway. For example, when a stock of mine drops, I find myself wishing that I were a child again, longing for the time when the only connection between the words "stock" and "market" was going to the market to buy food that eventually found its way into the stockpot. On those days, I cook something that I associate with my childhood.

Hot Pepper Jelly is a good recipe for me on blue days. It's a taste that I remember from my family home in Mansfield, and I use an old family recipe passed along to me by my cousin Virginia, an excellent cook herself.

HOT-PEPPER JELLY

8 to 10 half-pint jars

When we find ourselves depressed over an uncertain, bleak future, it's sensible to spend that rainy day preparing a dish that will always be on hand in the months to come. Any jam or relish will do for an all-day, preparing-for-the-future project, but this Louisiana favorite is good for perking up any meal, and with very little work or time. In addition, a taste or two of the finished product is bound to chase the blues—and bring sweat to the brow.

1 cup red or green sweet peppers, ground with the seeds
½ cup red or green hot peppers, ground (canned jalapeño pepper, drained, will do)
1 cup sugar
6½ cups cider vinegar
1½ cups white vinegar
¼ teaspoon salt
1 6-ounce bottle fruit pectin
red or green food coloring

Simmer the peppers, sugar, vinegar and salt for about 10 minutes, stirring occasionally. Pour in the pectin and bring back to a boil. Stir in the food coloring, then pour into half-pint jars and seal with paraffin. Use as a general condiment—on meats, fritters, even sandwiches.

All of us have fond memories of something that mother used to make. Recreating it can help motivate us toward doing something besides just being depressed, and can bring back, through aroma and taste, a feeling of the security of childhood.

There's nothing wrong with escaping. And for a doctor, at least *this* doctor, there's nothing worse than moving an office. It's happened to me once or twice because of urban renewal and a growing practice. I could hardly ask my patients not to get sick while I moved, so I've had to carry on my practice and move at the same time.

Those moves were real crises for me, and I got away from them physically when I finally got back to my apartment. But my mind was still on and in the office until I discovered that could "move" it. France, Italy, North Africa—any place I'd been on holiday I could revisit, at least in spirit. I cooked specialities of the places I liked, foods that I remembered liking. Both cooking and tasting the completed result made me remember happier, even idyllic, times.

Pasta alla Opal is such a dish—one that I first tasted in Italy, and then recreated in my own kitchen. It's simple, and while the opal is supposedly the "bad luck" gem, this recipe has been the most consistently successful, extravagantly complimented item in my cooking repertory. I use it to recapture the relaxation and pleasure of that trip to Italy when I'm depressed—and to remind myself this "bad luck" can help things change for the better!

PASTA ALLA OPAL

This recipe is for one portion; let the state of your social life dictate the proportions you use.

1 teaspoon salt	¼ teaspoon cracked
2½ teaspoons olive oil	pepper
⅛ pound pasta (shell	¼ teaspoon lemon juice
macaroni preferred)	½ cup sour cream
¼ cup chopped fresh	
basil	

Bring at least 3 cups of water to a boil, then add ½ teaspoon salt, the oil, and the pasta. While cooking as directed, blend the rest of the ingredients and warm. Drain the pasta thoroughly, add sauce and mix.

One needn't actually have traveled extensively to benefit from this form of basic escapist therapy. Let's suppose that rumors of bankruptcy are sweeping the company and you are worried about losing your job. Or maybe your husband is off on a business trip and you aren't happy about being alone. Why not think of a place you'd like to visit—anywhere from Jamaica to China—and cook up an ethnic dish that will give you, at least, the flavor of your dream vacation spot?

"But isn't it wrong to try to pretend that problems don't exist?" a friend of mine asked me when I explained this idea. "Isn't it really healthier to meet them head on?"

Escape often is the best natural antidepressant. And while it's good to face a crisis realistically—head on—there are times when our heads need a respite from attack. Nothing can be said in words to explain the "blah" feeling of a depression we can't quite link to a specific event or problem. All of us are familiar with it. Something is wrong, usually *everything,* or so it seems; but we can't quite put a finger on the source of the problem. The emotions are jumbled. Guilt, hostility, anger, and sadness all may be present, and these feelings are turned inward.

When this kind of mood strikes, involving primitive and basic feelings, respond primitively. Comfort, the comfort of recalling childhood or a pleasant experience such as a vacation, isn't needed so much as an outlet is. The kitchen is a perfect place to raise hell. Anxiety- and tension-reducing activities that we talked about work well here; depression is often part of an anxiety-depressive syndrome. Chop, cut, hack and grind to your heart's content.

Do all the things that your mother wouldn't let you do in the kitchen—or that convention frowns upon. Eat dessert first. Cook something your mother or father or Aunt Tillie prided herself on—and do it better. Eat with your hands. When I'm the victim of an anxiety-depressive mood, I like to roast some lamb shanks and gnaw at them, holding them in my hands as soon as they're cool enough to pick up. Ribs work well too. Perhaps the gnawing and gnashing and the sheer mess of this kind of eating makes me feel like a primitive man. I know that it helps me cope with primitive emotions I might not otherwise be able to express and release.

At the end of this chapter you'll find the recipes for what I call a "Henry VIII Dinner." It's composed of the following: Lamb Shanks, Eggplant Thumbs, Asparagus and Finger Salad. It's easy to make, and designed to be eaten completely "by hand."

A very common cause of depression in these days of an ever-climbing divorce rate is readjustment to single living. When a partner—husband, wife, or in these days of trial marriages, lover—leaves home, many of us want nothing more than to move. The instinct is easy to understand, and its manifestation can be summed up in one word: *run!*

We want to change our dwelling place, our job and

our friends. We need to share a bed with someone else; now we sleep alone and the other pillow seems twice as big. Friends may try to be helpful, but we may resent being pitied. Even more, we may hate the questions many well-intentioned friends and relatives ask, and having to answer them when they want to know "what went wrong." There are reminders everywhere, and they make the transition from being half of a couple to being a whole—and single—person all the more difficult.

Around the time that my own marriage broke up, Louise, a young copy editor whom I've treated ever since she came to New York from her native Chicago, broke up with a man she'd lived with just about as long as I'd lived with my ex-wife. I was glad that she was the last patient of the day. That way, there was no rush, and over the years we'd gotten to like each other as people. Now, I realized, we were going through a similar experience.

"Well," Louise said, "I had a trial marriage with Chuck all right. We tried and we failed!"

Depressed as I was about my own problems, I had to smile. "At least he didn't get custody of your sense of humor, Louise. It's a big asset at a time like this."

She shrugged her shoulders. "Excuse me for being frank, Dr. Parrish, but try cuddling up to your sense of humor on a cold night! What can I do, really? I mean life has to go on. In a way, I'm lucky that Chuck and I decided to split before we got married. At least we saved all that legal mess."

"It sounds to me as if you're coping very well," I told my patient. "You're aware that you have a lot of time ahead of you, time in which you'll be able to have other relationships that hopefully will be happier for you. You'd be surprised at how many people sit just where you're sitting now and begin talking about a divorce or the breakup of a relationship by telling me that their life is over."

Louise smiled. "Oh, I had a few days of feeling like

that, but I wouldn't give Chuck the satisfaction by staying *that* miserable. What I feel now, I guess, is just kind of nothing. Empty inside, if that makes sense. And you know what the worst thing is, the time when I get most upset?"

"When?" I asked.

"When it comes to eating. If I'm in the market, and it's crowded, I just want to get out as fast as I can. I find myself buying all the things that Chuck used to like. I even bought coffee the other day—and I don't drink it, he does! When I cook something, Doctor Parrish, it's even worse. I know enough to try to keep my mind busy, and I think about a lot of things just so that I won't be thinking about Chuck.

"And guess what happens—I end up making four eggs instead of two, or twice as much salad as I'd eat alone. I try to remember to cut all of my recipes in half, but I forget sometimes, and seeing the extra food— Chuck's portion—just makes me miserable."

Louise had stated her case very simply, and I could empathize with her fully. Her experience was hardly unique. Almost everyone who has had to readjust to a single life is familiar with it. After a given period of time, the length of which depends on the people involved, many things become instinctive. It's possible to find yourself cooking for two without thinking about it, or even preparing foods that a former partner preferred and which you learned to cook out of love.

As I told Louise that day in my office, and as I've discovered in my own life, one of the best ways to handle this situation is through change. Most of us can't afford to move or thoroughly redecorate or otherwise get rid of the thousand and one reminders of someone's presence, but the kitchen is one place where we do have control.

Instead of repeating all the recipes that John or Mary used to like, find new ones. Experiment with new kinds of food, and new ways of cooking foods you are familiar with. Instead of wondering if the meat loaf will be "just the way" a former spouse would have liked it, try a *pot au feu*.

Pot au feu, a classic French peasant dish, is easily adaptable to what you happen to have on hand. My version, found at the end of this chapter, is a therapeutic as well as a tasty one. It's designed to let you literally cook the day away. With luck, in the process, you'll get your mind off whatever is depressing you, and one thing is certain: you'll end up with a delicious meal that will keep for days, improve with each reheating, and wait patiently in the refrigerator to come in handy when you don't feel in a cooking mood.

Aside from novelty, cooking new things helps orient you toward the future. New beginnings, don't forget, have to start somewhere, and the kitchen is as good a place as any. If you concentrate on a former mate's favorite cuisine, you let yourself in for a meal plagued by painful reminders. You are much more likely, when you get ready to form new relationships, to appreciate your dinners and those whom you invite to them if you serve something that isn't psychologically linked to the past.

Should you make Louise's mistake and overcook in terms of quantity, think constructively. Many foods are better the second time around, and that extra portion will keep very nicely in the refrigerator or freezer.

Depression is a kind of psychological pain, and this is important to keep in mind. If you turned your ankle, you wouldn't want to aggravate the condition by going out dancing. In the same way, don't let what you do in the kitchen when you are in a blue mood make you feel worse. There's nothing like confusion and chaos— looking for that misplaced scraper when you urgently need it—for pure frustration. Or maybe there is: dull knives! On days when you're depressed, try to make the time you spend preparing food as pleasant as possible, avoiding problems rather than creating them.

A good way to begin is by taking out all the equipment, implements and ingredients you'll need. Make sure that all of your knives are sharp as can be, and that the utensils you'll be using aren't in the dishwasher.

As for the recipes you actually prepare, select them with an eye on the thin line between involving and boring. Activity is a good answer to the whirpool effect that so often compounds a depression. We are depressed, and depression is characterized by a lack of motivation. Therefore we sit and think about how we feel—which is *rotten*—and start to feel even worse. Cooking (like closet- or drawer-cleaning, or simple paint jobs or home improvements) can be an excellent motivating factor in terms of getting us involved with doing *something* constructive when we're depressed.

Be sure, however, that you don't create new problems for yourself when you cook. Stay away from recipes that look too challenging—if you're already feeling sad, you don't need the frustration of a failure at the stove. Look for recipes that sound like something you would like to eat and seem problem free. Read them through—always an important step—to make sure there is no hidden trouble spot: a direction you don't understand or an ingredient you don't have.

Times when you're depressed are good times to repeat proven winners. Recipes you've prepared for guests and received compliments on can help you to feel better. As you eat your specialty, you can recall how pleased you were when people praised it. If you are alone and feeling sad about it, try my Treat-Yourself-Like-Company Steak. Instead of making you feel depressed about being alone, it enhances the situation. You pamper yourself by buying the very best meat you can find, something you might not splurge on if you were cooking for two.

Guard, however, against boring recipes—those that are dull to prepare, require a task you find unpleasant or monotonous, or that simply aren't appetizing to you. Maybe you have a bunch of carrots in the refrigerator and feel that you should use them up. Fine, if you want to—but if you're really not in the mood for carrots and don't feel like cleaning them, it's better to let them sit for another day. And though I get depressed when I waste food, we're all different. If you're tired of looking at those carrots or something else that *could* be used if you felt like it (but don't), you might get a lift from discarding them (with apologies to humorless conservationists).

Sometimes depressions bring with them an almost overwhelming kind of inertia. As mentioned, involutional depression occurs frequently in older people. They can, at times, sink into a state that is characterized by withdrawal. Life, they feel, is over for them—it's easier to sit back and not get involved.

The most dramatic case of this type I ever treated involved two elderly sisters, spinsters who shared a single room in a dingy residential hotel. When Alice and Evelyn came to me, at the suggestion of a friend, I was shocked. They were underweight, suffering from malnutrition, and showing signs of other problems. The biggest problem of all, however, was their attitude. Evelyn and Alice were lethargic—totally uninterested in anything, including their own well-being.

"What do we have to be interested in?" Alice asked me during our first visit. "We're two old women. We don't have any relatives, at least none who care about us, and we don't have any money except our Social Security. We're old, and we know it, and we're waiting around until it's time for us to die."

I decided to try a little verbal shock therapy. "You seem to have taken that particular matter into your own hands," I suggested.

Alice glared at me—at least she was getting excited about something. "And just what is that smart remark supposed to mean, young man?" she asked testily.

"You two aren't waiting to die," I said. "You're slowly killing yourselves. You have many reasons to be disenchanted with life, legitimate reasons. But, by not eating, you're lowering your resistance and literally starving your bodies of the nutrients they need."

"But we do eat," Evelyn insisted. "We—"

"Sister!" Alice interrupted, leaving no doubt about who was the spokeswoman for the family. Then she turned to me. "Young man, they have just raised the rate of our room for the third time in two years. Unfortunately, nobody is raising our checks! And while the food at the automat or the coffee shop where we eat isn't all that good, it costs money! And so, may I add, does this visit with you!"

Alice and her sister had too much spunk to just wither away, I told myself. As we talked further, I found that the two sisters shared a single room with no cooking facilities.

"Then you never cook at all?" I asked.

"Not in years!" Alice answered. "I don't think I'd remember how."

"Well," I told her, "you're going to find out. My first prescription for you is a hot plate. Get one today. And a skillet and a saucepan, along with a couple of plates. I want you to start cooking your own meals. You'll find that it's a lot less expensive than taking all of your meals at coffee shops, and the food you'll make —fresh food—is much better for you."

"But *sister,*" Evelyn said, finally getting a word in, "the management won't allow a hot plate—"

"Makes no difference," Alice insisted. "At the rates they charge us, we'll do just as we please."

I was relieved when she agreed to try my suggestion. I didn't delude myself or them for a moment—cooking meals on a hot plate wasn't going to turn back the clock for these two sisters. But it would improve their nutrition, and most important, it would get them interested in a positive approach to their own well-being. They began to come to me regularly, with each visit bringing me news of the latest culinary triumph they'd created on the hot plate.

One of my favorites was a product of their positive efforts at using up meat they'd have left over, either from a previous meal at home or one at a restaurant.

They even took to having a cocktail hour before dining each evening: one sister sipped sherry while the other enjoyed a martini, from which she never ate the onion. Both onion and sherry found their way into various left-over concoctions, like the one that follows:

DOGGIE-BAG STROGANOFF

Serves 2 elderly ladies

1 teaspoon oil	1 cup meat leftovers
1 cup broth, beef or chicken	½ cup long grain rice
¼ cup sour cream	4 martini onions, minced
	1 teaspoon sherry

Heat the oil in a saucepan. Quickly sauté the rice. Add all additional ingredients, and bring to a boil. Simmer covered for about 20 minutes, then turn off the heat and let steam for five to ten minutes.

My two patients at last had something to do, and creating economical meals, searching the markets for sales and bargains, became their favorite pastime. I've had few professional experiences as rewarding as watching these two old women, who previously were waiting to die, rediscover the pleasure of living.

And as a man who has to cope with the realities of daily life, with both the trauma of events and the biochemical mood swings that can be equally souring to the mind and disposition, I've found that while there is no single recipe that can serve as an antidote for depression, the kitchen is a place where I can take a comforting refuge on my personal rainy days.

CLAM BISQUE

Serves 2

It's fun to pick up exotic new recipes on faraway travels—and to recreate them, and their origins, in your own kitchen—but some of the best dishes can be found, as the song goes, "right in your own back yard." This soup, a specialty at a restaurant near where I spend my summers on Long Island, reminds me not only of the restaurant where it originated, but the funny story that accompanies my discovery of their recipe. A neighbor of mine on Long Island who shared my delight at this soup spent years attempting it at home with occasionally frightful results. Then one night I met the chef of the restaurant at a party and he revealed that his "secret" began with a can of minced clams. When I prepare it now, I remember not only the many sky-blue summers but also that depression—like "gourmet" cooking— can often be the trees because of which we can't see the forest.

1 medium potato	2 cups (16 ounces)
1 carrot	canned clam juice
½ leek (white only)	6 peppercorns
2 8-ounce cans minced	1 teaspoon paprika
clams	1 cup medium cream

Peel and slice into chunks the potato and carrot. Add leek. Put the chunks into a saucepan with the clams (juice and all), the extra clam juice, pepper and paprika. Simmer covered for 30 minutes. Pour into the blender, and run at a low speed for thirty seconds. Stir in the cream and reheat.

POT AU FEU

Cook the day away. When one of those days comes
along—and they do—my therapeutic version of the
classic *pot au feu* will have the day over and a delicious
meal waiting for you before you realize it. Shopping,
organizing, washing, peeling, chopping, tying, cooking,
skimming . . . and serving. The cooking alone should
take about 5 hours. The sizes and amount of ingredients
vary, of course, on the number of people you're having
in to cap your day—or the number of days following
you'll be happy not to have to cook. This is one dish
that truly does get better and better each time it's reheated.

1 gallon (at least) stock,
  salted to taste
1 to 3 pounds beef
  brisket
2 to 3 pounds fresh ham

2 to 3 pounds stewing
  chicken
1 to 2 pounds smoked
  sausage

Soup Vegetables:

6-8 each of carrots,
  turnips, celery stalks,
  leeks, onions—all

washed and
quartered

Herbs:

a fistful of parsley
1 bay leaf
3 garlic cloves
6 peppercorns

a sprig each of fresh
  thyme and marjoram
  (½ teaspoon each if
  dried)
1 teaspoon mustard seeds

Serving Vegetables:

1 per person each of
  peeled onion, carrot,

scraped parsnip,
turnip
½ cup green beans

Bring the pot of stock to a boil. Bind the brisket of beef with butcher's cord, leaving a loose end of string to hang out of the pot. Drop into the stock. Prepare the soup vegetables and throw into the pot. Wrap the herbs in washed cheesecloth, tie and add. (The stock should cover the ingredients by at least six inches at this point.) Simmer for about an hour, skimming the grease from time to time.

Meanwhile, bind the ham like the beef, leaving a string so that it may be pulled from the pot if necessary. Truss the chicken, leaving a string trailing. Add the ham and the chicken, and simmer for another hour and a half. Skim the top occasionally. Wrap all the serving vegetables except the beans in washed cheesecloth and tie. (Don't forget the string.) Add the serving vegetables to the pot and simmer for another hour.

Tie the beans in washed cheesecloth and throw into the pot. At the same time, add the sausage (tied with a string or not). Simmer for another thirty minutes. Each of the ingredients may be lifted from the pot by its string and untied for serving.

A delicious gravy is easily prepared allowing one cup of stock for each person to be served. Thicken the stock (with butter and flour) and add one half a chopped boiled egg per serving. Serve with noodles.

TREAT-YOURSELF-LIKE-COMPANY STEAK

For yourself

I'm a firm believer in fighting back the depression of loneliness by preparing an elegant dinner party for one. For me, that spells *Tournedos Rossini* for an entree— the dish that Julia Child says "takes the filet steak about as far as it can go." When I'm not feeling quite up to going that far, I've developed a simplified version of this most elegant steak with the ingredients all within easy reach of the can opener. And should your loneliness end one fine evening, you'll be proud to double the recipe.

1 filet mignon, about 1¼ inches thick, fat trimmed	1 slice thin dark rye bread, crusts trimmed
1 slice bacon	1 5-ounce can bamboo shoots
2 tablespoons butter	¼ teaspoon cornstarch
¼ teaspoon salt	2 tablespoons Madeira
⅛ teaspoon pepper	2 shallots, minced
2 ounces goose pâté	

Turn the oven on to about 275 degrees. Place the bacon in a pan of shallow water and boil out some of the fat, then wrap it around the filet and bind with butcher's cord. Heat a skillet with the butter, salt and pepper, then sear the steak brown on both sides. Meanwhile, spread the pâté onto the bread and cover with sliced bamboo shoots, reserving the juice from the can. (You'll have bamboo shoots left over, as an impetus for finding yourself a partner for this meal.) Place the seared steak on top of the bamboo shoots, and place in the oven for 10 minutes. While waiting, prepare the sauce, first dissolving the cornstarch into the Madeira. Pour this mixture into your original skillet, and sauté the shallots. When the sauce begins to thicken, it's ready to serve.

HENRY VIII DINNER

For 2, of course

The Henry VIII Dinner satisfies our most basic instincts; it's food you can pick up and eat with your hands. When you feel depressed, there's nothing like a little primitive munching and gnawing to break us out of our rut. After all, how much time could our Neanderthal ancestors have had to feel depressed? This dinner saves on the laundry bill, too; don't even bring napkins to the table, just lick your fingers clean!

Lamb Shanks

2 lamb shanks, about
  1½ pounds each
2 teaspoons salt
2 teaspoons pepper

1 tablespoon cumin
  powder
4 teaspoons soy sauce
2 teaspoons vegetable
  oil

Slice off the "flap" of meat from each shank and save for a stew. Then trim as much of the fat and membrane as possible; puncture the meat with the point of your knife. Mix the rest of the ingredients and rub into the meat. Bake covered in a 200 degree oven for 20 minutes.

Eggplant Thumbs

From McDonald's country to, more recently, France itself, the deep-fat-fried potato is the most common of all finger foods. Here's a fresh alternative, utilizing one of our most unappreciated vegetables, as well as an item I never know what to do with—beer that's gone flat.

1 egg
⅔ cup all-purpose flour
½ teaspoon salt
¼ teaspoon pepper
½ tablespoon butter
⅓ cup beer, fresh or stale

2 eggplants (roughly 2
  pounds), peeled and
  sliced into thumb-sized
  pieces
16 ounces olive oil

Separate the egg white from the yolk, and set aside. Mix the yolk thoroughly into the flour, salt, pepper and butter; then slowly add the beer. Set aside for at least an hour, or an hour and a half, out of the refrigerator. When ready to begin again, beat the egg white and add to the batter. Dip the eggplant into the batter and deep-fat fry until the crust is golden brown.

Asparagus

Preparing asparagus not only offers the pleasure of scrubbing all the recalcitrant grits of sand out of the heads, but also a satisfying noise. Snap off the bottoms rather than cut them.

1 bundle asparagus, large spears	butcher's string

Tie the bundle of asparagus with string and place upright in a steamer. Cook until just tender, 8 to 10 minutes. Serve with a simple lemon butter. Then lick your fingers!

Lemon Butter

4 tablespoons (½ stick) butter	¼ teaspoon salt
1 tablespoon lemon juice	¼ teaspoon ground pepper

Heat the mixture until the butter is fully melted.

Finger Salad

Our choice of greens for this hands-on salad begins with watercress. This seriously underrated delight is available almost everywhere and—more important—is easy to pick up. Continue with any or all of the ingredients listed.

1 bunch watercress, left in branches

whole cherry tomatoes

scallions, trimmed to leave an inch or so of leaves

radishes

mushrooms

celery

cucumbers, sliced lengthwise

Mix, add salt and pepper to taste—and eat.

BREAKFAST MUFFINS

Getting *into* the day can often be more depressing than getting through the night before. But mornings can be made a little brighter if you have some of these in the breadbox to help you get started.

First prepare the fruit-peel flour, with the leftovers from your morning orange juice (and the night before's leftover lemons!):

12 squeezed orange halves

12 squeezed lemon halves

Cut each half into quarters and dry on a cookie sheet in a very low oven for 2 hours. Chop in a blender. Spread back on the cookie sheet and keep in the low oven until dry. Then pulverize in an electric blender, or with a mortar and pestle.

2⅔ cups all-purpose flour

½ teaspoon salt

4 teaspoons baking powder

1 cup sugar

½ cup fruit-peel flour

4 eggs

4 tablespoons melted butter

2 cups milk

Sift together the flour, salt, baking powder, and sugar. Mix. Stir in the fruit-peel flour.

Beat the eggs well, then add the milk and melted butter and beat. Combine with the dry ingredients and give the mixture a dozen or so strong strokes with a wire whisk. Bake in a muffin tin at 400 degrees for twenty minutes.

COCONUT CHIPS

Sometimes with depression over a romantic involvement, or any mood directed at a single individual, it's best to take the direct approach. So buy a coconut, paint the appropriate face on it, then go at it with the hammer. When you're finished, use the meat for this delicious appetizer. The chips are a terrific alternative to salted nuts.

meat of 1 coconut   1 tablespoon salt

Chop the coconut meat into bite-sized chunks and place on a cookie tray. Sprinkle with salt, then roll the chips around to assure all-over salting. Bake in a 200 degree oven for 30 minutes, then turn off the oven, leaving the tray in until cool. (For those of you who might be depressed at wasting the coconut milk: substitute the milk for the appropriate amount of water the next time you boil rice.)

WHISKEY PIE

Dessert for 6 to 8

Until now, this recipe was a closely guarded secret of my cousins, the Durhams. It wasn't that they were intent on keeping the recipe to themselves, but being good Baptists, they were not supposed to partake of alcoholic beverages. Even Baptists can get depressed, of course, but a slice of this pie can make anyone feel better!

3 cups brown sugar	½ teaspoon nutmeg
1 cup butter	1 prepared pie crust (or
8 egg yolks	see page 47)
½ cup whiskey (bourbon preferred)	

Cream together the sugar and butter, then add in the egg yolks, beaten until thick. Add the whiskey and the nutmeg. Pour the mixture into a partially-baked pie crust (you can, of course, make your own, but since pie crusts, from my experience, can be very depressing and frustrating, a prepared crust works equally well). Bake at 300 degrees for 15 to 20 minutes.

CONFLICT CAKE

The beginning of some sorts of depression can also be the end. I refer to our recognition of what, for lack of a better term, we think of as the "bittersweet" nature of life. "Every cloud has a silver lining"—and vice-versa. It's the "versa" part that gets us down, the feeling that everything good that happens to us will inevitably be followed by something bad. Like most prophecies, this one can be self-fulfilling. So we find ourselves depressed for no particular reason, but simply because there seems to be no rhyme or reason to life itself.

I can offer no logical cure for this species of depression—logic and depression mix like oil and water—but I can provide a cooking therapy that will at least symbolize the dilemma. My Conflict Cake is truly the bitter and the sweet; each taste is balanced with a conflicting taste—sour milk with sugar, lemon with syrup. Act out this depression in the kitchen, and reward yourself with a delicious piece of cake (two pieces for serious cases).

2 sticks (½ pound) butter	2 tablespoons water
2 ounces (usually two squares) bittersweet chocolate	1½ cups all-purpose flour
	⅛ teaspoon baking powder
1 tablespoon instant coffee	⅛ teaspoon baking soda
¼ cup sweet syrup (maple, pancake or corn)	½ teaspoon salt
	½ cup sugar
	¼ cup Angostura bitters
2 tablespoons lemon juice	¼ cup buttermilk
1 teaspoon grated lemon rind	½ cup chopped nuts, preferably walnuts
	2 eggs

Set aside one stick of butter to soften; melt the other stick with the chocolate, instant coffee, syrup, lemon juice, lemon rind and water in the top of a double boiler. Sift the flour, baking soda, baking powder, and salt; then cream in the first stick of butter and the sugar. Add bitters and milk, and stir in the chopped nuts. Beat the eggs and stir into the batter. Pour into well-greased (glass) baking dish. Then take melted sauce and pour over the top; cut into the batter with a plastic spatula a time or two to distribute the sauce. Bake in a pan of water ½-inch deep for 35 minutes in a 400 degree oven. Scoop out with a spoon.

JUNIPER BEEF

For more than one

1½ tablespoons juniper berries	1 tablespoon cornstarch
1 cup white wine or beer	¼ teaspoon pepper
2 pounds thick shoulder steak	2 tablespoons butter
	½ teaspoon salt
	¼ tablespoon sugar

Pulverize the juniper berries. Add the wine. Place the beef in a bowl just big enough to hold it; marinate as long as you like but at least 3 hours. Drain off marinade and reserve.

Grill steak on top of stove for 5 minutes on each side. Keep in warm oven for 15 to 20 minutes. Slowly stir cornstarch into the marinade. Add pepper, butter, salt, sugar. Simmer until thickened. Pour over warm slices of beef.

The juniper berries might turn vodka into gin. But, it also helps to turn an inexpensive cut of beef into a taste experience.

MAGIC CAKE

2 squares unsweetened chocolate	½ cup sugar
⅔ cup honey	½ cup butter
1 cup sifted flour	¼ cup orange juice
½ teaspoon salt	¼ cup milk
2 teaspoons baking powder	3 eggs

Melt chocolate and honey in the top of a double boiler. Cream flour, salt, baking powder, sugar and butter, adding orange juice and milk; mix well. Beat eggs until light and gently stir into batter. Pour into well-greased, floured baking dish. Pour melted chocolate and honey over the top. Bake in a 325 degree oven for 35 minutes.

If you are depressed, you are probably counting on a little magic. This might do the trick. Even if it doesn't turn out to be white—or even black—magic, it is still sweet.

ICED SLICED CAKE

When your cream solidifies instead of whipping, don't be down-hearted. With a little ingenuity you can likely use it with the same dish, made a little differently. Like strawberry shortcake. Heat the whipped butter, half the strawberries, the sugar you intended to use, and a little orange juice. Cook and stir until well blended. Cool. Spread on the shortcake and decorate with the remaining berries.

Or here is a recovery recipe that will make you happy if the cream turned on you and you don't have any fruit on hand. You might even want to make the mistake again. This is not difficult: just have the cream and the beating bowl at a warm room temperature and beat until you see it begin to solidify. Keep beating, drain off the "blue john," and reserve the whipped butter.

⅓ cup sugar   a pound cake
the whipped butter that
   has come from ½ pint
   of heavy cream

Caralmelize the sugar in a saucepan. Set aside. Cut the cake lengthwise into 5 or 6 slices. Mix the whipped butter, the caramel, and ice the slices. Put back into shape of loaf. Chill.

6

Ruts and Remedies

A DOCTOR tends, not surprisingly, to think of "cases" in terms of his professional practice. However, I realize that one of the problems I frequently treat is more familiar to me in my personal than my professional life. I admit it. Sometimes I will leave my office on a Friday afternoon and take immediately to my bed—not to venture forth until it's time to leave for work Monday morning.

Maybe I'll turn the television on, but only as background noise. And now and again I'll consult my bedside refrigerator to check on the choice of beverages. But I won't hear the phone, unless it's my emergency line. Even food—my one life-long possession—doesn't tempt me. I'm not ill—not really. I'm not even particularly depressed. Unscientifically speaking, my ailment is a form of apathy compounded by a severe case of boredom.

What I'm doing, of course, is escaping from life. I'd be better off escaping to the kitchen instead of the bedroom—at least the kitchen would offer a chance for some productivity during my day or two of withdrawal. But, with the perversity that always characterizes this condition, I choose the bed. I unilaterally declare myself *non compos mentis.* I refuse to make any decisions save one: I decide to decide nothing.

But, while I may be alone in my self-styled "sick" bed, I'm anything but alone in my condition. Unfortunately it's all too timely, and its proportions in today's society are epidemic. Treating "abulia" poses a number of problems. There is no simple prescription that can make it go away. And patients don't do much to help matters.

"What difference does it make?" a woman whose obesity problem I'd been treating for several months asked. Susan, at thirty-four, had spent most of her lifetime being overweight and going from diet to diet, and when she first came to me, I felt that if I could just channel her energy and enthusiasm toward controlling her weight, we'd have the problem conquered. Susan had managed to get rid of 40 excess pounds, but in follow-up visits, I began to realize that she'd also lost something else: her interest in living.

"I'm going to run some tests," I told her, "just to make sure that losing that weight hasn't changed anything in your metabolism."

"Why bother?" she asked me.

"Well, I do have a professional responsibility," I reminded her. "That's one reason. But what's more important is *you,* Susan. When you came to me to lose weight, you were full of life. You knew that you were obese, but it didn't temper your enjoyment of the world around you. Now you've lost the pounds you've been trying to lose for years, and you seem to be doing very well on your maintenance diet. I'm very proud of you, and you ought to be proud of yourself."

"You know," my patient said nostalgically, "I almost miss being fat. To tell you the truth, Dr. Parrish, I really *do* miss it. I tried out dozens of diets, but at least it was something to do. Now that I've lost weight, I feel . . ."

Her voice trailed off, and I knew that Susan was

searching for the right words to express her emotion, or rather the lack of it. "Bored?" I suggested. "In a rut? Empty?"

She nodded. "It's like—well, this probably won't make sense, but when I sit down to a meal, I don't even want to eat. Me! And you know how much I love food, or at least used to. I know what I'm eating now is better for me than the junk I used to stuff myself with, but I keep wishing for a potato or a piece of bread—"

"Now wait a minute," I interrupted. "If you remember, we spent a good deal of time on what you should or shouldn't eat, Susan. And I specifically remember telling you that there was nothing wrong with a potato. It's the butter and the sour cream that cause the problems."

Susan told me that while she remembered our discussions, she'd heard from a friend that the best way to keep weight off was to avoid everything white—bread, potatoes and rice included. That piece of information provided at least a clue to the problem. Many times over the years I'd seen patients avoid "white foods" either to lose weight or to keep it off, and the effects often seemed to be averse, at least on the personality.

The reason for this, I've come to believe, is in part due to the absence of carbohydrates, but there's a visual element involved too. The absence of a light-colored food in a meal, and particularly in meal after meal, seems to be psychologically disturbing. My first recommendation for Susan was that she investigate some of the many recipes that use "white foods" in a positive manner.

I shared the recipe for one of my favorites, Crab Boil, which includes a tasty, flavorful potato that stands on its own merit, without the aid of fattening additives. Besides, the recipe is so large that you're almost forced to invite over a friend or two to share your meal—if not your mood!

CRAB BOIL

3–4 servings or more

2 tablespoons crab boil
  (shrimp spice)
1 gallon water
4 tablespoons salt

12 new potatoes
24 crabs, as large as
  possible

Add crab boil to water and simmer for 15 minutes in large enamel pot. Add salt, potatoes, and crabs. Boil until potatoes are tender. Serve with Diet Tartar Sauce.

DIET TARTAR SAUCE

½ cup diet mayonnaise
2 tablespoons fresh dill,
  chopped

2 kosher dill pickles,
  minced
¼ teaspoon salt

Mix the ingredients. Chill. Serve.

Helping Susan to realize that she could still enjoy her favorite foods—though not in the exact manner or quantity as she'd enjoyed them before—made her feel better, but it was by no means the full answer to her problem. Susan was in a rut: a state of emotional inertia. The psychiatric term is "abulia," (from the Greek *aboulia,* meaning irresolution: *a*—without, *boulê* —will). Susan herself called it "the blahs."

Though we tend to associate such moods with disappointment or frustration, success, particularly success that results when we set out to accomplish a goal and then achieve it, is often followed by an emotional letdown. An extreme example of this, of course, is the postpartum depression. After nine months of expectancy, birth can be almost anticlimactic in emotional terms.

Biochemistry can also contribute to the blue mood that often takes a new mother by surprise—as can the body's need to rest and replenish itself.

In the same way, giving birth or fruition to a project or goal can have an aftermath of disappointment. The executive who gets the promotion he worked hard for, the writer whose long worked-on masterpiece becomes a success, the man or woman who has waited and planned for a new house or apartment and finally moves —all of us, in one way or another—are subject to ruts and those empty, let-down feelings.

When a tragedy strikes and we react to it by becoming depressed, we give vent to our sadness and are consoled, to some extent, by the sympathy and understanding of friends. When we find ourselves in an emotional rut that seems to have no basis in recent events or external factors, we often compound our problem by keeping our feelings bottled up.

"I can't tell my wife how I feel," a patient of mine confided to me just a few months after becoming a full partner in the law firm where he'd worked for a number of years. "I wish I didn't have to admit it to myself. Here I am, a successful guy, making good money. I have a nice house, a wife I love, and great kids. Why do I feel so rotten?"

Howard, I knew from past experience, was an articulate man, and I gently urged him to express the emotions that I could see were troubling him. "Why do you *think* you feel bad?" I asked him. "I'm sure you've tried to find the answers yourself. Why don't you tell me any of the reasons you've come up with, even if they don't seem like good ones."

"It's very selfish of me to feel the way I do," Howard said, punishing himself. "I know there are a lot of people who'd be very grateful to be in my position. I try to look ahead, but I keep feeling that I've made my life —that the future is already there for me, if that makes any sense."

What Howard was feeling was a realistic emotion. He

was coming to terms with his maturity, facing as all of us have to at some point in life the fact that not all of our dreams will come true. We're all due, at some place in the emotional life cycle, to come to terms with this realization, and our appreciation of what we do have (and will have) is tempered to some degree by the knowledge of what we don't (and won't) have, or achieve.

I wish that we were better able to accept our own humanity and the broad range of human emotions to which we are all subject. Like Howard, many people simply cannot accept *not* feeling one hundred percent one hundred percent of the time. And even if we can be honest enough with ourselves about our feelings, we tend to remain reluctant to admit them to others, including those we like or love.

Result: ruts. Things have gone either too well or not as well as we would like. Often the world around us and what's happening in it, both in the broad sense and in our private lives, doesn't seem important. We're melancholy. We may be nostalgic for the past, or long for some present that exists only in our imagination. We're not really unhappy, but we're not happy either.

The individual who finds himself in this position can be further confused by his very inability to function. "Sometimes I think that I must be a mental case," Howard told me during one of his visits. "I know I feel a lot worse than I should feel, but I still go to my job every day, and put in a good day's work. I come home and spend time with my family, and I don't even think they suspect what's in my mind. It's as if I was going through the motions, acting."

I understood just what he meant. Someone once put it in terms of a TV game show, describing the feeling as "being a mystery guest in my own life." If its any consolation, doctors are as susceptible to ruts as anyone else, and the root of the problem can be equally mystifying. Every winter, it seems, I find myself in just such a mood. It can last for days, or for weeks—and I'm sure that if I let the mood run rampant, it could go on for months. Part of my problem, I've come to realize, has to do with the gray monotony of New York winters. With all the recent interest in the environment, the word "ecology" has been widely used. We think of it in terms of pollution and nature, but we forget another meaning: man's relationship to his environment.

As the winter drags on, I want the environment to change—but it has ideas of its own. One dreary day passes after another, and the only change that takes place is dirty snow turning to even dirtier slush. The worse the weather gets, the deeper in a rut *I* get. I'm sure that my friends wonder why, during these moods, I refuse invitations and do very little entertaining. I have learned to tell my closest friends the simple truth: my mood is so rotten that I don't want to inflict it on anyone else.

At least that's part of the truth. Another reason why I stick to myself is that I've discovered at least a partial remedy. On those dark, gray days when I seriously begin to think about moving—giving up my practice and my apartment and fulfilling my fantasy about getting a little house in Virginia—I can at least alleviate some of my glumness by cooking myself out of my troubles.

My Fowl With Fennel is a simple dish (I find that when I'm in a rut, I like to cook things that don't require too much time), but it's also a kind of culinary escape. Tasting this particular favorite never fails to remind me of the time I spent in Italy—in weather much more cheerful than what New York offers in the winter.

(WILD) FOWL WITH FENNEL

Per serving

1 tablespoon fennel seeds	½ teaspoon pepper
1 tablespoon oil	1 teaspoon lemon juice
1 tablespoon meat sauce (See recipe, p. 52)	1 small chicken, Cornish hen, or several gamebirds

Pulverize the fennel seeds; combine with oil, meat sauce, pepper and lemon juice, and blend.

Improvise a roasting pit by placing a grilled rack (like a refrigerator shelf) over a large shallow pan with ¾ inch of water. Wash the bird and coat with the sauce. Roast in a 425 degree oven for 30 to 45 minutes, depending on size. It should be turned occasionally in order to brown easily. The drippings in the pan make a very nice gravy.

SICILIAN RABBIT

Serves 2 to 4

Another favorite of mine for those gloomy days also comes from Italy; but instead of Northern Italy, where the spaghetti dish originated, one of the best tasting forms of rabbit I've ever had is Sicilian in origin. Fresh rabbit isn't always easy to find, though it's showing up increasingly in markets these days. Sometimes I frankly welcome the search—even if it means walking through slush-filled streets, it helps to get my mind working.

And when I eat Sicilian Rabbit, the mildly gamey taste is invigorating as well as satisfying. Besides, I tell myself, I may not be in the best mood, but at least I'm more fortunate than the rabbit . . .

2 pounds rabbit, quartered	2 cloves garlic, minced or pressed
1 6-ounce can pitted ripe olives	1 teaspoon salt
1 tablespoon vinegar	½ teaspoon pepper
⅔ cup chopped fresh mint	2½ cups stock
	1 cup water
	2 tablespoons flour

Put all the ingredients except the flour in a Dutch oven and simmer uncovered for 1½ hours. Remove rabbit and let cool. Make a paste with flour and 2 tablespoons cool broth. Slowly stir into the pot. Pick the meat off the rabbit, making sure to remove small bones. Add to the pot and simmer covered for ½ hour.

In cooking (and eating) your way out of a rut, try to avoid your usual repertory of menus. There may be many factors in your life that you can't change, but there are others, including the food you eat, that you can vary to your heart's content. Take advantage of this freedom.

Recall, as suggested, a trip you enjoyed. Take down those photographs of your trip to Paris, or South America, or wherever. If you're like me, chances are that you're much bigger on taking them than you are on actually looking at them. Create a meal that duplicates one you ate on the trip, or that is at least suggested by the kind of cuisine you enjoyed. It won't solve all your problems, but it will certainly provide a different and enjoyable departure from "just another" night at home.

Investigate new kinds of cuisine. The doldrums that strike my emotions in the dead of winter may strike you during some other season. Go to foreign restaurants. Try recipes from international cookbooks. And when you cook tried and true favorites, use herbs and seasonings to give them a new, fresher taste.

Growing your own herbs, as I've said earlier, allows

you to exert at least some power over nature. In addition, herbs offer medicinal properties that, while not exactly endorsed by the American Medical Association, have been recognized for centuries. Try using some of your dried herbs in tea form. Simply crush ½ teaspoonful for each cup into a teapot and add hot (not quite boiling) water in proportion. Allow to steep for at least five minutes.

Peppermint, sassafras, ginger, and marjoram are well-known stimulants, and their use might be a welcome change for the constant coffee drinker. And for those who love coffee after dinner in the evenings but are afraid of the insomnia that can result, various herb teas are terrific calmatives. Dill and anise make delicious teas, and while they won't *put* you to sleep, they should get you in the mood for a good night's slumber.

Herb lore offers more than simply pulling you up or setting you down. Chamomile tea has been used for centuries to calm the stomach. Try it some night when you've overindulged—it's cheaper than seltzer and infinitely more pleasing to the palate.

Rose hips are the most concentrated natural form of Vitamin C, and they make a delicious dark pink tea. The current vogue of massive doses of Vitamin C has produced no incontrovertible evidence of its value, but there seems to be no reason *not* to use it. So if you don't like the highly acid taste of the pill form, try brewing a cup of rose hip tea several times a day, from real rose hips.

I have a persistent sweet tooth, so I often put a dab of honey in my herb teas. There are those who swear that honey, not milk, is nature's most perfect food—thus I satisfy my craving for sweets and get "perfection" in the bargain. Try it yourself.

You may also wish to try basil, either in a tea form or straight off the branch. Italian men believe it a stimulus to the sex drive. (The basil may produce a slight irritation in the urethral tract, which can be confused with sexual desire.)

We should probably take our herb folklore with a grain of salt as well as a dash of honey. I wouldn't *prescribe* any of these remedies to my patients—but I might suggest them. Perhaps the suggestibility is the source of their power. However, the proof is in not only the pudding, but also the cure. In other words, if it works, use it.

The most effective remedies are often those that we most believe in. I know that mild arthritics are able to maintain themselves quite well on aspirin. They believe in it, and it works for them. But more important, I think, is that remedies make sense to us. I've tried to suggest throughout this book that the therapeutic value of food comes not only from the food we eat, but from the manner in which we prepare that food. Some recipes, for example, allow us to put our emotions—those same emotions that we may be hard pressed to put into words—into a pot or pan. One reason, I think, why I like Sweet and Sour Pork is that it's not unlike life itself. But a recipe like this one is edible proof that sweet and sour, in terms of taste as in experience, mix well together.

SWEET-AND-SOUR PORK

2 servings

1 pound pork tenderloin	¼ teaspoon pepper
4 tablespoons cooking sherry	5 tablespoons cornstarch
	3 tablespoons soy sauce
½ teaspoon salt	oil for frying

Cut the meat into bite-sized pieces. Toss these in a sauce made of sherry, salt, pepper, 3 tablespoons cornstarch and 1 tablespoon soy sauce. Then fry them in medium hot oil until brown, 7 or 8 minutes. Drain on a paper towel and keep warm.

Sauce:

⅔ cup sugar	2 tablespoons cornstarch
½ cup vinegar	1 tablespoon oil
½ cup orange juice	⅓ cup water
juice from 1 pressed clove of garlic	1 cup (fresh) pineapple bits

Mix in a bowl the sugar, vinegar, 2 tablespoons soy sauce and orange juice. Set aside. Heat the juice from the garlic in the oil. Add the vinegar and sugar mixture and bring to a boil. Dissolve 2 tablespoons of cornstarch in ⅓ cup water; add to saucepan and cook until thickened and clear. Add pineapple and bring back to a boil; add the warm pork pieces.

I'm a firm believer in trying anything that will get me through—and out of—the "blahs." And I've found few things that work as well as sheer indulgence. Granted, this particular antidote must be tempered by some restraint, but pampering myself with foods that I don't eat all the time is a never-fail cure.

When you feel that you are in a rut, you may, like me, find yourself preferring your own company. Chances are that you don't go out as often as you do when you have more of a feeling of well-being; well, at least you don't spend as much on entertainment. In any case, why not entertain yourself with delicacies? Shad roe, caviar, champagne and good wines—you deserve them as much as anyone else, remember, and you can and should feel free to enjoy them when you need an emotional boost. Force yourself to go to the local gourmet shop and see what strikes your fancy. Bored and apathetic as you may feel, the odds are good that a good Brie, a tasty pâté, or some boxed or bottled delicacy will be surprisingly appealing.

Whatever you eat, try to make your meal an experience. Don't—whatever you do—take the "what difference does it make since I'm the only one here" approach and eat out of your kitchen pans, as many people do.

You may not be feeling your best, but you're alive. That alone is reason for celebration. Bring out the good linen, the silver and the best china. Invest in some fresh flowers for the table. Enjoy your meal and at least you'll have enjoyed *something*. And enjoying your meal can be a first step in helping you to enjoy other things.

All of us respond to "events." When somebody remembers our birthday, or sends us flowers, or shows an interest in our lives, we're stimulated. But the fact is that we have the capacity to make our *own* events and occasions, to turn the ordinary into the extraordinary. All it takes is a little effort.

Here are some recipes that offer new tastes, and new ways of cooking old favorites.

RICE PUDDING

For you alone, two or three times

High blood pressure? On a sodium-free, high-potassium, low-cholesterol reducing diet? Take heart. This dessert not only conforms to what you should eat, but has nutritious raisins and soy nuts.

1 teaspoon cornstarch	1 pinch salt substitute
1 cup skimmed milk	¼ teaspoon imitation
½ cup egg substitute	butter flavoring
2 tablespoons honey	½ teaspoon vanilla
½ teaspoon sugar	extract
substitute	1 ripe banana
1 tablespoon lemon juice	3 cups cooked rice
⅔ cup raisins	2 teaspoons allspice
¼ cup crumbled soy nuts	

In the top section of a large double boiler dissolve cornstarch in milk and add egg substitute, honey, sugar substitute and lemon juice. Stir until it begins to thicken; then add the raisins, nuts and two flavorings. Stir again until thick. Turn off the flame and mash in one very ripe banana. Add rice and stir gently. Sprinkle with allspice. Refrigerate.

LEG OF GOAT

4 to 6 servings

It is different. And a young goat, though not as tender as a baby lamb, is as tender as a pig. You may consider making a gravy with the marinade, but it will need a lot of help: there will be no juices from the goat leg.

2 tangerines	1 teaspoon powdered
1 cup red wine	cardamom
2½ to 3 pound leg of	1 teaspoon salt
baby goat	½ teaspoon pepper
4 cloves garlic	1 tablespoon meat sauce
	(See recipe, p. 52)

Peel the tangerines and separate into sections. Mix with the wine and use as a marinade for the goat, preferably overnight. Discard the liquid but reserve the tangerine slices.

Grind the garlic, cardamom, salt and pepper together. Add the meat sauce and make into a paste. Make holes in the meat and stuff with half of the paste. Coat the meat with the remainder.

Bake in a preheated oven at 225 degrees, for 1½ to 2 hours on a rack in a Dutch oven. Cover with tangerine sections. Remove cover and increase to 350 degrees for 15 minutes.

SHERRY KIDNEYS

2 servings

Sometimes, when I'm looking for a change of pace, I'll remember dishes I've discovered on holidays over the years. Sherry Kidneys, a Spanish favorite, is just the thing to get me out of a rut.

2 veal kidneys
4 teaspoons vinegar
1 clove garlic, finely minced
1 teaspoon salt
¼ teaspoon pepper

2 tablespoons bacon drippings
5 teaspoons flour
⅔ cup stock
¼ cup sherry

Soak kidneys for a few hours in 2 cups of water and 2 teaspoons vinegar. Trim off the fat and membrane and cut into small slices. Sauté in bacon drippings, garlic, salt and pepper for 5 minutes. Sprinkle on the flour and stir for another 5 minutes. Add the stock and simmer until sauce is thick. When ready to serve, add the sherry and bring back to a simmer.

RED ONION SALAD

Maybe you're not tired of salads, but just tired of the same old salad greens. There's nothing "same old" about this crunchy salad.

⅔ cup olive oil
¼ cup herb vinegar
1 teaspoon salt
½ teaspoon pepper
1 pickled beet, chopped
½ pound cooked wax beans

2 red onions (about ½ pound), chopped
6 stalks celery, chopped
2 tablespoons mayonnaise

In a blender make a dressing of the oil, vinegar, salt, pepper and chopped beet. Toss with the other ingredients.

IMPROVISATIONAL BRUNCH

Serves 6

This is the remedy my patient R. F. proudly reported he'd used to cope with a morning-after depression. He awoke, hung over, to the shattering realization that he had invited five people for brunch. They were due in an hour and he hadn't a clue what was in the refrigerator, let alone what he was going to serve. This is what evolved.

1 pound frozen sausage	3 cloves garlic
1 large onion	1 teaspoon basil
4 sweet green peppers	½ teaspoon oregano
1 pound fresh mushrooms	1 teaspoon pepper
1 dozen eggs	1 teaspoon salt
1 pint mayonnaise	1 pound sharp cheddar
½ cup milk	cheese, grated
1 4-ounce can taco sauce	

Thaw the sausage as quickly as possible, and brown. Add the onions and peppers and cook until soft. Remove sausage and vegetables to a large, well-greased casserole.

Beat the eggs in a large bowl; then stir into them the rest of the ingredients. Mix this with the other ingredients in the casserole. Bake at 350 degrees for 20 to 30 minutes, depending on how firm you like your eggs.

THERAPEUTIC RED SNAPPER

Serves 4

A patient of mine never ate fish because she was afraid she would swallow a bone. One evening she found herself in a situation where she couldn't refuse, but she asked as politely and as forcefully as possible that she be given a piece with no bones. She took the first bite with trepidation. No bone in it—or any of the others. Surprised, she asked if red snapper didn't have bones. It was then, at age 35, she learned that filets of fish, like filets of beef, have no bones. Her phobia, if not cured, had at least become controlled.

Her experience was also therapeutic for me. As healthful as I knew it was, I couldn't learn really to like fish. But I tried the recipe, and now I long for fish—this red snapper with olive oil dressing at any rate. (I'm not sure I would like it with butter.)

1 4-pound red snapper with head and tail but cleaned and ready to cook	¾ teaspoon pepper
	½ teaspoon oregano
	½ cup olive oil
	¼ cup lemon juice
1½ teaspoons salt	¼ cup chopped parsley

Preheat the broiler to 450 degrees. Rub the fish inside and out with a mixture of the salt, pepper and oregano. Starting at the base of the head, make an incision down the backbone to the tail. Broil for 10 minutes on each side and remove to a hot ovenware platter. Cover with a sauce of the olive oil and lemon juice that have been whipped in a blender and heated. Spoon some of the sauce onto each serving of fish, and sprinkle with parsley.

SWEETBREADS

Serves 4

On the subject of sweetbreads, I'm in a twenty-year rut. When I eat out I invariably scan the menu for sweetbreads. If it is there, that is my entree. But I don't mind this rut; I've become something of an authority on sweetbreads—eating them and, more lately, preparing them at home.

2 quarts water	¾ tablespoon pepper
2 tablespoons vinegar	½ cup chicken stock
2½ pounds sweetbreads	½ cup light cream
¼ cup shallots, chopped	1½ teaspoons anise
¼ cup butter	extract (or 3
¼ cup flour	tablespoons pernod)
1½ tablespoons salt	

Boil water and vinegar, add sweetbreads and bring back to a boil. Turn off flame and set aside to cool. Take out the sweetbreads and strip off the membranes; they should separate into good-sized chunks. In a large casserole, sauté the sweetbreads and shallots in the butter. Sprinkle with the flour, salt and pepper and stir until chunks are well coated. Stir in the stock and bring to a boil. Simmer uncovered for 15 minutes. Add the cream and anise extract and bring to a boil. Serve over rice.

SEAFOOD COQUILLE

4 to 5 servings

2 tablespoons butter	1 pound cooked shrimp
2 teaspoons salt	1 pound mushrooms,
½ teaspoon pepper	sliced
8 whole scallions,	3 tablespoons paprika
chopped	4 tablespoons flour
2½ tablespoons fresh dill	¼ cup dry vermouth
1 pound scallops	1 4-ounce jar pimientos
2 tablespoons lemon	1 10-ounce can oyster
juice	stew

Melt butter in an enamel pot; add salt, pepper, and chopped scallions and dill. Sauté over medium flame until scallions soften. Add the scallops and sauté for 5 minutes. Remove with a slotted spoon to a large bowl. Sprinkle with 1 tablespoon lemon juice.

Poach the shrimp in the butter and scallop juice for 2 to 3 minutes. Remove with a slotted spoon to bowl with the scallops. Sprinkle with 1 tablespoon lemon juice.

Poach the mushrooms up to the point where they are beginning to turn dark. Turn off the heat. Add mushrooms to seafood and sprinkle with paprika.

Make a paste of the flour and vermouth. Drain the pimientos and add the juice to the paste.

Chop the pimientos and add to the seafood. Slowly stir the paste into the sauce and simmer until it is blended and thickened. Add the can of oyster stew, 1 tablespoon lemon juice and the juice that has collected in the bottom of the bowl. Simmer, stirring from time to time until the sauce is not runny (about 15 minutes).

Transfer the seafood mixture to four well-greased ovenproof dishes and sprinkle with Tomato Croutons. Warm in the oven, then place under the broiler for 3 minutes.

TOMATO CROUTONS

8 slices bread   ground pepper to taste
1 7-ounce can tomato
  paste

Toast bread in low oven for 15 minutes. Coat each slice with paste, then grind pepper over it. Gently trim off crusts and cut into as small squares as possible. Return to oven and bake for 10 minutes.

    Serve this combination as a first course with a meat entree—or as a light lunch.

SUPPER IN A DIFFERENT RUT

For 4

Hearty Cream Soup

3 cups beef stock   1 cup chopped cabbage
2 tablespoons beef   1 cup light cream
  extract   ¼ cup Madeira wine
1 cup chopped onions   (optional)
1 cup chopped   salt and pepper
  mushrooms

Simmer everything but the cream and wine for 15 minutes. Liquify in a blender. Add the cream and Madeira and salt and pepper to taste.

Grilled Hot-Dog Sandwich

Per person

8 frankfurters
8 pieces of white bread
4 slices cheese

butter, mustard and
mayonnaise

Split the franks in half and grill until the ends start
to curl. Remove and reserve. Put butter on one side
of a slice of bread, and mustard on the other. Place
on the grill, buttered-side-down, and cover with the
split franks, then the slice of cheese. Butter one
side of the other slice of bread and place mayonnaise on the other. Place on cheese, mayonnaise-
side-down. Grill each side until golden brown and
crunchy.

The soup can be prepared ahead and warmed
when ready to serve. The sandwiches are made to
order.

FRESH GREEN SOUP

3 cups vegetable or
chicken broth
½ teaspoon salt
¼ teaspoon pepper

1 cup chopped
watercress
1 cup chopped bean
sprouts
1 cup chopped parsley

Simmer for 15 minutes covered. Liquify in a blender.
Serve with a dab of yogurt, hot or cold.

I always find this soup refreshing when I am weary.
And when it is available, I add ¼ cup tender worm-
wood leaves, which are supposed to be stimulating.

BROCCOLI RABE SALAD

Serves 3 or 4

1½ pounds broccoli rabe   ½ teaspoon salt
2 teaspoons lemon juice   ¼ teaspoon pepper
¼ cup olive oil

Wash and steam the broccoli rabe for 5 minutes,
then chill. When cold, wrap in a paper towel and
press dry. Toss with a dressing made from the other
ingredients.

Cold vegetables with an olive oil and lemon juice
dressing are an interesting change. You can cook the
vegetables by intent, or you can use leftovers. Just ask
your greengrocer for broccoli rabe—if you haven't
heard of it before now.

BRAISED BREADED ASPARAGUS

4 to 6 servings

Traditionally the correct thing is to steam the largest
stalks of asparagus. For a change pick the thinnest.

2 pounds thin asparagus   ½ teaspoon pepper
¼ cup butter   2 tablespoons bread
1 teaspoon salt   crumbs

Steam, clean and dry the asparagus. Combine the
butter, salt and pepper in a hot skillet and stir-fry
the asparagus for 3 to 4 minutes. Sprinkle on the
bread crumbs. Cook for another minute or two.

SOS SUMMER SQUASH

This particular squash looks pretty and is almost synonymous with summer. Its taste appeals to millions of other people, but I think it needs help.

3 strips bacon	½ teaspoon pepper
1 pound summer squash	1 teaspoon vinegar
1 cup chopped onions	1 pinch powdered cloves
4 cups chopped celery cabbage	¼ teaspoon curry powder
1 teaspoon salt	

Cook the bacon crisp and drain on paper towels. Pour off all except one tablespoon of the grease from the skillet. Stir and fry the rest of the ingredients in it for 5 minutes.

Crumble the bacon over the vegetable mixture, and serve.

SHAD ROE

Single serving

To celebrate the coming of spring—or just to remind yourself that winter has an end—nothing works like Shad Roe. It's a true *spécialité* for any *maison*.

1 shad roe	¼ teaspoon salt
1 teaspoon lemon juice	1 dash pepper
3 cloves shallots, minced	⅛ cup brandy
1½ tablespoons butter	

Pour the lemon juice over the shad roe and reserve. Sauté the shallots in the butter, salt, and pepper until they are soft. Add the roe and saute for 3 minutes on each side.

Have the brandy warmed, and pour over the roe. Flame.

ROSE PETAL PUDDING

6 servings

A truly unique dish, both for taste and texture. So the next time those roses you received start to wilt, don't throw them away, eat them!

4 cups rose petals	2 teaspoons arrowroot
1¼ cups water	(or 1 tablespoon
¼ teaspoon salt	cornstarch)
¼ teaspoon nutmeg	2 egg yolks
2 teaspoons lemon juice	⅓ cup honey
	1 cup heavy cream

Wash the petals and put in the top of a steamer. In the bottom put the water, salt, nutmeg and lemon juice. Steam the petals for 30 minutes. Reserve them and the liquid. Dissolve the arrowroot in the liquid.

Beat the yolks; mix in the honey then the rose liquid. Place in a heavy saucepan.

Bring the heavy cream up to a boil then stir slowly into the egg mixture. Cover over low heat until it thickens. Try to keep from boiling and stir frequently to keep from sticking.

Chop 1 cup of the steamed rose petals and stir into the pudding. Chill in individual dishes.

SAGE AND VEAL ROAST

2 teaspoons salt	2 teaspoons oil
4 tablespoons fresh sage	1 teaspoon soy sauce
1 clove garlic	3½ pounds veal roast
½ teaspoon ground pepper	

Make a paste of the salt, sage, garlic, pepper, oil and soy sauce. Take a paring knife and make slits in the roast. Stuff the slits with the paste. Use the remainder to coat the piece of meat.

Place ¼ cup water in covered roaster and roast in 275 degree oven for 1 hour. Remove the cover and roast for another 30 minutes. All the while, the paste gives veal a new flavor—sage.

LAMB STEAK

For the steak lovers, a new taste in the time-tested filet.

¼ teaspoon salt	¼ teaspoon cracked pepper
½ teaspoon soy sauce	1 teaspoon crushed rosemary leaves
1 tablespoon sweet vermouth	1½ pounds lamb steak

Blend the first five ingredients together to prepare your marinade. After you have completed this task rub the meat with it. Place in a small container to marinate overnight.

Cook it the way you normally would a thick steak or try a new way for any cut of lamb except prime chops. Allow 45 minutes per pound at 175 degrees. Then 4 minutes per pound at 275 degrees.

7

Weight Control
in the Kitchen

"HOW about this one, Dr. Parrish? I have a friend who worked with a girl who went on this diet, and she said . . ."

This familiar refrain, familiar not only to me but to every doctor in the world, is repeated several times each month in my office. A patient with a weight problem comes in waving a piece of paper torn from a newspaper or magazine, or the latest diet book to sweep the nation, proclaiming the supposed merits of the new reducing plan. The public's enthusiasm for every new diet that comes along points to a phenomenon of our time: dieting, for many overweight men and women, is a hobby.

I have seen some patients go from the Mayo Diet (which, for the record, has nothing to do with the clinic of the same name) to the Grapefruit Diet to the Banana Diet without losing more than a pound or two. They are so busy playing "musical diets" that they never stick with any one plan long enough for it to do any good.

"I was *going* to stick with it, but somebody told me it didn't really work," Grace, an obese secretary confessed to me after her weekly weigh-in. Seven days before, she'd been full of enthusiasm for the Ice Cream Diet, assuring me that "this time it'll be different."

Now, a pound heavier than she'd been the previous week, Grace was quick to point out that she was about to join the revolution—the latest diet revolution, that is.

"It works, doesn't it?" she asked me, hopping off the scale as lithely as a two-hundred-pound woman can.

"Grace, the facts of life haven't changed since last week," I said. "Just about any diet that's reasonably sensible works—providing you follow it. But I don't think you have the temperament to stick to a diet—"

Grace's big brown eyes looked hurt. "How can you say I don't have the willpower?" she challenged. "I lost ten pounds on the Egg and Tomato Diet."

"Yes, until you got bored with it," I reminded her. "And I didn't mention willpower. You did. I said temperament. You just aren't the type of person who can follow somebody else's regimen."

My patient sighed. "Well, it isn't my fault," she insisted. "I liked the Ice Cream Diet, but I felt like a big idiot ordering a sundae at lunch. Besides, how much ice cream can a person eat?"

That, of course, is the question the Ice Cream Diet—and all fad and novelty diets based on one food or food groups—ask and propose to answer. You're supposed to become bored with ice cream or eggs and tomatoes, and then you're supposed to moderate the amount of food you eat as boredom sets in.

To better understand how this principle works, think of your favorite food, no matter how fattening it may be. Let's suppose that cheesecake is your personal favorite; you may have said, as many people do of the food they like best, "I could *live* on it . . . I could eat cheesecake and nothing else for the rest of my life."

This may well seem the case as you bring a forkful of the dessert to your mouth, but suppose you were to go on the Cheesecake Diet—which dictates that you can eat as much cheesecake as you want as often as you want, but no other solid food is allowed. For the first few meals you'd feel happy, and you'd stuff yourself. Soon, ennui would set in. The taste would be repetitive and monotonous. If you followed the diet principle strictly—eating your favorite food (or any *one* food only), you'd begin to notice that your portions get smaller and smaller. Soon you might decide to skip a meal rather than have yet another piece of cheesecake.

This, in essence, is the dynamics of the idea, and as a concept it is viable. We're accustomed to a variety of tastes. When we're restricted to just one taste, we soon lose interest in it and feel deprived of the variety that we take for granted under normal circumstances. The theory is that we become so bored and deprived that we react by not eating much of the central diet food.

Novelty diets are most effective for quick weight loss, and they can produce fast results for the man or woman who wants to lose a few pounds. People such as Grace, who have a serious weight problem, may become bored with ice cream or whatever, but they all too quickly become interested in something else—like chocolate cake—and interest sparks the appetite. I hadn't wanted to hurt Grace's feelings, I assured her, and I by no means thought her case was hopeless. But I told her what I tell many of the overweight patients I work with.

After letting them experiment with various fad diets, I find they're more ready to accept the truth. And that truth, to put it as simply as possible, is that if you've spent a lifetime getting fat, you can't expect a "miracle" to happen in just a few weeks of dieting. "You don't need diversion," I told Grace that day. "The Ice Cream Diet and those other fads are supposed to take your mind off food. You need to think about food, but in a new way."

The individual who likes to eat, whether he gorges himself on gourmet delights or stuffs his face with junk food, isn't likely to lose interest in his appetite, or his interest in eating as an activity. The importance of food in his life may be out of proportion to other interests, but often it is much more effective to head him on the road toward weight control before helping him to understand why he eats.

One of the best places to lose weight isn't likely to be in the pages of the latest diet bestseller (especially if you also read the diet bestseller before that) or at a spa; it's in your own kitchen. Contrary to what some people think, staying out of the kitchen isn't the best idea for the individual who wants to tip the balance on the scales. Not in these days, where there are fast food outlets on almost every corner!

Staying out of the kitchen and the monotony of most diets offer the would-be weight loser constant punishment (deprivation of one of his favorite pleasures, namely food) and very slow reward. He may stick it out for a while, but too often he'll rebel, overeating as a reaction to the tediousness of the diet.

The good plans for long-term weight control are those that offer a wide variety of foods. The best diets of all are those that we can make up and follow ourselves, and the key component isn't any particular food group, but common sense.

I love to eat, and I overdo it at times, just like everyone else. The holidays are my particular downfall. It begins before Thanksgiving, early in November, when I experiment with new recipes that I *may* want to incorporate into my Thanksgiving dinner. The seasonal round of parties doesn't help much—I'm too easy a victim for the plates heaped high with specialties that friends hand me when I visit. I top it off not simply with Christmas Day, but with the New Year's Eve Black-Eyed Peas—see page 90 (not to mention the rest of the meal) that are a tradition in the South. I'm big on traditions, and once the traditional holiday season is over, I'm just plain big!

One saving grace of holiday meals, as far as the figure goes, is turkey. It's low in calories (white meat, as mentioned, has fewer than dark) as well as in price, and besides serving as a delicious main course, leftover turkey can be used in a number of ways—salads, casseroles, etc.—throughout the holiday season, for slimming meals.

Here's a recipe I fall back on when my belt starts getting too tight midway through the holiday season. Though I make it with turkey legs (each one is a generous serving, and turkey legs are sold separately in most markets all year round, and are inexpensive), it could also be made with turkey wings or slices of meat.

This recipe came about when I was trying to use up some food I had on hand. I've since discovered that the combination of clams and turkey is a great taste match, and that the juice from the canned clams helps keep the meat moist and tasty.

TURKEY OFF THE HALF SHELL

1 or 2 servings

2 turkey legs	¼ cup soy sauce
1 8-ounce can minced clams	1 teaspoon lemon juice
	⅓ cup water

Strip off the skin and place turkey legs (meat-side-down) in a baking pan. Add juice from can of clams and bake in a 325 degree oven for 30 minutes. Mix clams, soy sauce, lemon juice and water. Turn the oven up to 450, pour the blend over the turkey and bake for another ten minutes.

I try to make the start of a new year a season of discovery in the kitchen. Having just made two months' worth of recipes that I use year after year, I'm psychologically ready to move on to new taste experiences. All I do is temper my selection with common-sense knowledge of what is and is not fattening. One needn't be a physician or a nutrition expert to figure it out. As a matter of fact, the first rule of weight control in the kitchen is simple: if you're overweight, the most fattening food for you is probably the one you eat the most of.

When I've been on an eating binge, I have no interest whatsoever in a scoop of cottage cheese and a wedge of tomato. I want a *meal,* and I put my creativity to work making up one that is interesting, appealing and suitable to the purpose.

Food that is low in calories—lower that is than the food you are accustomed to—doesn't have to resemble something that a rabbit might consider eating in captivity. Miniscule portions of unappetizing foods are enough to send even the best of us in search of the closest fast-food shop. Though several days of fad dieting may have some value at the start of a reducing program, in showing a chronically obese individual that he *can* lose weight, it's much better to approach weight control as an exercise in education.

Perhaps that sounds like the opening line for a nutrition-course recruitment drive. It isn't. I do, however, believe that it's a good idea to keep a book of calorie and carbohydrate listings on your cookbook shelf. Several are available, both for general food items and specific brands. I know very well that the average person isn't going to look up every item he eats, and I'm not going to suggest it. But these books can be useful tools in deciding what you want to eat when you're of two minds. Perhaps you're planning a meal that could benefit from the addition of an orange vegetable. The choice may come down to carrots or sweet potatoes—check a simple food value directory to make your decision, particularly if you're watching your weight.

The best reducing plan, I've always believed and told my patients, is the one that works. In years of practice, I've seen some very unusual programs take the pounds off—and I've also seen many excellent diets, well balanced in nutritional components, fail dismally. Nothing is more discouraging than going on a diet, losing weight, and then finding yourself putting the pounds, slowly but surely, back on once you go off the diet. Discouraging it may be, but it's a common experience. One reason this happens, of course, is that we let diets do too much of the work.

Maria, a suburban housewife who comes to my office on days when she visits Manhattan for shopping, was a victim of the let-the-diet-do-it syndrome. She faithfully followed a diet for a month, losing 10 pounds. Yet within three weeks of post-diet eating, she was complaining, and rightly so: the scale showed that seven of the pounds she'd lost had already found their way back.

"Something's wrong with my body," Maria insisted. "I must have a condition, doctor."

"Maria," I began, after checking her chart, "you've just had a checkup, remember? There is no indication of any thyroid trouble or glandular imbalance. There's only one condition that you have, and it's called eating too much of the wrong foods."

"How can you say that?" she asked. "I followed my diet to the letter!"

"I know you did," I told her. "And it was a very commendable effort. I'm proud of you. But now you're off the diet, and you still have a problem. Tell me, what did you have for dinner last night."

"Just the regular things," she said.

"What kind of regular things?"

"Well, my husband and I are both Italian, and we love the food we grew up on. I made some sauce the other day, and we had it with shells . . ."

Maria, it turned out, served pasta as a main dish several nights a week. Her menu, combined with a hearty appetite, was her downfall, but I thought I glimpsed a possible answer.

"If you like Italian food so much, why not look into

it further?" I suggested. "I'm not talking about pasta, Maria, but about all kinds of Italian food. How about rugola and some of the other marvelous greens that Italians use in those delicious salads? What about northern Italian cooking—things like lean veal chops, pounded thin and sautéed in garlic and lemon? You can still have your sauce, but why not try pouring it over a piece of broiled fish instead of pasta?"

Maria agreed to try enlarging her repertoire of specialties, and I tried to steer her toward foods that were authentically ethnic, but less fattening than the pasta that was a staple of her cooking. The result wasn't a sudden and dramatic loss of weight, but a gradual slimming process. Over the next two months, Maria began to lose a pound or so a week. Finally she had shed nine pounds, and she'd kept them off for three weeks.

"It's amazing," she said. "I'm spending more time in the kitchen than ever, but I'm losing weight instead of gaining it. And my husband has lost five pounds too. He'd never have gone on a diet, but this way he's losing weight without knowing it!"

One family member's desire to lose unwanted pounds can motivate the rest to lose weight as well—painlessly. The secret is learning how to substitute slimming foods for fattening standard fare, and to make these foods as appealing as possible. The woman who prepares two or three meals each day for her family would undoubtedly have a hard time being the "only one" in the house on a diet. Limiting her own eating to a restrictive diet while having to cook normal meals for her husband and children is asking too much. It's much better, I believe, to incorporate new, slimming dishes into family menus. This way, the woman who is on a weight-loss program can eat what she prepares *with* the family. She can take pride not only in her own weight loss, but in the fact that she's helping her husband and children discover new, more healthful foods.

Many of us eat too much buttered white rice, and although it's filling and economical, it can really put the pounds on. Why not, instead, try using celery in place of rice? Every would-be weight loser has heard that celery is low in calories, and we all know, too, that it provides good roughage for regularity. The trick, as far as I'm concerned, is turning the prosaic celery stalk into something one really wants to eat a lot of. This version (figure on a half cup of chopped celery per serving) could really be called "mock fennel," and has a decidedly Italian taste.

SASSAFRAS CELERY

2 servings

2 cups chopped celery
¾ cup chicken stock
¼ teaspoon salt

1 teaspoon powdered sassafras root

Combine all the ingredients in a saucepan and simmer for ten minutes. If you are unable to find sassafras root, substitute a few drops of imitation anise flavoring, or use diet root beer instead of stock.

Even fattening family favorites can be served in less fattening ways. Potatoes, for example, are an American institution. We all like them (I confess that pasta is my personal favorite in the starch category, though) and we eat a lot of them. It is a popular misconception that potatoes, by definition, are the downfall of the individual who wants to lose weight. In fact, it's not so much the potato that does the dieter in as what we do to it—frying it, mashing it with milk and butter, or topping it off with sour cream when we bake it.

My Slash-Brown Potatoes are an alternative to French fries or hash browns. They have the crispness and "buttery" taste most people like with potatoes, and while they aren't as slimming as a serving of spinach, they are better for the body and figure than the standard potato dish alternatives.

SLASH-BROWN POTATOES

For 2

2 medium-sized baking potatoes	paprika
	salt
2 tablespoons diet (imitation) margarine	pepper

Preheat the oven to 500 degrees. Wash and dry the potatoes, then rub the skins with ½ teaspoon of diet margarine per potato. Sprinkle "buttered" potato skins with paprika and salt, then pierce the potatoes in several places with a fork or skewer. Place them in the oven for one hour, or until the potatoes are done and the skins are crisp and dark. Then, using a chopping knife, slash the potatoes on a cutting board, chopping them—skin and all—until they are cut into fork-sized pieces. Add the remaining diet margarine, and season with pepper and salt. Serve in a dish, family style, allowing one potato per serving.

Even some of the usual diet foods that are so dull on their own can take on new appeal if you approach them with creativity. I'm the first to admit that it's very hard to get excited about the idea of a few carrot sticks. But it's easy to get interested in a first course relish tray of raw vegetables, nicely arranged and served with an interesting sauce. Don't, *please,* limit yourself to carrots! Radishes, mushrooms, zucchini, celery, new tomatoes, onions, and peppers are just some of the possibilities.

Try a relish tray instead of the usual chips and dips with cocktails, and if there are vegetables left over, don't even think about throwing them away. Instead, mix them in the blender as I do with chicken or beef stock (instant stocks, by the way, have an average of just 10 calories per packet) and you'll end up with delicious, slimming soups. The possibilities are limited only by your imagination, but possibilities include mushroom and onion, and zucchini and tomato.

Gazpacho is another blender project. This marvelous cold soup can be made in quantity and kept in a large jar or covered pitcher in the refrigerator. It's filling and interesting enough to serve as a light lunch; or the weight-conscious individual can pour it over ice and sip it all day long.

BLENDER GAZPACHO

Serves 3 or 4

4 medium tomatoes, peeled and seeded
1 sweet green pepper
3 cloves garlic, peeled
1 medium onion, peeled and chopped
1 cup cucumber, peeled, chopped and seeded
1½ teaspoon salt
2 cups vegetable juice
½ cup fresh herbs
(coarsely chopped parsley, tarragon, chives, oregano, basil, thyme and/or marjoram)
¼ cup olive oil
3 tablespoons lemon juice
1 pinch cayenne pepper
4 dashes Tabasco

Throw everything into the blender, and chop briefly —don't "over-blend." The truly calorie-conscious can substitute diet mayonnaise for the olive oil.

Remember that an occasional day of fasting or sticking to liquids doesn't hurt the figure or the body, providing you are in good health. This form of judicious stress may well stimulate the metabolism.

When we think of diets, we think of taking food away, of depriving ourselves. Creative weight control, on the other hand, has a beneficial psychological side effect. Instead of doing something to ourselves, we're doing something *for* ourselves. Our minds and our taste buds welcome the difference.

Some substitutions in our basic shopping lists can also help in keeping weight down. Today low-calorie substitutes for a wide variety of foods can be found on the shelves of the market, though it's important to read labels carefully and make sure that manufacturers' claims are substantiated. When I shop, I always buy low-calorie soft drinks to serve my guests. Very few, if any of them, know the difference between a typical cola and its low-calorie cousin.

Some of my patients complain that the sugar-free sodas leave an unpleasant aftertaste. I experimented at home, and discovered that a squeeze of fresh lemon (lemon cokes are popular throughout the South) cuts the aftertaste and perks up the beverage. Other patients have complained that low-calorie foods just don't have the taste of the so-called real thing.

Bill, an artist who wanted to get rid of fifteen pounds in time for an exhibition at a gallery, was one of these. "I admit that I'm something of a freak when it comes to my eating habits," he told me. "I really like tuna salad, and I practically live on it when I'm working on a painting. You told me to try a low-calorie mayonnaise substitute, Dr. Parrish, and I bought a jar. I stuck my finger in and had a taste—yuck! And as for that water-packed tuna . . . well, I tasted that and I hated it."

At least Bill was honest. But he hadn't given the things a chance. "A mayonnaise substitute isn't the same as real mayonnaise," I concurred. "But, Bill, it's not supposed to be eaten out of the jar. If you want to give it a fair chance, try it in one of your tuna salads. And use that water packed tuna, too. Slice and chop some tomatoes and green peppers and see what happens when you add them."

Bill later admitted that while the low-calorie substitutes didn't taste like much in their original containers, there was a definite improvement in combining them. The peppers and tomatoes added another taste dimension.

The sandwich, as we know it in this country, consists of two pieces of bread with something in between. In other parts of the world, though, people are much more adventurous. Open-faced sandwiches are a good, slimming idea. To get rid of the feeling that something —namely the top piece of bread—is missing, decorate with a bit of crumbled bacon, sliced olives, or whatever goes best with what you're eating. Don't forget that it's possible to do away with not only one piece of bread, but two: if you don't believe it, try a bit of your favorite cheese between two thin, crisp, slices of apple.

We have to remember that the lifestyles we live make it virtually impossible for most of us to stick to a regimen of prescribed eating even if we want to. The executive who has to have a big lunch with a client or associate isn't about to risk losing an account because he's on a diet. The woman who is joining friends for a club meeting or bridge game may not have any control over what her hostess serves. If you watch what you eat *most* of the time, you can afford to close your eyes and eat blindly *some* of the time.

The man or woman who is trying to lose some unwanted pounds often believes that losing weight means a curtailed social life. This belief, quite naturally, is another reason why so many people don't get around to tackling their weight problems—they don't want to be cut off from friends and the rest of the world, or missing all the fun.

I often advise obese patients to entertain while they are on a weight-loss program. Dinners and cocktail parties aren't fattening: the food that is served at them might or might not be, depending on the menu. Nothing generates interest in experimenting with creative, low-calorie cooking as much as compliments. Serve good food, interestingly and well prepared, and people will be too busy savoring to even notice that what they are eating is slimming.

Chinese cooking has become extremely popular over the past few years, and the Chinese have a number of interesting ways to deal with vegetables. Most involve use of the classic Chinese frying pan, the wok (or wock). Stir-frying in a wok is quick and easy, and though a bit of cooking oil is used in this form of cooking, the amount is very, very small. You need deprive yourself of all fried foods no longer; vegetables aren't overdone, but instead come out full of flavor and freshness. (The wok is ecology-minded as well—the design makes for maximum use of small amounts of heat.)

STIR-FRY VEGETABLES

Serves 2

½ cup green beans, sliced lengthwise and chopped in half
½ cup cauliflower buds
½ cup onions, coarsely chopped

½ cup carrot slices
2 teaspoons vegetable oil
½ teaspoon soy sauce
½ teaspoon pepper

Stir-fry all ingredients together in the wok for 7 or 8 minutes. (If you like its taste better, substitute ¼ cup chopped sweet potato for the carrots.)

This is just one of many dishes that a would-be weight loser can take pleasure in introducing to friends and guests; and the therapeutic value of a continued social life cannot be overstated. Instead of limiting the foods you eat, as with a diet, you enlarge the number and variety when you take a creative approach to weight control. Each success stimulates the mind onward to new dishes, and each new dish can help you move downward on the scale.

Salads offer excellent ground for experimentation, not only salads themselves, but salad dressings too. A good spinach salad, made with fresh, crisp leaves, some Bermuda onion rings and a bit of bacon makes an excellent main dish for lunch. The dressing can be simple—even fresh lemon juice alone does it justice.

Remember there's never anything wrong with being original. I'd often wondered why I'd never had a salad made with fresh zucchini, one of my favorite vegetables. The other night I stopped wondering and sliced some, very thin, combining the slices with greens and an herb dressing. The result was delicious, and the answer was apparent: I hadn't had it before because I hadn't tried it.

I find that a mortar and pestle is very useful in getting the full flavor of herbs into my salad dressings. Basil, oregano and countless others can go into a fresh dressing, or they can be used to pick up the flavor of a low-calorie bottled dressing from the market. Yogurt, too, makes a good dressing on its own, or as a base.

Whether you are serving low-calorie meals to friends or eating alone, the way food is served makes a difference. I once had a secretary who was on a diet. At lunch time, she'd take out her brown bag and carefully unwrap the two stalks of celery or whatever she was allotted on a given day. The image of that girl's face as she took out her lunch is etched in my mind—in assorted shades of gray. She looked about as interested in what she was eating as a man serving a life imprisonment might be in a calendar.

"What do you eat for dinner?" I asked her, knowing that she lived alone.

"Oh, let's see," she said without any excitement. She consulted the copy of her diet in her bag and made a dismal face. "Four ounces of broiled fish. This diet is dull, but it sure saves on dishwashing."

I asked what she meant, and she explained: the food she was allowed was so dull that she wanted to get her meager meals over with, and so she ate right out of the pan, standing at the stove. And knowing her as I did, I was certain that she spent the rest of the evening longing for a piece or three of cheesecake.

A meal should be an experience, as pleasant an experience as possible. This is never more important than when an overweight man or woman is relearning eating habits and experimenting with new foods. Just as we have to learn to be comfortable in the kitchen, we have to learn how to be guests in our own homes.

Anything looks better when it's served in a pleasant environment. Even if you live alone, there's no reason to save your best china and silverware for guests. Prepare and serve slimming meals as if they were made for someone important. Who, when you come right down to it, is more important than you?

A piece of sole, broiled, baked, or poached, may look very plain. It is, but it becomes much more inviting if you top it with some freshly grated carrot or finely chopped parsley. Attractive surroundings and a pleasant atmosphere, be it at home or in a restaurant, make us much more receptive to new tastes. Put on some of your favorite music, dim the lights, and spend the dollar or two that would have gone to the bakery on some fresh flowers for your table. When you finish a meal, don't rush right in to do the dishes. Instead linger over a cup of coffee or tea and think about your double accomplishments: the new dish you've created, and the positive step you've taken for your own well-being.

Keeping one's weight down, it should be remembered, is beneficial in many ways. Aesthetics are important, certainly, in that how we look influences how we feel about ourselves and how others feel about us. But do not forget also that statistics prove that people who maintain a normal weight live longer than those who are obese and that a weight problem can be a factor in heart disease, as well as in other conditions, including diabetes and high blood pressure.

Another reason why I so avidly recommend a creative approach *to low calorie cooking, as opposed to dieting,* is that diets tend to repeat themselves. A man or woman who sticks with a regimented diet for six weeks may lose 15 pounds; but as indicated by some of the examples above, once the diet period is over, he or she may put those pounds right back on. Or perhaps weight will increase gradually. In either case, the natural response of this individual is to go back on the diet. It worked before, is the reasoning, and it will work again.

It may well work a second time around—or a third, fourth and fifth. But the actual problem, namely the individual's eating habits, hasn't been dealt with. A diet can be a stalling measure, though few people realize it. Nor are they aware that constant weight fluctuation is not healthy.

As we get older, our skin loses elasticity—the ability to stretch and shrink back when we lose weight. A constantly fluctuating weight therefore not only puts stress on various organs of the body, but can also result in a saggy, flabby look that is unattractive at any weight. This, of course, makes still another argument for gradual weight loss and careful maintenance.

The kitchen is a perfect place to illustrate a point that I find I have to make to patients time and time again. A desire to slim down is essential to any kind of weight-loss program, but a realistic goal is also essential. A roasting chicken is going to have more meat on it than a Cornish hen—we all know that. In the same way, a person with a large frame is going to weigh more than an individual whose bone structure is smaller. It sounds obvious, and it is—to everyone except the large-framed man or woman who wants to look like a model.

As you begin a weight-loss/weight-control program, think in terms of a goal that is realistic for *you*. Forget the insurance company charts that allegedly tell what a man or woman of a given height and age should weigh. Most make no allowance for body type, and this fact, determined by heredity rather than what we eat, is very significant. Your doctor can best advise you on the proper weight to strive for, and it's always best to check with a physician before starting any kind of reducing plan.

Not only is it possible to lose weight in the kitchen, but it's possible to use *your* kitchen to lose the weight you've picked up via someone else's. All of us, no matter how calorie-conscious we are, find ourselves in situations from time to time when it's impossible to say "no" to a meal that we're well aware is too fattening. But excess can be balanced in terms of afternoon or evening "after eating." For that matter, you can take an evening or afternoon "before" approach, too.

The idea works this way. If you know that you're going to dinner with friends and that you'll be eating a rich, calorie-packed meal, eat a light, slimming lunch. A spinach salad is a good bet, or the low-calorie Tuna Salad recipe you'll find at the end of this chapter.

If lunches are your problem, keep dinner light—try my Cheese Toast and a bowl of Relish Tray Soup for something slimming and yet filling. A weekend of watching your weight can help to make up for a week during which you overate—a few weekdays of low-calorie eating can, in the same way, help to balance a weekend spent with friends who love to cook and serve food without regard to calories.

Remember, too, that watching your weight is much more than a matter of vanity; it's a matter of taking a positive interest in your health. Your creativity with low-calorie cookery can benefit not only you but other family members, too. Children, siblings, and spouses of overweight men and women often tend to be over-weight themselves.

The following recipes are just a sample of what can be done with inventive, weight-conscious creativity in the kitchen. The possibilities are limitless—and you'll live a longer, healthier, and more attractive life in which to enjoy them if you think of the kitchen as a place where weight can be lost

There is a new *haute cuisine* that is low calorie, low cholesterol. It began in France, but you can introduce it in your community. For an idea, see my Souffléd Pear.

TUNA SALAD

3 or 4 servings

A low-calorie version of an old favorite—and a particular favorite of those who seem to have more of a desire to shed pounds than they have success at it.

1 7-ounce can water-packed tuna, drained
½ cup chopped dill pickle
1 hard-cooked egg, chopped

1 4-ounce container pimientos, drained and chopped
½ cup chopped onion
½ teaspoon freshly ground pepper
¼ teaspoon salt

Use a fork to break up the tuna and combine with the other ingredients. Serve on a bed of lettuce, or packed into half a steamed acorn squash.

OLIVE OIL DRESSING

For 1 salad

Popeye's ever-slender mate can dash this tasty dressing on her spinach salad without a worry about her figure. Utilizing martini by-products provides the taste of olive oil with none of the calories.

1 teaspoon dried bell pepper flakes	1 tablespoon vegetable oil
1 teaspoon diced parsley	1 egg
1 teaspoon dried basil	⅓ cup juice from a jar of olives
1 teaspoon dried dill	
½ teaspoon cracked pepper	

Place everything in the blender for a moment. Any leftover dressing can be blended with some sour cream dressing for a "party dip" at least the equal of the packaged version.

SLIM SLAW

3 or 4 servings

Cole slaw is one of the by-the-quart downfalls of overweight people, along with ice cream and orange juice by the same measure. This is a slimming slaw recipe that stands by itself, or makes a good base for main-dish meat and cheese salads. It can, of course, be stored in the refrigerator—and be sure to save some for the recipe that follows, a hot dish that uses Slim Slaw as a base.

1 tablespoon olive oil
½ teaspoon salt
¼ teaspoon mustard
  seeds
¼ teaspoon ground
  pepper
½ teaspoon dried basil
  leaves
1 tablespoon cream of
  tartar
1 package dried
  vegetable broth

4 cups chopped cabbage
1 teaspoon dried parsley
  flakes
¼ teaspoon
  Worcestershire sauce
½ teaspoon vinegar
⅓ cup low-fat sour
  cream (a.k.a. sour-
  cream dressing)
1 grated carrot
1 chopped green pepper
1 tablespoon celery seed

Pestle-ize the olive oil, salt, mustard seeds, pepper, basil, and parsley into a paste. Add the Worcestershire sauce, the vinegar, low-fat sour cream, cream of tartar and the vegetable broth, stirring until all ingredients are well combined. Pour over the remaining ingredients, toss, and refrigerate. Toss again before serving.

CHOPPED FUEY

1 serving

This is a quick and unusual meal that's prepared in minutes. The chopping is minimal—and the "fuey" is on excess calories!

¾ tablespoon diet
  (imitation) margarine
1 cup Slim Slaw (see
  recipe above) drained

¼ cup water-packed
  sardines, chopped
¼ cup low-cholesterol
  egg substitute (or
  1 egg)

Melt the imitation margarine in a skillet over a low heat, watching it carefully as it has a tendency to burn. When it is melted and hot, add the drained Slim Slaw and sauté for 5 minutes, stirring frequently. Add the chopped sardines and scramble for 1 minute, then add the egg substitute and scramble rapidly for 2 minutes. Serve hot, with Cheesed Toast.

CHEESED TOAST

1 light supper

Melba toast is another of those things that is less than exciting unless something creative is done with it, and if I say so myself, this treatment turns it from something blah and bland into something with an interesting taste and texture. A note here on "imitation" cream cheese and sour cream, and assorted "imitation" products in general. Often they are not so much imitations of the real thing as low-fat versions. And usually the "imitation" name is a lot less desirable than the taste. Don't be afraid of them.

3 ounces imitation cream cheese	⅓ teaspoon Worcestershire sauce
¾ teaspoon dried tarragon	¾ teaspoon paprika
	4 slices melba toast

Mix the cream cheese and seasonings and spread them onto the 4 pieces of melba toast. Turn the oven to low, and set the spread pieces of toast on a cookie sheet or a piece of foil. Let the cheese toast bake for 10 minutes—just long enough for the cheese to moisten the toast and the baking to give it a chewy texture.

RELISH TRAY SOUP

2 servings

One of the best ways to keep unwanted weight away is to keep fattening snacks out of the house. Stock up instead on fresh vegetables that can be served with cocktails, or munched on during the day. For variety —or to use up leftovers—create this tasty soup.

1 cup chopped celery	2 cups vegetable or
1 cup chopped radishes	chicken stock
1 cup chopped scallions	salt and pepper

Simmer vegetables and stock in a 2-quart saucepan for 20 minutes, covered. Pour into blender and blend until stock and vegetables are liquified. Sample, and add salt and pepper to taste. Serve hot with a chopped onion garnish, or refrigerate and serve cold, topped with chopped olive. This soup can be reheated, frozen, or poured over ice and sipped as a cold liquid meal.

SPRING CREAM DRESSING

For 2 salads

Frequent dieters often begin to hate even the thought of another salad. Some of the blame must go to their lack of imagination—variety in the choice of salad greens can make a world of difference. Add fresh mustard greens to an otherwise ordinary salad, or splurge one night and serve yourself nothing but the sliced hearts of romaine. No matter what the greens, this salad dressing is sure to perk up interest.

4 scallions
2 tablespoons chopped
   green pepper
¼ cup chopped parsley
2 tablespoons chopped
   basil leaves (fresh)
   or 1 tablespoon dried
2 tablespoons tarragon
   vinegar

¼ cup sour cream
   dressing
¼ teaspoon sugar
   substitute
¼ teaspoon ground
   pepper
¾ teaspoon salt

Chop the scallions, leaves and all, and throw them, along with all the other ingredients, into the blender. Adding the rest of a cup (¾ cup) of sour-cream dressing makes a terrific sauce for dipping into with raw vegetables—flowers of broccoli and cauliflower, as well as the usual carrots.

ICE-CREAMED COLA

For 1

Many of my patients who go on weight-loss programs find their Waterloo at the soda fountain. I can't blame them—I get an occasional craving for something with a fountain taste myself. Here's a drink that satisfies both the taste buds and the slimming program. And best of all, it can be made with that last bit of diet cola that you think has gone flat and may be tempted to pour down the sink!

½ cup diet cola
½ cup yogurt

1 tablespoon instant
   coffee or cocoa

Blend all the ingredients and then freeze the blended mixture. About a half hour or so should do the job—the longer you freeze the Ice-Creamed Cola, the longer you'll have to leave it out of the freezer before enjoying it. It should defrost, helped along by an occasional stirring, so that it's partly thick and sippable, and partly crunchy. Serve with a straw and a spoon.

DIET PIE CRUST

For a 2-crust pie

¼ cup diet margarine
¼ cup boiling water
½ teaspoon imitation
  butter flavor

1 cup sifted flour
½ teaspoon salt
½ teaspoon baking
  powder

Mix the margarine, water and butter flavoring. Stir in flour, salt, and baking powder; mix well. Form into a ball and refrigerate. When cool, roll out and proceed as per your recipe.

PIZZA

4 to 6 servings

Prepare Diet Piecrust as instructed above. Roll out to line the bottom, sides, and edge of a lightly-greased and floured baking dish about 9 inches in diameter and 1¼ inches deep. Prick. Bake in a very hot oven for 10 minutes. (The crust will keep its shape better if an ovenproof dish is placed atop the crust while baking.)

1 pound Italian sweet
   sausage
½ pound (2 cups)
   chopped mushrooms
¾ pound (2 cups) sliced
   tomatoes (preferably
   plum)
¾ pound (2 cups) sliced
   sweet green peppers
2 teaspoons salt
2 tablespoons tomato
   puree
2 cloves garlic, minced
anchovy paste

pepperoni, sliced
1 tablespoon Italian sea-
   soning
1 teaspoon marjoram
1 teaspoon dried anise
   (or 1 teaspoon ground
   star anise seed)
2 teaspoons cornstarch
¼ teaspoon crumbled
   hot red pepper
2 tablespoons tomato
   paste
¼ cup grated Parmesan
   cheese

Prick the sausage and simmer in a Dutch oven with 1 cup of water for 15 minutes. Pour off all the liquid except for the light coating of fat that will stay on the bottom of the Dutch oven.

Add the mushrooms, tomatoes, green peppers and salt. Simmer slowly until the vegetables are soft. Add the seasonings, cornstarch, tomato puree and garlic. Simmer and stir for another 30 minutes or until no liquid is left. Spoon into baked pie shell.

Decorate with spokes of anchovy paste, thin slices of pepperoni (⅛ pound yields 16 slices), the tomato paste and the grated cheese. Place in a very hot oven for 3 to 5 minutes. Serve immediately, or refrigerate and serve chilled.

POACHED FLOUNDER

2 servings

1 pound flounder filets
½ cup vegetable stock
2 tablespoons grated carrot
½ teaspoon grated lemon peel
2 tablespoons chopped scallion greens

2 tablespoons chopped celery leaves
½ teaspoon salt
¼ teaspoon ground pepper
2 teaspoons lemon juice

Grease lightly the bottom of a baking dish with diet margarine and place the filets in it. Cover with the stock, then the grated carrot and lemon peel and the chopped scallion greens and celery leaves. Sprinkle with salt, and pepper and lemon juice.

Bake in a 375 degree oven for 5 to 7 minutes.

BRUSSELS CASSEROLE

Serves 2

1 cup brussel sprouts, cooked
1¼ cups chicken, cooked
½ cup cottage cheese
¼ cup Parmesan cheese
½ teaspoon ground coriander seeds

¼ cup stock
3 tablespoons diet margarine
½ cup bread crumbs
¼ cup sour-cream dressing
2 tablespoons water

Chop the sprouts, dice the chicken, blend the cheeses, pulverize the coriander seeds; mix all with the stock. Put into a casserole greased with margarine. Sauté the bread crumbs in the remaining margarine for 3 minutes. Stir in the sour-cream dressing and water. Spread on top of the sprouts and chicken.

Bake at 325 degrees for 15 minutes. Run under the broiler for 3 minutes.

SOLE VERONIQUE

2 servings

3 teaspoons diet margarine
1 pound sole filets
2 tablespoons dry vermouth
½ teaspoon salt
¼ teaspoon ground pepper

2 teaspoons flour
½ cup vegetable stock
½ cup seedless white grapes
4 cloves shallots, chopped
1 teaspoon lemon juice
¼ cup diet mayonnaise

Grease a baking dish with a cover with 1 teaspoon diet margarine. Layer the filets in it. Add the vermouth. Sprinkle with salt and pepper. Bake in a 375 degree oven for 5 to 7 minutes. Remove and reserve.

In a saucepan combine 2 teaspoons diet margarine and the flour over low heat until blended, but not browned. Slowly add the juice from the baked fish and the stock. Simmer covered for 10 minutes. Add the grapes, shallots, lemon juice and mayonnaise and simmer another minute or 2.

Pour the sauce over the filets. Cover and return to a warm oven for 3 to 5 minutes.

ACORN SQUASH

1 or 2 servings

Acorn squash is an often neglected nicely textured vegetable that lends itself to a number of uses. It's a good taste to introduce into your life during a weight-loss program; and for weight-control maintenance.

1 acorn squash	2 thin strips of bacon, fried
2 teaspoons diet margarine or butter substitute	

Cut the squash in half; clean out the seeds. Steam the inverted halves for 10 to 15 minutes, until almost tender. Cool. Rub with 1 teaspoon of margarine or butter substitute. Crumble 1 thin strip of bacon, fried crisp and drained, on each half.

PLAIN PORK CHOPS

2 servings

Pork may seem a peculiar item in a group of dietary recipes. It is high in both fats and calories, but if you are not on a strict reducing diet, it is not all that bad for you, and the taste is almost always good. Of course, one of the things that makes it taste good is the fat. But pork fat about balances out in saturated (bad) and unsaturated (not so bad) fatty acids. So very little harm is done to your arteries.

The problem is the calories, but this can be compensated for by buying good lean chops, trimming off the loose fat, and cooking so that excess fat, which does not contribute to the taste of your chop, is thrown away. The remaining fat can be cut away at the table. The average lean chop, cooked in the manner described below, will cost you about 255 calories, but nothing in cholesterol.

4 lean chops, excess fat trimmed away	salt and pepper to taste

Wash chops and rub generously with salt and pepper. Place on rack in roasting pan in 300 degree oven for 20 minutes on each side.

CHICKEN TARRAGON

Serves 1 or 2

¼ teaspoon salt
¼ teaspoon pepper
1 teaspoon dried tar-
  ragon

1 teaspoon lemon juice
½ teaspoon oil
2 chicken breasts

Put salt, pepper, tarragon, lemon juice and oil into a mortar and pestle and grind. Peel back the skin from the chicken and rub the meat with this mixture. Recover with the skin. Broil for 15 minutes with door open. The skin side of the breasts should be up. Turn, broil for another 10 minutes with door closed. Remove the skin before serving.

MUSSELS

For 1 or 2

2 finely chopped scal-
  lions
1 clove garlic, minced
¼ grated carrot
½ stalk of celery,
  chopped
2 tablespoons chopped
  parsley
1 tablespoon tomato
  paste

1 tablespoon diet mar-
  garine
½ cup dry vermouth
1 teaspoon lemon juice
¼ teaspoon thyme
2 dozen mussels,
  scrubbed and "de-
  bearded"

Put all ingredients but mussels into a heavy casserole dish with a tight cover. Blend over very low heat. Add mussels and steam for 10 minutes. Serve immediately, piping hot.

DIET CHEESECAKE

1 9-inch cake

Whenever we're dieting, we always find ourselves craving the worst possible dishes. So when the craving hits for cheesecake, don't run out for the frozen commercial variety; make it yourself and enjoy it. Guiltlessly.

Crust:

2 tablespoons diet margarine
14 slices melba toast
¼ teaspoon imitation butter flavor
¼ teaspoon vanilla
¼ teaspoon sugar substitute

Melt margarine; crush toast; mix both with the flavorings and sugar substitute. Press into 9-inch pie plate.

Filling:

3 tablespoons lemon juice
2 eggs, well beaten
2 8-ounce packages diet cream cheese, soft
1 cup sour-cream dressing
½ cup honey
3 tablespoons minced orange rind
1 tablespoon orange liqueur (optional)

Mix lemon juice and eggs. Add cream cheese, sour-cream dressing, honey, orange rind and liqueur. Blend. Pour into pie crust. Refrigerate.

SOUFFLÉED PEAR

Per person

This is a treat for the dieter, who can omit the sugar and enjoy the natural sweetness of the fruit. The recipe can be multiplied, but will take longer to cook.

1 egg, separated	1 pinch of cream of tartar
1 teaspoon arrowroot	
1 ripe pear	1 pinch of salt
	sugar

In the top of a double boiler, beat the egg yolk with the arrowroot until blended. Core the pear and cut into slivers. Mix together and heat over warm water until thickened. Beat the whites with the cream of tartar and salt until dry and stiff. Stir a quarter into the pear mixture. Then gently fold in the rest. Spoon into a soufflé dish that has been greased and coated with granulated sugar. Bake in a 375 degree oven for 20 minutes.

ASPARAGUS HOLLANDAISE

2 or 3 servings

1 pound thin asparagus spears	¾ teaspoon salt
1 beaten egg	½ teaspoon ground pepper
2 teaspoons lemon juice	½ cup diet mayonnaise

Steam asparagus for 5 to 7 minutes. Blend and heat the other ingredients in a double boiler, stirring constantly with a wire whisk. When your mock Hollandaise is completely blended, pour over the asparagus, and serve.

MARMALADE TART

5–6 servings

This delicious tart has only about 135 calories per serving.

Prepare Diet Pie Crust as instructed (see page 202). Roll out into an oblong, large enough for it to cover the bottom of a bread loaf pan and two inches up the sides. Trim off about ¾ inch all around. Reserve. Pinch the corners and the edge. Prick the pastry. Bake in 450 degree oven for 15 minutes. Cool and remove crust.

4 oranges
4 lemons
1 cup water

2 teaspoons sugar substitute

Cut 2 oranges and 2 lemons into thin slices. Halve. Put in saucepan with water and sugar substitute. Simmer for about 10 minutes, stirring occasionally. Remove slices with slotted spoon and reserve on a plate.

To the remaining liquid add the juice of 2 oranges and 2 lemons. After cleaning the white from inside the skin of ½ orange and 1 lemon, mince and add to the liquid. Add sugar substitute. Boil moderately fast until liquid is reduced to about 1½ cups. Liquify in an electric blender.

Layer the reserved slices of oranges and lemons in the tart. Pour over this layer the blended liquid. Cut the reserved pastry into thin strips and arrange on the tart. Bake in 350 degree oven for 15 minutes. Run under the broiler until strips are brown.

8

Cooking Together

MOST of us, for one reason or another, cook alone; and some of us like it that way. After a busy day in my office I welcome a quiet kitchen—temperamental as my stove can be at times, unlike my patients it has never forgotten to take its medicine or to show up on time for an appointment. Because my kitchen is organized the way I want it, I feel very much in control.

After a good eight to ten hours of trying to control diseases and health problems, I need that feeling. Talking about my feelings recently at a dinner where the subject of attitudes toward cooking arose, I noticed a woman near me nodding her head in agreement.

"I'm with you a hundred percent!" she told me. "I have three children, and I love them dearly. But two of them are pre-schoolers, and they require a lot of attention. I love being alone by myself in the kitchen while they're napping. It's a special kind of privacy, and I relish it!"

Single man and mother of three, we had a lot in common. But another guest that evening, a young wife who worked in the public school system, had a very different point of view.

"I think that there's nothing I hate more than being alone in the kitchen," she explained. "When Charles, my husband, and I get home from work, it's usually around six o'clock. We want to see each other, to relax, unwind, and enjoy each other's company. I hate having to go into the kitchen and fix a meal, so I usually cook the fastest things."

I appreciated her feelings, and I know that many people feel the same way. Not only do married men and women sometimes resent the time that preparing meals takes away from their time together, but single people often feel *most* single when it comes to cooking.

"You never feel more alone than when you go to the market to buy one lamb chop," a patient of mine once observed, "unless it's when you cook it."

If you like cooking by yourself, there's no problem. If, on the other hand, you don't like it, the situation can be easily remedied. Cooking, though it is often a solitary experience, doesn't have to be a one-person activity. Cooking with someone else can be productive, and it can be fun.

My own attitude, I'm sure, would be much different if I always cooked by myself. Though I usually cook by and for myself during the week, I often entertain on weekends. I don't hold formal dinners in my kitchen, needless to say, but when close friends come over, I frequently fix them a drink and invite them into my kitchen. Some people are content to sit, sip, and watch me do my work. Others offer to help, and I have had no reluctance about taking them up on their offers: some of my best dishes have been created this way, and some of my best friendships cemented.

Cooking involves a good deal of busywork, and, as indicated, the chopping, cutting, peeling, scraping and such can help to take our minds off the problems and tensions of the moment. But the line between busywork and monotony can be thin—boredom is the greatest enemy of creativity, in cooking and elsewhere. There's no reason why the full responsibility of preparing meals should be placed on one member of the family or one-half of a marriage.

Certainly the size of a kitchen is an important factor in determining how many people can work in the room without getting in one another's way. Most kitchens in apartments tend to be small, but frequently a pantry or dining room can be used for some part of meal preparation.

Who do you cook with? That depends, to a large extent, on personality. If you are living with a husband, wife, lover or roommate, he or she is the logical choice. But don't exclude children—bringing them into the kitchen is an ideal way of instilling in them an appreciation of the food they eat. Family cooking can help children understand the basic principles of good nutrition, and equally important, it can offer a chance for total family activity, in which each member shares in both the responsibility of the work and the pride of accomplishment at the finished result. Besides, my own experience has taught me that the earlier in life you learn how to cook, the better!

Growing up in Mansfield, Louisiana, I was raised in what now seems to be a bygone world. I'm not pining for the "good old days" and wistfully imagining the scent of magnolia blossoms; I pride myself on being an adaptable man, and my professional training has taught me that memories are usually much more picturesque than the realities they recall. But for most of my early life we had a cook in the kitchen. She, rather than my mother, prepared the meals. Later, when our cook left and my mother went into the kitchen, I remained outside, seeing meals only when they reached the table. I'd have had an easier time later on, I think, if I'd learned about cooking before I had to cook for myself.

A possible answer to this problem is my Family Dinner. Designed for a family of four, it can easily be adapted to families of any size. The menu consists of four dishes, each prepared primarily by one person. Facing the reality that Mom, in most cases, does most of the cooking, this dinner is also designed to give her a change of pace. Her contribution, a Lime Refrigerator Pie, is made ahead of time and left to chill in the refrigerator.

With her actual cooking out of the way, the mother is free to supervise other family members. Barbecued Spare Ribs are prepared by Dad on the grill (though the oven can be used in colder months). Little Sister takes charge of Stuffed Zucchini, stuffing the vegetable, wrapping it in foil, then handing it over to her father to cook on the grill for 20 minutes.

Boys, as every mother and father know only too well, love to play with knives, and my Young Man's Salad offers a load of ingredients to cut up—under supervision, of course. Besides creating a course of his own, the young man has a good chance to learn one of the safe, proper uses of a knife.

FAMILY DINNER

For 4

Barbecued Spare Ribs

¼ cup oil
1 onion, minced
1 green pepper, minced
2 cloves garlic, minced
½ teaspoon salt
¼ cup herb vinegar
1 8-ounce can tomato
    sauce
½ lemon, sliced
½ teaspoon sage
½ teaspoon cracked red
    pepper
½ teaspoon ground
    ginger
2 teaspoons dry mustard
1 teaspoon Worcester-
    shire sauce
1 teaspoon celery seeds
5 pounds spare ribs

Place oil in a saucepan; add the onion, green pepper, and garlic. Sauté until onion is soft. Add all other ingredients but ribs and simmer for 20 minutes, stirring occasionally. Coat ribs on both sides with sauce. Barbecue over glowing coals for about an hour and a half, turning and basting constantly. (For indoor chefs, about 45 minutes on a cookie sheet in a 350 degree oven should do almost as well. Before baking, though, boil the ribs in water for about 15 minutes to get out the fat that ordinarily would drip out on the grill.)

Stuffed Zucchini

4 large zucchinis, sliced crosswise
6 mushrooms, chopped
4 tablespoons chopped parsley
1¼ teaspoons salt
½ teaspoon pepper
¼ teaspoon rosemary
2 tablespoons butter oil

Cut the zucchinis in half. With a grapefruit knife scoop out the bullet-shaped zucchini halves, reserving the shells. Chop and combine the pulp, mushrooms, and parsley. Sauté the vegetables and seasonings in the butter, then simmer uncovered until almost dry. Lightly oil the outside of the zucchinis and stuff the mixture inside. Wrap in aluminum foil, and Dad can put them toward the back of his grill for about 20 minutes. (Or bake in a 250 degree oven for about the same length of time.)

Young Man's Salad

¼ cup yellow ("ballpark") mustard
½ cup mayonnaise
1 stalk celery, chopped
2 small green peppers, cut into rings
1 red onion, sliced into rings
1 carrot, cut into 2-inch strips
1 tomato, cut into wedges
1 dozen stuffed olives, sliced
1 dozen radishes, carved
1 head lettuce, shredded

Any would-be surgeon (girls, too, after all!) will get plenty of practice with this salad. The dressing is simple: combine mustard and mayonnaise in a small jar, and shake the daylights out of it. So much for the surgeon's delicate touch. . . .

Now wield the knife, as indicated, on everything else. Pour on the dressing and toss the whole thing 100 times.

Lime Refrigerator Pie

1 8-ounce box graham crackers
2 tablespoons butter, melted
3 eggs, separated
½ cup lime juice
1 teaspoon grated lime peel
1 14-ounce can, sweetened condensed milk
¼ teaspoon cream of tartar

Crush the graham crackers into crumbs. Mix in the butter with a fork. Line a 9-inch pie plate with the mixture.

Beat the egg yolks until light yellow. Slowly add the lime juice while continuing to beat. Stir in the condensed milk and lime peel and beat more. Pour this mixture into the graham-cracker crust.

Beat the egg whites and cream of tartar until stiff. Spread this over the other layer of the pie. Put under the broiler in the oven until the peaks of the egg whites are barely browned. Put the pie into the refrigerator to chill, if possible, for a full 24 hours.

I can't stress enough the importance of a family approach to cooking. Besides sharing the work load and instilling responsibility in children (and some fathers, for that matter), cooking is one thing that the whole family can do together on a regular basis. Unlike painting the house, cleaning the garage or attic, or seeding the lawn, cooking isn't a one-time task; it lends a sense of continuity to family life. I recommend that the family cook together once a week, perhaps on Saturdays or Sundays.

You'll find, if you are a parent, that involving children in the preparation of meals broadens their horizons. Junior may turn up his nose at canned peas, but he'll be more favorably disposed toward peas if he has the "fun" of shelling them. Beets, carrots and beans, let's admit, are not as popular with young people as hamburgers and hotdogs. But let the children have their own garden where they can "make" these vegetables grow, and chances are that they'll be so pleased with their accomplishment that they will be eager to eat the fruits (or vegetables in this case) of their labors!

It is important to remember that the foundations of good nutrition are laid in childhood. Tendencies toward obesity, and poor eating habits often show themselves early in life. And the earlier they are spotted, the earlier they can be dealt with. A balanced meal is one thing when it miraculously appears on the table; but the child who plays a role in preparing a balanced meal can better understand the concept of good nutrition, and carry this concept into adult life.

In addition to cooking with your children, try shopping with them. Don't make the excursion on a day when you are in a rush—pick a day when you are feeling relaxed and unpressured, and then take the children to the supermarket. They'll undoubtedly have a hundred questions, but you can teach them a lot by explaining why certain foods are bought and others are not. Make out a shopping list and follow it, rather than roaming the aisles at random. After a few such visits, the children will be able to help you shop rather than hinder your visits to the store.

Some people, of course, manage to reach maturity without knowing very much about food or cooking. Unlike children, uninformed adults may have very strong opinions even if they don't have facts—and they are more difficult to teach than are young people. When it comes to cooking with other adults, roles *have* to be played in the kitchen. The old cliché about too many chefs need not be true as long as these roles are defined.

If restaurant kitchens can function without falling victim to the "too many cooks" syndrome, so can yours. In the professional kitchen, the assistant doesn't intrude on the master chef, the salad chef sticks to his specialty. The pastry chef sticks to his, as does the sauce chef, and so on. When you begin cooking with someone else, don't start by doing. Instead, start by talking. In order to form the most effective kitchen partnership, if it's only for one meal, see what specific talents each partner can bring to the joint venture. It isn't merely a matter of who knows what—how each of you *feels* and your basic personality types also determine the role you play.

For openers, accept the premise that one of you is going to be in charge, though the degree of "kitchen dominance" is determined not so much by decision (most of us, given the opportunity, have an innate desire to be in charge, in the kitchen and out of it!) as by expertise.

If, for example, you are an expert cook and you are cooking with a novice, your kitchen partnership may take on a master/slave aspect. I'm not suggesting that you beat your partner with a meat tenderizer, or that you throw eggs or garbage at him. But if you know what you're doing and he doesn't, then you will have to give the orders. If he or she is to help effectively, and to contribute, then these orders will have to be followed.

Jambalaya, a traditional Southern favorite, is a perfect dish for an experienced chef and an apprentice to make together. The apprentice, following instructions, can prepare all the ingredients, from the sausage to the chopped celery, the peppers, scallions, etc. This is a good deal of work, which the master chef can supervise, and then the apprentice's ingredients can be combined by the expert into a tasty, filling dish.

JAMBALAYA

4 ample servings

1 pound ground sausage meat
1½ teaspoons salt
1 bay leaf, chopped
¾ teaspoon thyme
¼ teaspoon Tabasco
1 cup chopped celery
1 cup chopped onions
1 cup green pepper, minced

1 cup chopped scallions (greens and all)
½ cup chopped parsley
1 cup tomatoes (fresh or canned)
3 cloves garlic, minced
1 6-ounce can tomato paste
2 cups rice
2 pounds shrimp
3 cups stock or tomato juice

Sauté the sausage in a Dutch oven until almost brown. Add the spices and herbs, then the celery, onions, green pepper, scallions, parsley, tomatoes and garlic. Sauté until all are soft. Stir in the tomato paste, then add the rice, the shrimp and the stock. Cover and bake in a warm oven (325 degrees) for about 30 minutes, or until the rice is tender. Stir from time to time; if it looks too juicy, remove the cover for a while.

CHOCOLATE AMARETTO MOUSSE

Should feed 4

In this dessert, the roles are not so much a matter of who gives the orders as who does what. This recipe is an ideal way to utilize basic personality traits or, for a change of pace, to reverse the roles that are played in broader, out-of-the-kitchen, relationships. Let the usually more passive partner whip the egg whites and the cream. The customarily more aggressive individual does the blending and the folding. Here's how it's done:

1 envelope plain gelatin	1 pinch salt
6 eggs, separated	½ cup sugar
2 squares unsweetened chocolate	1 pint heavy cream
1 cup milk	2 tablespoons grated lemon rind
3 ounces Amaretto liqueur	

Soften gelatin in specified amount of cold water. Meanwhile, beat egg yolks until light yellow. Add the salt and sugar; mix well in a large enamel pot. Melt the chocolate with the milk in a small enamel saucepan. Add to it the yolk mixture; blend well over low heat, stirring constantly. Cool this thoroughly. Add amaretto to the softened gelatin—make sure all the gelatin is dissolved. Stir into cooled sauce and beat briskly with a small wire whisk until smooth. (If this mixture is not smooth, you'll need to strain it through a sieve.) Beat the egg whites and fold into previous mixture. Then beat the cream and fold it in. Transfer to a soufflé dish for chilling. Garnish top with lemon rind.

Besides providing a chance for shared activity, cooking together affords a chance to examine, explore and perhaps better accept the roles we play in life—and to appreciate them for what we are. So often we feel that being ourselves is, somehow, wrong.

Marilyn, a patient of mine, came into my office one day with a worried expression on her face. I knew that she was in good health, having given her a checkup the week before, and was puzzled—particularly when

I remembered that she'd told me how well her husband, Gary, was doing at the company where he'd recently been promoted another notch up the executive ladder.

"What's the problem?" I asked my patient.

Marilyn sighed. "I think it's me, Dr. Parrish. I just spent a few days talking with my sister, who was visiting with us, and she told me that my marriage is in real trouble."

"Your sister told you?" I asked, wanting to be sure I hadn't missed something. Marilyn nodded. "Doesn't that strike you as a little bit odd? I would think that if you had a serious marriage problem, you and your husband would know about it long before she did."

"Oh, Gary is happy," Marilyn explained. "That is, he seems happy. But Lorraine—my sister—says that he's secretly miserable. I hate to say it, but I guess that I'm one of those bossy, dominating wives. I always tell Gary what to do. Lorraine says that he probably has all kinds of hostility bottled up inside himself, and that he resents me—"

"Now let's get one thing straight," I insisted. "Did your husband confide these feelings to your sister, or was she just offering her opinion?"

Marilyn informed me that her husband, in fact, hadn't complained at all. But she felt sure that her sister was in a position to judge. "She reads a lot of books about psychology."

I tried to explain that both armchair and professional psychologists can speak about generalities, but that specific realities are what really count. I asked Marilyn what had brought about her sister's "diagnosis" of the marriage.

"It was a number of things," Marilyn revealed. "I usually remind Gary about things that have to be done in the house . . . and we talk about his business a lot, and I offer suggestions. But Lorraine said she really saw the writing on the wall one day when we were getting dinner ready. Gary likes to help out in the kitchen. He says it relaxes him after a day at the office, especially with all the tension he's under. Anyway, I was telling him what to do with whatever we were cooking—chicken, I think—and later on my sister said that I was castrating my husband!"

It took some time, but I managed to explain to Marilyn that unless she felt her husband was unhappy, or unless he expressed displeasure, the only problem was in her sister's mind. Having treated this patient for a number of years, I was familiar with her personality, and her husband's. The truth was that Marilyn's strength and encouragement had helped motivate her husband to move ahead in his work. She was bright, aggressive, and a very vigorous personality.

Gary was hardly a passive lamb. As an executive he had a lot of responsibility, with a large department to supervise. If in his marriage he wanted a "dominating" wife, it was hardly up to Marilyn's sister to make judgments. Marilyn, I told her, had to learn to accept the fact that she liked telling Gary what to do at home as much as he liked being told what to do. The marriage worked, and that was what mattered. Questioning our personalities is very constructive, and we can all benefit from examining ourselves; but while it is sometimes nice to be a leader, it's equally pleasing to be a follower, if that's what we want.

Knowing who you are is essential to psychological well-being. And the kitchen offers many clues to personality types. Take for example the Spinach Salad, an ideal course for two people to prepare. The two principal steps involved are washing the spinach and tossing it. Given free choice, the individual with a compulsive personality will instinctively take to the sink, where he can channel his obsessiveness on washing the last trace of grit from the leaves. The free-spirited person, on the other hand, will probably prefer the tossing and taste-testing. Try the Spinach Salad recipe at the end of this chapter—and you can experiment yourself!

Good relationships can be made better by doing

things together. And cooking is something that two people can share beautifully. Examine one of my favorite pasta dishes, Vermicelli with Salsa Marinara, which follows immediately. This is a dish that has to be better for joint effort. The thin vermicelli cooks almost immediately, and it must be watched. While one person handles the pasta, the other prepares the sauce. This way, both can be ready at the exact same moment, solving the problem of timing: togetherness at work!

VERMICELLI WITH SALSA MARINARA

Feeds 4 or so

3 tablespoons butter	¾ teaspoon salt
3 tablespoons flour	1 pound vermicelli
½ cup milk	ground pepper
2 cups strong fish stock	chopped parsley

In a small enamel saucepan over low heat, blend the butter and flour with a wire whisk until thick. In another pan bring the milk and fish stock to a boil and stir into the roux. Add the salt, and continue to stir until blended—keeping it very hot until the vermicelli is ready.

The other partner should have boiled the vermicelli until it's, as the Italians say, *al dente*—gives slight resistance to the teeth. Drain the vermicelli. Toss vermicelli and sauce lightly. Sprinkle with pepper and parsley to taste.

Good relationships and not-so-good relationships can both suffer from a common problem: taking the other person for granted. Women frequently complain that they spend hours on end in the kitchen and receive little appreciation—the meal is eaten in a fraction of the time it took to prepare it, and their husbands and children leave the table.

"I get so damn mad I want to scream!" said one wife who came to me with her husband to discuss their marriage problems. "I spend three hours cooking, and Tom wolfs the food down then leaves me with the dishes on the table and a mess in the kitchen!"

"What am I supposed to do?" Tom, the husband, asked. "I tell her that I like her cooking. Isn't that enough?"

Obviously for this woman it wasn't. And when you come right down to it, why should it be? Particularly today, when we are recognizing that careers in the home are just as demanding as careers in business or professional fields (and when more and more women are working outside the home), responsibilities of family life *should* be shared.

A romanticized version of this concept is my Dandelion Salad. One person gathers dandelion greens in the wild, or finds a place where he can buy them. The other person is pleased with the gesture—and in return fixes the salad.

DANDELION SALAD

For 2

½ pound dandelion leaves	½ teaspoon salt
¼ cup oil	1 pinch pepper
1½ tablespoons vinegar	1 teaspoon dry mustard
	¼ teaspoon sugar

The dandelion leaves should be washed well and dried. Combine the other ingredients into a jar or the blender and shake (or blend) well. Dress the greens with this mixture.

Less romantic but very practical is extending kitchen cooperation outside the physical kitchen. Not every meal has to be prepared by two, or by the whole family.

Some of us, let's face it, prefer to do our cooking by ourselves; and others prefer not to cook at all. But that doesn't mean that help can't be enlisted in setting the table, clearing it, and in cleaning up the kitchen.

If hobbies and pastimes can be put to constructive use, the effect on a relationship can be marvelous. I spent some time last summer at the Long Island home of some married friends, and each morning by the time I woke up the husband was long gone.

"That Mark!" Karen said. "Every morning it's the same. He gets up at the crack of dawn to go fishing!"

"Do you mind that much?" I asked innocently.

"Mind?" she answered, astonished. "Of course I mind! It's bad enough that we haven't had breakfast together since I don't know when; but then those fish of his take up all the space in my refrigerator and freezer until we can find someone to give them to!"

As we talked some more, Karen told me that she had never learned how to cook fish. Though she ordered it from time to time in restaurants, she confessed that the prospect of cleaning fish was disgusting to her. "I was the girl who fainted when we had to do the dissections in biology class," she told me. "I just couldn't stand cutting them and taking all that *stuff* out!"

I suggested that her husband was probably not quite so squeamish. If he could bait a hook, no doubt he'd be pleased to clean the fish as well. Sure enough, when Mark returned with some fresh striped bass, he had no reluctance whatsoever about cleaning it. He told me that he'd have offered before—if Karen had shown any interest!

There's something about catching a fish or getting one's own fresh food that is very satisfying, and not only because of the superior taste. It's a kind of throwback to living off the land that gives us a sense of our own ability to provide for ourselves. And it's particularly enjoyable because we don't have to do it all the time. The fisherman who provides a tasty catch, the scuba diver who brings up a lobster, the hunter who captures fresh game—increases his satisfaction a hundredfold if the catch is turned into a meal.

Gardening is a pleasant activity, and an equally viable form of "providing." But as much fun as puttering in the garden may be, there is an immense pleasure in sitting down to a salad made from tomatoes and greens you've grown yourself. As mentioned, city dwellers, like myself, can find fulfillment in growing their own herbs.

Kitchen activities in partnership work best when we use our knowledge of personality traits to full advantage. Some of us are more energetic than others, and some of us are lazy. The less energetic individual should set his sights on one simple task—paring carrots, washing vegetables or creating one simple dish. Realistic goals help to avoid tension and pressure, and one completed project will be far more appreciated than myriad uncompleted starts.

Some of us, too, are more patient than others. The impatient man or woman is not the ideal choice for preparing Hollandaise sauce for eggs Benedict, or anything else that requires constant watching and slow, careful cooking. Instead, his or her personality is better suited to getting the English muffins and poaching the eggs.

There are those of us who thrive on precise work, and those of us who don't. My Chicken Cutlets Marsala provide a good opportunity for the would-be surgeon to bone chicken breasts (an activity that I don't particularly like because I get too compulsive about it) while someone else prepares the artichokes and sauce.

CHICKEN CUTLETS MARSALA

2 servings

2 chicken breasts	1 teaspoon lemon juice
1 6-ounce jar artichokes	¼ cup chopped shallots
1 tablespoon butter	1½ teaspoons flour
¼ teaspoon salt	3 tablespoons water
1 pinch pepper	¼ cup Marsala wine

Bone the chicken breasts (see below). Drain the liquid from the artichokes into a skillet. Add to this the butter, salt, pepper, lemon juice and shallots; heat over medium flame until butter bubbles. Sauté the chicken in this mixture, about 5 minutes on each side. Remove the breasts to a plate and keep warm in the oven. Place artichokes in the same saucepan and sauté them for just a minute or 2, then place them with the chicken breasts.

Scrape loose all residue in the skillet; mix the flour and water and add to the skillet, stirring over low heat until the mixture thickens. Slowly stir in the water and Marsala wine. Pour the sauce over the chicken and artichokes. Serve.

BONING CHICKEN BREASTS: Take a very sharp knife and first cut the meat away from the ribs. A slash then at the wishbone and it should all come out in one piece. Place the meat between two layers of wax paper and bash a few times with a mallet or the bottom of a heavy skillet. Presto: chicken cutlets.

There are those of us, it should be stressed, who would like to do more in the kitchen than we know how to do, and wanting to contribute without being able to is a frustrating experience. But decorating food requires little or no knowledge of cooking, and there are many imaginative garnishes to choose from.

Then, too, there are also Everybody Cookies—a

simple easy-to-handle pastry that can be shaped into anything the group desires. This is an excellent activity for the whole family to share, and it's easy, too, on whoever is preparing the cookie pastry.

EVERYBODY COOKIES

A family-sized batch

6 tablespoons butter
1 cup sugar
1 egg
¼ cup milk
1 teaspoon lemon juice

½ teaspoon lemon rind, grated
¼ teaspoon vanilla
2½ cups flour
1 teaspoon baking powder
¼ teaspoon salt

Soften the butter, sift the sugar into it and cream well. In a separate bowl beat the egg, milk, lemon juice, lemon rind and vanilla. In a third bowl sift the flour, baking powder and salt together. Add alternately one-third of the liquid and dry mixtures to the butter, blending until all is well mixed. Chill.

Roll pastry out ¼″ thick.

The pastry can be cut or molded into any form, then sugared or decorated. Place on a lightly-oiled cookie sheet and bake in a 400 degree oven until brown (about 15 to 20 minutes, depending on the size of the cookies).

If cooking with someone else is productive, it is also fun: mistakes are easier to laugh at when you have someone with whom you can share the humor as well as the responsibility. A friend and I frequently cook together on weekends, and I always look forward to spending weekends at his house in Amagansett, Long

Island. We've created some delicious meals over the years—but we've made our share of mistakes as well.

I remember the time we decided that we'd make a bouillabaisse. I wrote the recipe down on a paper on which I'd already written a recipe for something completely different. Somehow I managed to fold the piece of paper so that we had the right ingredients, but the incorrect proportions. Common sense should have told us that 15 pounds of fish was a little excessive for a "serves four to six" recipe—but as it so often does, common sense failed us.

The result was that several hours later we ended up with a washtub full of bouillabaisse. Realizing our mistake wasn't going to get rid of the excess, which would have served 20, so we decided to play a game. Since we had 20 portions, we each made up a list of the nine people we'd each most like to invite to dinner. Our respective guest lists turned out to be very different, and the only guest we had in common was Raquel Welch. We needed an extra man, and tossed something—a fish head, no doubt, since there was such an abundant supply—and Arthur won. He invited Westbrook Pegler, whom we decided we'd seat next to Eleanor Roosevelt. We paired Pearl Bailey off with George Wallace, General de Gaulle drew Martha Raye as a dinner partner, and so on. It was good for some laughs, that game of ours—and I know that if I'd overcooked so much on my own, I'd have been muttering and bad-tempered rather than amused. As for the bouillabaisse, we ate it for a *long time*, and each of us took some back to New York City.

Here are some recipes to be cooked by two or more. And please—read the proportions right . . . or have an imaginary guest list ready.

MAKE-THE-BEST-OF-IT-CAULIFLOWER

Sometimes you'll want to admit, at least to yourself, that you hate dieting, and "diet" foods. Go ahead: admit it. Maybe even feel sorry for yourself. But then go ahead: make the best of it. Admit it to your kitchen partner too. Then let him or her help you make the best of it. Let the cauliflower be steamed, and the sauce prepared. Then you come in, perform the required surgery on the buds and administer the sauce.

1 bunch cauliflower	grated Parmesan
1 cup yogurt	cheese
1 teaspoon cornstarch	¼ teaspoon salt
1½ ounces chopped	⅛ teaspoon pepper
Swiss cheese	⅛ teaspoon paprika
1 tablespoon freshly	

Steam the cauliflower for about 15 minutes, until it is almost tender. Meanwhile, place yogurt and cornstarch in top of double boiler and stir until it begins to thicken. Add cheeses, salt and pepper and cook until the mixture is smooth.

Remove the cauliflower and cool long enough to handle. Cut off the buds and arrange in baking dish, which has been lightly greased. (Grease with a dieter's conscience; diet margarine will do if you'll both feel better for it.) Pour on the sauce and serve.

CONTRIBUTION BOILED DINNER

Feeds 6 to 7

A big meal that a houseful of guests can pitch in to prepare. The hostess gets the meat started, then her guests throw their contributions into the pot. One can prepare the herb bouquet; another the vegetables. Any leftover guests can help put together a few before-dinner drinks.

10 cups water
6 teaspoons salt
1 tablespoon vinegar
2 cloves garlic
4 teaspoons allspice
½ teaspoon mustard seed
3½ pounds fresh pork butt

¼ teaspoon peppercorns
1 tablespoon celery seed
3 onions, halved
2 beets, peeled and halved
3 sweet potatoes, halved
1 cabbage, quartered

Put water, salt and vinegar in a deep pot. Tie the spices and herbs in clean cheesecloth. Bring to a boil and add the pork; boil for 1½ hours. Add the vegetables and more water, if necessary, to cover. Bring gently to a boil and continue boiling for 45 minutes, until potatoes are done.

Remove the solids from the pot, place in a tureen and keep warm. Reduce the stock to about 8 cups. Pour stock over the solids in tureen. Serve with horseradish sauce on the side.

HORSERADISH SAUCE

½ cup prepared horse-radish

¼ cup mayonnaise
1 teaspoon lemon juice

Mix ingredients together in a small dish and serve with a small spoon.

CHICKEN TETRAZZINI

Serves 4

Cooking together need not always be a kitchen version of "roles people play." Chicken Tetrazzini, for example, has so many little steps—removing the meat from the bones, preparing the sauce, cooking the pasta —that it's true togetherness. My cousin Hall and his wife Ann rate this recipe as one of their favorites, and their long and happy marriage must be a testament to their kitchen partnership.

8 large chicken breasts
¼ pound fresh mushrooms
½ pound butter
1 cup flour
4 cups milk
1 pound extra-sharp cheddar
1 12-ounce bottle of imported beer
1 8-ounce package vermicelli
½ cup cooking sherry
½ cup grated Parmesan cheese
¼ teaspoon salt
1 pinch paprika

Place chicken in a large pot, cover with water, bring to a boil and cook until meat can be easily pulled from bones. Sauté chopped mushrooms in ¼ pound of butter; then put cooked mushrooms aside. Pull meat from bones; keep meat aside and discard bones.

In a heavy enamel saucepan melt ¼ pound butter. Stir in 1 cup flour with wire whisk. Heat four cups milk to boiling and pour in flour-butter mixture all at once beating vigorously with whisk. The mixture should be so thick that it is almost solid. Chop or grate 1 pound extra-sharp cheddar cheese and stir into flour butter mixture until cheese is melted. Do this over low heat. When cheese is melted, pour beer in a little at a time until sauce is about the consistency of medium thick gravy. You may not need all the beer. Measure 16 cups of liquid to which you will add the boned chicken and the sautéed mushrooms. Cook vermicelli until *al dente*. Mix this with chicken mushroom sauce while blending in ½ cup sherry. Spread mixture into large flat casserole dish, sprinkle with salt, paprika and Parmesan cheese, and cook for 20 minutes in a preheated oven at 350 degrees.

The remaining sauce may be used for vegetables or frozen for next week's leftovers.

SPINACH SALAD

2 or more servings

½ pound fresh spinach (whole leaves)	2 eggs (not quite hard cooked)
½ pound bacon (fried and drained dry)	1½ pounds fresh mushrooms (optional)
2 tablespoons salad oil	¼ teaspoon pepper
4 tablespoons lemon juice	

Wash the spinach leaves and place in a salad bowl. Crumble the bacon and slice the eggs and mushrooms over it. Prepare a dressing of oil, lemon juice, salt and pepper. Pour over the greens and toss.

Here is where two personalities can complement each other. The compulsive can make sure the spinach leaves are well washed and dried, without being bruised. He can also fry the bacon and drain. He can time the boiling of the eggs so the yellow is still slightly soft and can peel it so that no white sticks to the shell. This is no easy task, but a challenge!

Place the eggs into cold water and bring to a gentle boil: reduce heat and let simmer for 15 minutes.

Immediately place them under cold water. When cool, roll between the palms to crack. Gently but thoroughly peel under running cold water.

The other partner then crumbles the bacon, adds the sliced eggs and mushrooms to the salad, shakes the dressing and tosses the salad.

9

Sex in the Kitchen

IN the process of working on *Cooking As Therapy*, I've found that writing a book is similar in many ways to creating a new dish. A variety of thoughts must be put into some reasonable order, the "ingredients" being treated in a manner and amount that will determine the degree of their emphasis in the final result. Shortly after starting this book I showed my outline—the equivalent of a recipe—to a writer friend.

"Sex in the Kitchen," he read aloud, his tone questioning and critical. "What is there to say about it? Don't you just do it?"

Some people, I'm sure, do, I explained—adding that I was more concerned with curry and other features of Indian cuisine than in adapting the positions of the Kama Sutra to fit in between the range and the blender!

My friend, like so many people, didn't see the connection between food and sex—at least not at first glance. Too often the only way sex and the kitchen are related is in the term sexism. The kitchen, I admit, is its bastion. The sexual revolution and the women's movement have changed things to some degree, but there is still a long, long way to go.

In the American family as at present constructed, there is little equality in the kitchen. It is still the "woman's place," and many women can and do feel imprisoned there. Why not? When a wife cooks a meal, its considered par for the course, part of the "job." But when a man prepares something, it's a special event.

How unfair—and how unrealistic. The sexist stereotype images we hold of our roles are far from "natural," or "traditional," as all but the most chauvinistic individuals agree. There is nothing feminine or dainty about standing over a hot stove—and chopping, cutting, and moving heavy pots and pans around is hard ("masculine" if you will) work! I firmly believe that if you examine the real reason why our cherished image of a family cook brings to mind a heavyset woman, it's not that she's overweight from enjoying her own cooking: she *needs* to be big and strong to do her job.

Men often fail to see this. "Masculine" cooking, in sexist terms, means reaching into our primitive past and doing something that involves fire—the grill or barbecue having replaced the front of the cave. Cooking with liquor is also considered "men's stuff."

The Shah of Iran recently teased a feminist interviewer by telling her that for all the cooking women do, the world's greatest chefs have been men. He remembered, I hope, that the professional kitchens of the world are the most sexist of all. Women have never been given the chance to succeed. The professional message, in every culture and language is this: *Leave the pressed duck to the men, lady, and stick to your tuna-noodle casserole!*

But if traditional sexist roles are unfair, some aspects of outdated thinking have at least some validity. Perhaps not *the* way, but *a* way to another person's heart is through the proverbial stomach. Let's face the facts: if you've had a hard day, or for that matter not such a hard day, and someone prepares an enjoyable, satisfying meal for you, you're going to be pleased.

We admire not only the expertise of the cooking, but the gesture—the consideration, attention, and effort that have been expended in our behalf. Whether this overture is sexual or not, or the meal conducive to sexuality, depends on two primary considerations: first and foremost is who is doing the cooking; second is what is being served.

I can't begin to count the times when patients in my office, often on some totally unrelated matter, have paused to ask me if there isn't some food that has aphrodisiac properties. "You know, doc," a typical inquiry begins, "I know it isn't true, but this friend of mine told me that if you eat raw meat, it kind of sexes you up, you know?"

I know, I tell my patients. I know the stories about raw meat, as well as those about shellfish, game, green vegetables, herbs, spices and assorted seasonings. Almost everything that can be eaten, I'm firmly convinced, is considered an aphrodisiac by somebody, somewhere. As is so often the case, amid all the old wives' tales and folk remedies there is a modicum of truth. But it is founded in simple fact rather than any "magical" properties that science has yet to discover. "If there was a food, or a seasoning, or a dish that really improved people's sex lives," I frequently tell my patients, "you wouldn't have to ask me about it. Believe me, whatever it is would be sold on every street corner!"

A varied diet is, not surprisingly, the best "menu" for a good sex life. Sex is an activity involving both the mind and the body. The loss of sexual interest, or the inability to function sexually, can be a sign of sickness or a health problem, or it can be—and *is*—a "pause" in our individual biochemical cycles. During some periods, we are more sexually active than others: this is a fact of life.

Obviously the individual who is in good health is going to function better in sexual terms than someone who is not in good health, and a varied diet supplies the nutrients that good health demands. Research studies linking various *specific* vitamins to sex are incomplete. While Vitamin E may well be found, at some future date, to be clearly linked (as many believe) to our libido, the other vitamins and minerals are also necessary.

As a general rule, you have to feel good to have a good sex life. Colds, flus and viruses "turn off" sexuality, and anxiety and tension can do the same. What turns *on* sexual interest is a very personalized matter. I remember being very surprised when an internationally known gourmet told me that a good, *big* meal aroused him. "I'm always in the mood to make love after a big dinner," this gentleman told me, "particularly if it's done well. I don't know why you find this so surprising."

"I think it's because I want to go to bed, too, after a big dinner," I answered, "only the last thing I want to do is make love. I want to go to sleep!"

For many people, this latter reaction is natural. After a heavy meal, we feel lazy. Our bodies need time for digestion. Perhaps the gentleman I spoke with so enjoys the pleasure of food that eating itself is almost a sexual experience for him. But most people find a modest midnight supper "sexier" than a big Sunday dinner.

"Don't tell me that seasoning doesn't make a difference," a patient of mine insisted. She prided herself on her cooking, with good reason, and I wasn't about to argue—at least not until I heard her out. "Dr. Parrish, it's a fact. Highly seasoned food always excites people. It's some kind of chemical reaction. There's this special type of pepper that I buy, and the secret is in the freshness of the peppercorns."

The supposed secret is very simple to understand. Spices can stimulate the body's sexual apparatus in that, as mentioned, they often produce a mild irritation in the urinary tract. This sensation can be interpreted by the nervous system as a sexual stimulus. That doesn't mean that red pepper is a guarantee for a happy sex life. Let's not forget that seasonings, particularly in quantity, can have a variety of effects. And indigestion and heartburn are, for many of us, among them!

A sexy meal is a matter of shadow as well as substance. How food is served makes a big difference. A candlelit table for two with attractive linens and glassware is a lot more romantic than a cafeteria line. Soft music and fresh flowers are more stimulating, in a sexual sense, than the clatter of dishes and the clutter of unwashed pots.

A picnic can be sexy. So can a meal of hot dogs roasted in the fireplace. Some find formal meals glamorous, luxurious, and exciting. But others find this type of dining uncomfortable and, in some cases, even threatening. Discomfort and a sense of obligation are not the choices of mood wanted for a romantic evening or afternoon.

A newspaper article about my cooking brought an interesting letter from the Midwest and I had to admire the candor of the woman who wrote to me. "It may sound foolish," she wrote, "but I thought I'd take the chance and ask you a question. My husband and I have been married for seventeen years, and we both feel very settled in our lives. Everything is routine, sex included. A friend suggested that by cooking new foods I could excite my husband, so I bought an 'international' cookbook. My friend said it worked for her, but it seems that foreign foods have no effect on my husband's sexual interest. Is something wrong with him —or with my cooking?"

One can't, of course, treat problems like this by mail, but the thinking behind the letter made sense. After a number of years together, many couples find that life becomes routine, and that sexual activity slows down. New clothes, hairstyles and surroundings can reactivate a sluggish sexual relationship for some people—why, then, shouldn't a new type of cuisine have the same effect?

For some people it does work; for others, it doesn't. Some people like new tastes. They are adventurers, always ready to try a new restaurant or a new kind of dish. Others are traditionalists, and they find security in eating the same things over and over. The man or woman who is apprehensive about snow peas and Chinese mushrooms is going to be so busy wondering what's on his plate when he or she is served an Oriental meal that there won't be time for the meal to encourage a romantic mood!

It is essential, therefore, to know for whom you're cooking when it comes to figuring out menus that are intended to arouse the appetite for more than food. And keep in mind, too, that even the most common, simple meal can have a surprisingly romantic flavor, as the patient of a colleague of mine found out. (Doctors, like everyone else, talk shop, and for some time I'd followed a case that a psychiatrist friend of mine was treating.)

Betty and Ron were a young, bright, successful couple. Both had careers, Betty working as a decorator and Ron working his way up the executive ladder of a brokerage house. "They're very well suited to each other in just about every way but one," their doctor told me. "For all their drive, ambition and compatibility in many areas, both husband and wife are very immature when it comes to admitting a mistake or giving an apology. Little arguments aren't resolved: instead they don't speak to each other for days on end."

The couple had wisely decided to seek professional help, and their doctor, in joint and separate sessions, was trying to help them understand themselves better as individuals in the hope of helping them as a couple. One day, my doctor friend and I had a drink after work. He seemed pleased with himself, and I soon learned why. "Well," he reported, "Betty still isn't quite able to come out and say, 'I was wrong and I'm sorry,' but she's making great strides. The other night they had a fight, and as usual they gave each other the silent treatment. It went on for two days. Then, last night, still not speaking to her husband, she cooked his favorite meal."

"And?" I asked.

The doctor laughed. "According to Betty, they never got around to eating it. He was so surprised and so pleased that they went off to bed—and both of them said they had an unusually good time there."

This story illustrates an important point. Meat loaf is certainly not the answer to the problems we face in our relationships, marital or otherwise. Neither can a single meal really change or improve our sex lives—it just isn't that simple. What food *can* do is act as a signal, depending on how it is served and prepared. An attractive looking table lets whomever you are serving know that you are interested in his enjoyment and anxious to please. A special effort—going out of your way to find Bibb lettuce or watercress for a salad instead of the usual, boring lettuce and tomato wedge, for example—is a non-verbal way of expressing a special feeling. A departure from the mundane even if it is only serving the same foods you usually do but this time on your best china, can be effective.

Taking one's partner for granted, I firmly believe, is one of the greatest enemies of a good sex life. We forget to appreciate; and therefore there is increasingly less stimulus to what will be appreciated.

Mealtimes are often ideal times for constructive approaches to the problems we face in our relationships; and the best way to approach solutions is to look at them realistically. It sounds a lot easier than it is, as I've discovered so many times in my practice. Frequently we tell ourselves, each other, and sometimes our doctors, that sex is the problem, when in fact sexual problems usually reflect other, deeper points of contention.

"John never wants to make love to me any more," Kay, a patient of mine, complained. "When we were married, we couldn't get enough of each other. Now that I'm going through the change of life, he thinks of me as an old woman. He doesn't want to touch me." She had had some problems with the climacteric, and she'd waited a while before seeking my help. She needed supplemental estrogen and some tranquilizers to help her get through this difficult time, but I felt that she also needed better communication with her husband.

"Did John tell you that he thought you were undesirable?" I asked.

"Of course not, Dr. Parrish. He doesn't have to say anything. He never touches me, so I know. And besides, I can tell that I'm turning into an old woman."

"Have you ever told John you feel this way?" I asked.

Kay replied that she hadn't. "I wouldn't know how to talk about it."

I suggested that she make the effort, and gave her a direction. "A quiet meal, Kay," I said, "can be an excellent place to discuss the feelings that should be shared between a husband and wife. We all need reassurance from time to time, and we certainly need to air our problems, fears and doubts. Why don't you try preparing a nice, leisurely meal—make it something like a roast or perhaps a chicken or duck, something that you can serve and then sit down to enjoy. The idea is to make something that won't demand your running into the kitchen every five minutes, so fix everything ahead of time. Salad, main dish, and dessert, too.

"Serve a nice wine," I suggested. "Not too much of it—you're not trying to escape from your problems, but you'll probably find that after a glass or two, you'll be less inhibited. Enjoy your husband's company, and let him enjoy yours. As you eat and relax, try telling John how you feel. And, Kay, don't be surprised if he shares some of his own feelings with you. He may have some problems that he wants to get out in the open as much as you do yours."

A few days later, when I was looking through some

test results, my secretary put through a call from Kay, who had insisted that her message was urgent. Her bright tone told me that for once, the important news was good! "For the first time in my life, Dr. Parrish," she said, "I let the dishes just sit on the table. I followed your advice and made a nice dinner. We had Cornish hens stuffed with wild rice, a nice salad, and an ice cream pie that's probably very bad for my figure, but one of my husband's favorite desserts. We sat and talked like we haven't talked in years, finishing a bottle of wine. After dinner we moved into the living room to talk some more. And you know what? John feels much the same way I do about our lack of communication. I guess we just had forgotten how to talk."

Obviously, Kay and John couldn't make up in one meal for all the time they'd spent not communicating, but that start helped to improve the marriage. As doubts and insecurities were shared, communication became better and easier. Opening minds and emotions is essential to a good relationship. In this case, as in many others, good communication led to renewed sexual interest.

For many families, quiet, leisurely meals are a rarity. It's difficult to discuss intimate emotions if junior and his sister are squabbling at the other end of the table. And the complete play-by-play description of Billy's little league game may be fascinating—but not if you're trying to have a romantic dinner. My advice is to set aside an evening or two a week. On those nights, serve the children at the usual time, or perhaps a little earlier than usual. Eat with them, if you wish, but eat lightly. This might make an excellent time for *whole-family* communication; later, when the children are in bed (or perhaps spending the night with friends, if it can be arranged) enjoy a leisurely late night supper with your wife or husband. Restaurants, of course, are another solution.

At home or eating out, make the meal a total experience. Make it as pleasant and relaxed as possible.

Though "sexy" foods are a matter of personal choice, some foods are more *sensual* than others. In planning menus, think of textures. You might, for example, serve crisp green peas. Nothing is more sensual than an ordinary taste made spectacularly extraordinary; instead of mushy, overcooked peas, cook them only lightly—and add the fresh taste of mint.

MINTED PEAS

Serves 2

2 to 3 cups shelled green
  peas
¼ cup chopped fresh
  mint
¼ teaspoon salt

dash of pepper
2 tablespoons cream
  cheese
2 tablespoons sour
  cream

Cook the peas as directed on page 78—or use your favorite recipe—but cut the cooking time down to a minimum . . . just enough to make them edible, but still crisp. Add half the mint to the peas as they cook. Mix the other half with the salt, pepper, cream cheese and sour cream. Combine this sauce with the cooking liquid and reheat. Or refrigerate, and serve chilled.

Use the same approach to flavors, incorporating a wide range of them in your meal. Stimulating several senses—sight, taste, feel and smell—certainly can't hurt your sex life. Include a sweet taste, and instead of a heavy dessert, try serving a sorbet (or frozen punch) to "refresh the palate" midway through the meal. A sherbet or ice will do, but you can make your own sorbets. One of my favorites follows.

NECTARINE FREEZE

2 to 4 servings

1 pound nectarines, chopped	⅓ cup lime juice
1½ cups water	2 tablespoons instant coffee
⅓ cup sugar	

Mix all the ingredients together and simmer for about 15 minutes. Liquify in a blender. Freeze. Let sit in the refrigerator for at least a half hour before you serve. To use as a creamy dessert, thaw sufficiently to blend in some heavy cream. Refreeze until just mushy, and serve.

Try ending your meal with espresso. Besides adding an astringent wind-up taste to your dinner, the caffeine will help perk up you and your companion. And you can always move on to the living room for an after-dinner drink, and whatever else may follow.

The time was, we should remember, when seduction was an art. For some it still is, but nowadays the artistry is more often needed to seduce a wife or husband than a stranger. The "singles" subculture and the new permissiveness so prevalent in our society have tolled the final bell for old-fashioned seduction, and these days if a man asks a lady friend up to see his etchings, he probably *has* a collection.

Still, social games are played—and despite all the talk of personal liberation, we shouldn't be too quick to shun them. Games, after all, can be fun, providing that you aren't trapped into playing them because you feel you have to. Like so many older games, Seduction Supper can be fun to play. The food itself isn't what does the trick. Instead it's the atmosphere of relaxation and enjoyment. Like bathroom towels they come in both His and Hers.

The old sexist approach called for a man to get a lady intoxicated in the hope that she would "give in." Men didn't know, of course, that women could enjoy sex as much as men, and women were wise not to let on— a seduction supper was probably one of the few meals that they could expect a man to prepare!

A traditional Sexist Seduction Supper that a man might prepare consists of dishes that include some form of alcoholic spirits in each course. "Liquor is quicker," or so they say. And the proportions on my menu have been created with the playboy image in mind; there will be plenty left over, so he can try again the second night!

Please don't be misled by my sexist menu; it is not an effort to keep chauvinism alive and well. I believe the playboy premise is so far behind us that we should now be able to laugh at our social past. Besides, the recipes are good!

HIS SEXIST SEDUCTION SUPPER

For 2, twice

Succotash Soup

The man does not prefer to be a master chef. The meal he prepares is simple and uses pre-packaged shortcuts. But the one thing he wants to do is get his date a little high without obviously forcing highball after highball on her.

1 16-ounce can suc-cotash	2 pinches powdered nutmeg
2 individual packages instant vegetable broth	1 teaspoon lemon juice
1½ cups water	⅓ cup tequila

Combine everything except the tequila in a saucepan. Simmer for 10 minutes and blend. Add the tequila and reheat to boiling. (Boiling will not change the flavor of the soup, but it will evaporate the alcohol.)

Beef Vermouth

His main dish is a heady stew. He should prepare it the night before so it can marinate and he can be with his date until he is ready to serve. While the stew warms he fixes the noodles. Invited to join him in the kitchen, she can see the meal was not ordered in and he may earn a few points for being handy in the kitchen.

3 strips bacon, cut into small pieces
½ teaspoon salt
¼ teaspoon pepper
¼ teaspoon thyme
1 crumbled bay leaf
2 pounds lean chuck, in large cubes
3 tablespoons flour

1 8-ounce can peeled tomatoes
1 8-ounce can julienne carrots
1 8-ounce can small onions
1 4-ounce can button mushrooms
⅓ cup sweet vermouth
⅓ cup dry vermouth

In a large enamel pot brown the bacon over a medium heat. Add salt, pepper, thyme, bay leaf and beef. Sauté for 10 minutes, stirring to prevent sticking. Sprinkle with flour and sauté for an additional 5 minutes. Add the can of tomatoes, then the juice from the carrots, onions, and mushrooms. Simmer covered for 45 minutes to an hour . . . or until juice is quite thick. Add the carrots, onions and mushrooms. Simmer for another 5 minutes. Turn off the heat. Stir in the vermouths.

Tipsy Trifle

1 package ladyfingers
1 8-ounce can sliced
  peaches
2 3½-ounce packages
  instant vanilla pudding
½ pint heavy cream
¼ cup brandy
¼ cup cointreau
¼ cup kirsch

1 8-ounce jar mara-
  schino cherries
cold milk
¼ cup blackberry
  brandy
1 2-ounce envelope
  whipped topping mix
¼ cup chopped walnuts

Line the sides and bottom of a medium-sized soufflé dish with the ladyfingers. Drain the peaches and cherry juices into a measuring cup. Add enough cold milk to make 1 cup and pour into a large mixing bowl with the contents of 2 packages of pudding. Beat for 1 minute. Add the heavy cream and beat for another minute. Measure all the liquors into a cup then slowly beat into the pudding. Let stand while in a separate bowl you beat until thick ½ cup cold milk and the topping mix.

Add the fruits to the pudding and stir in gently. Spoon in slowly half of the topping mix. Stir once and pour pudding into soufflé dish. Spoon the rest of the topping onto the pudding. Sprinkle with chopped nuts. Chill.

Spiked Coffee

The effect of his coffee is more powerful than suggested by the hint of rum.

1 cup strong coffee
1 clove
1 allspice berry
1 large slice lemon peel
½ stick cinnamon

½ teaspoon rum extract
1 ounce vodka
sugar and cream
  (optional)

In a saucepan bring the coffee, clove, allspice, lemon peel and cinnamon almost to a boil. Let simmer for 10 minutes. When ready to serve, add rum extract and vodka. Bring quickly to a boil. Sugar and cream to taste.

It should be remembered that not only men are sexists—women too have a sexist past. Each sex undeniably forces a role upon the other; men, traditionally, have done more forcing. Probably one of the most sexist things women have done to themselves, however, is listening to their mothers. Old wives' tales too frequently get confused with fact. In planning seduction dinners, more than their male counterparts, ladies of the past often incorporated ingredients that supposedly triggered desire. Here's an updated menu for Her Sexist Seduction Supper—complete with a dessert that includes Vitamin E capsules!

HER SEXIST SEDUCTION SUPPER

For 2 (she doesn't want to try again tomorrow!)

Oysterfeller Soup

To speak in the vernacular, oysters are supposed to put "lead in the pencil." If the old wives knew what they were talking about, this first course should suffice.

1 package frozen chopped spinach	2 dozen oysters, thinly sliced
3 tablespoons butter	1 whole scallion, chopped
2 tablespoons flour	½ pint light cream
¼ teaspoon salt	3 tablespoons anisette liqueur
1 pinch pepper	2 tablespoons butter
1 clove garlic, crushed	
1 pint chicken broth or stock	

Thaw spinach, drain and reserve. Melt the butter in a saucepan, add the flour and, over low heat, stir until blended. Add salt, pepper and garlic. Slowly stir in chicken stock and simmer until thickened. Add oysters, scallion, spinach and cream; bring to a boil and turn heat very low. Add anisette and butter. Serve hot.

Lamb Balls

1 pound ground lamb	1 cup yogurt
¼ cup wheat germ	1 teaspoon cornstarch
1¼ teaspoons salt	4 tablespoons butter
¼ teaspoon pepper	4 teaspoons chopped
½ teaspoon cumin	fresh mint
¼ teaspoon ground allspice	

Blend lamb, wheat germ, salt, pepper, cumin and allspice together. Mold into balls. (There is no better implement than the hands.) Cover the bottom of a large skillet with ¼ inch of water. Heat and add the meat balls. Simmer, turning from time to time, until the water has evaporated and the balls begin to brown in their own grease. Continue to sauté until lightly browned all over. Remove and drain on a paper towel.

Mix cornstarch with yogurt. Place butter in small enamel pot. Add yogurt, mix in chopped mint, salt and pepper to taste. Heat sauce until thickened. Add the lamb balls and place in a warm oven for 10 minutes.

Pilaf

½ cup uncooked pilaf
  white or brown
1 onion, chopped
1 green pepper,
  chopped

1½ teaspoons butter
¼ teaspoon salt
1 pinch pepper
1 cup water

Sauté pilaf, onion, and green pepper in butter until onion is beginning to brown. Add salt, pepper and water and simmer until all the water is absorbed, about 15 minutes.

Grapefruit Flip

Utilizing the whole capsules, this dessert provides the (unproven) aphrodisia of Vitamin E. Don't worry about being Found Out: the capsule dissolves in the juice entirely.

10 400 I.U. Vitamin E
  capsules
juice of 1 grapefruit,
  freshly squeezed, pink
  preferred
2 eggs, separated and
  whipped

½ cup sugar
1 pinch salt
2 teaspoons cornstarch
¼ teaspoon lemon juice
1 4-ounce container
  creamed cheese,
  whipped

Simmer Vitamin E capsules in grapefruit juice until completely dissolved. In top of large double boiler, beat egg yolks; add sugar, salt, cornstarch, lemon juice and whipped cream cheese. Heat over water, stirring with whisk until thick. Slowly add the grapefruit juice. Cool. Beat egg whites until stiff and fold into sauce. Spoon into compote dishes. Chill and serve.

HOMEMADE BREAD

If you've never made your own bread at home, you've missed one of the most sensual of kitchen delights. The rich aromas, the squishy art of kneading, the joy at finding your dough risen to an airy balloon—all combine to make homemade bread a unique (although time-consuming) occupation. And the results bear no resemblance to the foam rubber that passes for bread at the supermarket.

Invite someone you like into your kitchen for the procedure. Chances are they'll be so entranced they will join right in.

3 tablespoons bakers' yeast	3 cups warm water (not hot)
¾ cup honey	8 cups stone-ground whole wheat flour
¼ cup butter or margarine	1 tablespoon flour
	2½ teaspoons salt

Combine the yeast, water, and honey in a mixing bowl, and allow to stand for at least 5 minutes. The yeast should bubble on the top of the water. Add the butter, salt, and 5 cups of the flour, and beat about 150 strokes or 8 minutes with an electric mixer (low speed). Add in another 2 cups of flour and stir.

Shake the remaining flour over a pastry board. Place the dough on the board, and knead by pulling the back of the dough toward you and over the rest of the dough, then punch down. Continue to knead until the dough stops sticking to the board. (You may need to add another ½ cup of flour or so to get the dough to this point.)

Put the dough into a greased bowl, butter the top lightly and let rise in a barely warm oven, covered with a damp cloth. When double its original size, knead again. Then recover, return to a warm spot, and let the dough double in size again.

Knead down again to original size. Divide the dough into 2 parts and shape into loaves. Place each loaf into a well-greased 1½ pound bread pan. When dough has risen slightly again, place in a preheated 350 degree oven until well browned—usually at least an hour.

This bread is so delicious, you'll want to eat it just as is—even without butter. But share some with your kitchen partner!

With sexism out of the way, let's move forward. Suppose that you and your companion are enjoying a good relationship. After all, it does happen. So let's concentrate now on what you can cook up to make the evening more pleasant. Love and sex demand strength, and you have to eat sometime; so why not make eating as sensual as possible?

My recommendation is a Tom Jones Dinner. It's not an attempt to recapture the epoch that Fielding wrote about, but it has one thing in common with the eating habits of that time. Everything is eaten with the fingers. The meal invites hands to touch across the table, if only while dipping artichoke leaves or reaching for another chicken wing.

Once you get the basic idea, you can use your own imagination to come up with interesting meals that feature finger foods. Avoid, as a general rule, the obvious choice of deep-fried chicken. It's rather heavy to be conducive to romance.

THE TOM JONES DINNER

For 2

Artichokes with Lovage Butter

2 artichokes	4 dashes Tabasco or hot
2 teaspoons lemon juice	pepper sauce
4 tablespoons butter	1 tablespoon freshly
½ teaspoon salt	minced lovage leaves

Cut the stems off the artichokes to make a flat bottom. Peel off the loose outer leaves. Cut off ¼ inch of the top. Rub the artichokes with lemon juice. Place the artichokes in a large saucepan of boiling salted water. Sink the artichokes with a plate so that they will be evenly cooked. Boil for 30 to 45 minutes, depending on the size, until dark green. Remove and drain upside down. Serve chilled.

Melt butter, add 1 teaspoon lemon juice, salt, pepper sauce (and lovage leaves). Bring to a simmer. Serve warm, in little dishes the artichoke leaves can be dipped into.

Garlic Spaghetti

Who hasn't wanted to stop struggling with spaghetti and dig right in with the fingers? Here's your chance—and an opportunity to use that most sensual of kitchen utensils, the garlic press. Squish away!

⅓ cup olive oil	½ teaspoon fresh pepper
6 cloves garlic, juiced	1½ tablespoons butter
1 teaspoon salt	½ pound spaghetti

Heat olive oil; add garlic juice, salt and pepper. Melt butter. Cook spaghetti in salted water until desired texture is recognized. Drain off the water. Add the melted butter and toss; now add the garlic oil and toss.

Chicken Wings

1½ pounds chicken wings	1 tablespoon flour
1 teaspoon salt	¼ cup oil
½ teaspoon pepper	½ cup oyster sauce or fish sauce

Wash, singe, and cut off the tips of the chicken wings. Mix the salt, pepper and flour in a large bowl and roll the wings in it. Brown the wings in the oil over medium heat. Drain wings on paper towels; then place them in an oven-proof pan and baste with the oyster sauce. Bake in warm oven until the sauce is coated on the wings. Turn, baste and return to oven for a total of about 30 minutes.

Salad

Our hand-held salad is nothing more than finger-sized tomatoes with a great basil dressing.

2 tablespoons mayonnaise	1 tablespoon olive oil
2 tablespoons finely chopped fresh basil	2 teaspoons lemon juice
	½ teaspoon salt
	¼ teaspoon pepper

Anxious about the evenings outcome? Put the spices and oil in a mortar and pestle and grind. Combine this with the rest of the ingredients in a jar and shake. Pour over ¾ pound of cherry or small plum tomatoes.

MYSTERIOUS SOUP

2 or 3 servings

Two of the most novel textures in food are those of okra and avocado. This soup combines them, for a unique taste as well.

½ pound okra
1 onion, chopped
2 cups vegetable stock
½ teaspoon salt

¼ teaspoon pepper
1 teaspoon chili powder
1 avocado
sour cream

Simmer everything but the avocado and the sour cream for 20 minutes. Peel the avocado and divide. Place one half, sliced, in a blender with the soup. Liquify. Garnish with the other half of the avocado, chopped, and with a dash of sour cream. Serve hot or cold.

MANUAL MANICOTTI

For 2

The use of the hands in this recipe can be very sensuous, and the handiwork is greatly appreciated by the taste buds.

½ pound leftover meat
½ cup celery
½ cup green peppers
½ cup scallions
2 tablespoons fresh herbs (⅔ basil ⅓ thyme)
½ cup cheese
salt and pepper to taste

½ teaspoon allspice
lemon juice, to taste
½ pound tomatoes, sliced
1 cup stock
2 tablespoons flour
2 tablespoons butter
6 manicotti

Chop as finely as possible the meat, celery, peppers, scallions, herbs and cheese; add allspice. With the fingers, blend in a bowl. Salt, pepper and lemon juice to taste.

Boil the tomatoes in the stock until they are soft. Make a roux of the flour and butter. Stir in the stock. Cook until thickened. Put the manicotti in boiling salted water and cook for about 7 minutes, until not quite soft. Cover immediately with cold water and let sit until ready to use.

Stuff the manicotti with the meat-and-vegetable mixture. Place in a well-greased baking dish. Pour the tomato sauce over the manicotti and bake in a 325 degree oven for 20 to 25 minutes.

CAPRIKA

About 4 servings

The paprika you buy in a supermarket is bland. Help it! Add some cayenne pepper. Cayenne is known as a stimulant. (Also as a rubefacient, causing redness and local congestion of the blood vessels. So don't overdo it!)

2 pounds goat meat	2 tablespoons hot paprika (to which a dash of cayenne has been added)
1 quart water	
2 tablespoons vinegar	
3 tablespoons oil	
2 tablespoons flour	1 teaspoon salt
	¼ teaspoon pepper
	3 cups heavy stock

Cube the meat and marinate overnight in the water and vinegar. Drain and dry. In a Dutch oven sauté the meat in oil until brown (not too easy, the meat gets quite juicy). Make a mixture of the flour, pa-

prika, salt and pepper and sprinkle over the meat.
Stir and blend. Slowly add the stock, cover and simmer for an hour.

APPLE PIE

Makes a 9-inch pie

I credit my patient L.S.B. for introducing me to Granny
Smith apples and this recipe, which he guarantees to
reduce sexual frustration—if not the waistline.

1 piecrust, uncooked	2 teaspoons ground
2½ pounds green apples	allspice
2 tablespoons flour	¼ pound butter
½ cup sugar	juice of 1 lemon
½ teaspoon salt	½ pint heavy cream
	¼ teaspoon cinnamon

Line a 9-inch pie plate with your favorite piecrust.
Quarter and core, but do not peel the apples. Cut
them into thin slices and layer on the crust. Mix the
flour, sugar, salt, cinnamon and allspice. Sprinkle
over the apples. Dot with butter. Squeeze the lemon
juice over it. Repeat this several times to make
four layers. (The apples should be piled high.) Pour
in the heavy cream and sprinkle with cinnamon.
Bake for 1½ hours in 250 degree oven. Serve hot
or cold.

FLAMING BANANAS

For 2

My patient L. G. reported that this recipe successfully
ended an enchanted meal she prepared especially for a
very particular friend.

3 tablespoons brown
  sugar
5 tablespoons butter
4 bananas, peeled and
  sliced lengthwise

3 jiggers brandy
3 jiggers rum
½ cup chopped nuts

Melt brown sugar and butter in a chafing dish. Add
bananas and sauté until tender. Add brandy and
rum. When warm, light with a match and baste
until flame burns out. Sprinkle with nuts. Prepare
the dish at the table under dim lights.

MERINGUE KISSES

Again, for 2

It takes a good deal of motion—especially as applied
to rolls and egg whites—to make this airy, light after-
dinner sweet.

¼ cup bread crumbs
2 egg whites
¼ teaspoon salt
¼ teaspoon cream of
  tartar

1 cup sugar
4 tablespoons crème de
  menthe extract

The crumbs should be made from very stale hard
rolls, or white French bread. Take off the crust and
with the fingers grind into grains. Beat the egg
whites with the salt and cream of tartar. When they
are stiff, stir in the sugar, bread crumbs and mint.
Drop onto a well-greased cookie sheet in kisses as
small but as tall as possible. Bake in a 250 degree
oven for 15 minutes. Remove immediately with a
spatula, and cool.

10

Creativity in the Kitchen (Including Leftover Cookery): How Much, What and When

BEING creative in the kitchen, as in every other area of endeavor, is a highly individual matter. For some it's turning out a perfect Quiche Lorraine—something I've never been able to do. For others a masterpiece of creative cooking means Beef Wellington, or Peking Duck or Baked Alaska. The beginning cook may take pride in the most basic accomplishment—scrambled eggs, a hamburger—or well boiled water, for that matter; where the more experienced cook may set his or her sights on higher goals such as classic French cuisine or Viennese pastries.

I admit that the classic dishes are not my greatest successes, and frankly it's taken me approximately 20 years to turn out a decent Bechamel sauce. But when it comes to creativity, *what* you do isn't nearly as important as how you feel about it. All of us need forms of creative expression, both in our professional and our personal lives. As a doctor, my greatest satisfaction comes from treating difficult cases, cases that not only demand all the skills I've learned in medical school and in treating the more than 5,000 patients who've passed through my office, but also force me to think and rethink and innovate. As a cook, I find the greatest creative satisfaction comes from developing my own recipes.

Any job or task can become routine. One of the reasons that I went into general practice rather than specializing in just one area is that I thrive on constant challenge and on variety. It makes me function better and work harder. With cooking it's much the same. If I had to cook the same dishes, or stick to a basic repertory, I think I'd soon find cooking boring. Much as I enjoy cooking, I can sympathize with those individuals, particularly housewives, who eventually come to loathe it.

"When I first got married," a mother of four told me at a party, "I used to actually look forward to getting meals ready. I was the original Little Miss Homemaker, always clipping recipes from magazines, always trying something new. Now it's impossible. The kids demand so much of my time. Billy won't eat vegetables. Susie hates fish. My husband has colitis, and then there's the baby. Good luck with your book, Louis, but be sure to let me know when you write one about how to take the easy way out in the kitchen. I want the first copy!"

Time and the needs of those we cook for decidedly tax our ingenuity in the kitchen. But all of us can, and should, be creative to some extent—even if the possibilities aren't as readily evident as they might be. When a patient of mine developed an ulcer, it wasn't so much my diagnosis that troubled him as my prescription—particularly the diet that was necessary.

"My wife is in the waiting room," he said. "Do you think I could bring her into the office for a few minutes? It's going to be really rough on her."

"By all means, ask her to come in," I agreed. "But first why don't you explain that there's really nothing for her to be disturbed about? If you watch what you eat and take the medicine we spoke about, that ulcer shouldn't give you too much trouble."

My patient shook his head. "I don't think that Lorraine will blow the situation out of proportion. But she loves to cook. My having to go on a strict ulcer diet is going to take a lot of the fun out of cooking."

Lorraine came in and I explained her husband's condition and the treatment needed. She relaxed once she realized that he wasn't in danger; but as her husband predicted, she was a bit alarmed at the mention of a diet. "Whatever Hal needs," Lorraine promised. "But I guess I'll have to go through my recipes to weed out the foods he can't eat."

I sensed that this couple really enjoyed food and eating, and that Lorraine spent a lot of time in the kitchen. For Hal's treatment to be as successful as possible, I had to reassure him and do my best to be supportive. A feeling of deprivation, while it would be a natural response to the situation, wouldn't be in his own best interests, I knew—and I sensed that with Lorraine on hand, I had a good chance to offer some balm. "Your husband tells me that you're quite a cook," I told Lorraine.

She smiled. "All my life. I've built up quite a file of recipes. But I guess now I'll have to change them." Lorraine wasn't being selfish, just honest. Her husband's change of diet was obviously going to take almost as much adjustment on her part as on his.

"You know," I said, "if you're a good cook, why don't you approach Hal's diet as a challenge? After all, it's not that his diet is going to be all that restricted— particularly once we get him through these first few weeks. Mostly you'll be avoiding only spicy foods and anything cooked with wine. So instead of just adapting and changing the recipes you've enjoyed, why don't you see what you can come up with that's new! And be sure to keep me posted. Lots of my patients with ulcers would welcome some new recipes!"

Lorraine seemed pleased, and Hal smiled. In the following weeks, I learned that my idea had worked. Rather than feeling punished, Hal took a delight in the new dishes that Lorraine prepared. And Lorraine took a justifiable pride in the creativity she'd brought to the problem at hand.

This type of constructive use of the creative ability that is in every one of us can be brought to special diets prescribed for heart problems, weight loss and control, and many other conditions. If a patient is interested in cooking, I spend time with him, when I prescribe a special diet, trying to motivate him in this new direction. If he isn't interested in cooking, I encourage him to explore new tastes, and to look at the "outer boundaries" of his new diet as well as its limitations.

From a psychological standpoint, kitchen creativity can be an excellent form of do-it-yourself therapy. We too often measure accomplishment in quantitative rather than qualitative terms: the "achiever" is the man or woman who makes the most money, has the biggest office or has taken the most steps up the corporate ladder.

Yet the determined achiever, the individual who pushes himself constantly, is very susceptible to the anxiety-depressive syndrome. I've told many a top executive to take up cooking, not out of necessity but as a tranquilizer! Puttering with pots and pans and turning out even the most simple meal or dish can be a surprisingly rich and rewarding experience.

"I don't know if the merger I'm trying to arrange is going to work out or not," a harried bank executive confided to me during an office visit, "but at least that recipe for Marmalade Duck you gave me turned out terrific last night. And better than the duck was that while I was cooking, I didn't think about the merger once!"

But to derive the full benefits of creativity, one needn't be tense and anxious, or have a health problem. Talent, for that matter, isn't as much of a requisite as it might seem: many of the best cooks are *taught* (even self taught), rather than *born*. And in the kitchen, practice is the best teacher. We must realize that practice implies that not every attempt we make will be successful. If success every time we took a spoon or spatula in hand was guaranteed, creative cooking wouldn't really be very challenging—we need to be prepared to accept failure from time to time, in the kitchen as in other areas of life.

Every man or woman who has ever stood over the stove has been tempted, I firmly believe, to throw some half-baked, overdone or otherwise inedible culinary disaster across the room. Many of us give in to this temptation at one time or another, only to face the problem of a mess to clean up, on top of a ruined meal.

Failure can be instructive. We learn the obvious— that something went wrong—and we can examine the result with an eye toward success the next time around. But we can also learn about ourselves, and about coping with failures in other areas of life. Learning to laugh at our mistakes rather than crying over them is, for most of us, an acquired art.

It took almost more of a sense of humor than I could muster some time ago when I tried to invent a pie despite the fact that I had not yet managed a good pie-crust. But I worked at it for a while, and now my Mocha Meringue Pie features a crust that I've just about re-fined down to foolproof status. It's an exciting recipe, one that should brighten your day further if you're feeling confident enough in the kitchen to attempt it.

MOCHA MERINGUE PIE

3 eggs, separated
2 cups sugar
¼ teaspoon cream of tartar
⅓ cup finely-crumbled soda crackers
1½ squares unsweetened chocolate

1 tablespoon butter
⅓ cup milk
1 tablespoon instant espresso coffee
2 tablespoons grated lemon rind
1 pint heavy cream

Beat the egg whites until stiff. Sift together 1 cup of the sugar and the cream of tartar, and add to the whipped whites. Stir in the cracker crumbs. Spoon into a well-buttered, 9-inch pie plate. Bake in a 300 degree oven for 40 to 45 minutes. This is your crust. When it has cooled, push down the meringue sufficiently to allow room for the filling to be added.

For the filling, melt 1 square of the chocolate with the butter in the top of a double boiler. Scald the milk and add to the chocolate. Mix the egg yolks, the instant coffee, the remaining 1 cup of the sugar, and 1½ tablespoons of the lemon rind; add this mixture to the sauce. Cook, stirring frequently, until the filling thickens. Cool.

Beat the cream until stiff; stir half of the whipped cream into the chocolate sauce, reserving the other half on ice. Spoon the sauce into the meringue crust. Cover with the second half of the whipped cream and sprinkle with remaining chocolate (grated) and the rest of the lemon rind. Keep refrigerated.

I don't always choose to test my wits (and my patience) so rigidly in the kitchen. In fact, my favorite form of creative cookery is as far from *haute cuisine* as possible. My greatest satisfaction as a cook comes from using leftovers creatively—not merely reheating them, but using them to develop new dishes that simply could not exist if they didn't spring from leftover food.

Just why I'm so fond of leftover cookery has to do with what my friends call the "penny-wise and dollar-foolish" aspect of my personality. I delight in finding bargains, combing thrift shops, going to auctions. And I get a lot of satisfaction from rummaging through my refrigerator, trying to use up food creatively. Some of my experiments have been spectacular successes: others dismal failures. I've made it easier on myself, not to mention friends, by doing most of my experimenting by myself, repeating my recipes at a later date to share the successes—and to spare my friends the mistakes I've made (not to mention sparing myself the embarrassment!).

It may sound as though I come from a deprived background, which certainly would be a likely forerunner to a don't-throw-it-out approach to leftovers. In truth, food was plentiful in our part of the South throughout my childhood. But World War II, as those of us who lived through it know, was an all too dramatic illustration of shortages, both here and abroad. I know that it was a great influence on me.

Leftovers, too, are a great challenge. Once I decided that I enjoyed meeting it, I began intentionally to overcook—cook more than a meal's worth—the first time around. If I was preparing a roast, I always bought one that would yield an extra "serving" for the refrigerator. Instead of halving a chicken I'm fixing myself, now I always prepare the whole bird—and know I have something to play around with the next night.

I confess that sometimes when it comes to leftovers, I can be overly frugal. The only justification I have is the intense satisfaction (which, after all, is what creativity is all about) I get from waging my private war on rising prices. Rather than throw those extra peas out when they're not sufficient for another serving, I save them. I've found the perfect thing for those tiny portions of leftovers, my Stuffed Mushrooms. The recipe that follows uses little green peas, but a few bites of chicken salad, or even rice, could be substituted.

STUFFED MUSHROOMS

4 large mushrooms
2 tablespoons sour cream

⅔ cup leftover green peas
oil
4 dashes paprika

Remove the mushroom stems and core (scrape out the brown fringe). Mix the mushroom stems and scrapings with the peas and sour cream and purée in the blender. Rub the outside of the mushroom caps lightly with oil and stuff them with the purée. Garnish with a dash of paprika. Cook under the broiler for 7 or 8 minutes.

Successful leftover cookery demands a knowledge of the basic principles of cooking, and a willingness to take risks. My perpetual Casserole is more of a story than a recipe, and it began the night I looked into my refrigerator and found some leftover curried vegetables, some ground beef, and some cooked noodles staring back at me. Individually, these items didn't exactly spell an exciting meal. Collectively, they presented a challenge. So I mixed them in a casserole with a bit of leftover salad dressing, and a houseguest and I waited to see what would come out of the oven.

The result, if I say so myself, was delicious—but filling. The following night I combined the leftover portion of the casserole with another leftover: some lentil soup I'd made with leeks, onions and the carcass of a duck as the basis of a thick broth. There was some smoked pork butt—not enough for two but too much for one—and that too was mixed with the leftover casserole. Again the result was tasty, enjoyed but not all eaten.

My perpetual casserole was perpetuated again . . . and again. Chicken and rice, lamb and cauliflower au gratin, sweet spiced pork and cucumbers, and finally veal stew were added. The results were always delicious, and one night I grew so adventuresome that I invited another friend over to taste for herself. The third portion, that night, was eaten instead of put back into the refrigerator to perpetuate the casserole once more, and I said a silent and somewhat nostalgic goodbye.

The triumphant history of that casserole is a/ ence to be savored, in memory now rather th/

dinner table. The tastes and textures could never be duplicated, but I look forward to creating other casseroles that will have tastes—and lives—of their own.

Certainly in today's troubled economy, using leftovers constructively is an ideal pastime. Food costs have climbed considerably higher over the past years—and months—and few of us can afford to turn up our noses, or taste buds, at the idea of eating yesterday's leftovers. There are some people, however, who have a built-in resistance to the concept, either out of preference or, in some cases, because they grew up having to eat the same meals over and over again. I have several friends who have categorically refused to eat leftovers, so I don't tell them that the food they're eating had its start yesterday or the day before. Literally, what they don't know won't hurt them. Still, I wouldn't think of offering to a guest, whether he or she liked leftovers or not, a serving of yesterday's steak on a plate. But I have no qualms about turning it into Steak and Rice Cacciatore, which my guests seem to like as much as I do.

STEAK AND RICE CACCIATORE

About 2 servings

2 tablespoons flour	¼ teaspoon pepper
2 tablespoons oil	½ teaspoon dried
½ cup chopped onion	oregano
¼ cup chopped stuffed	1 teaspoon dried basil
olives	¼ teaspoon crumbled
⅓ cup chopped celery	bay leaf
2 tablespoons chopped	1 cup tomato sauce
parsley	4 cups stock
2 cloves garlic, minced	2 cups cooked rice
½ teaspoon salt	⅔ pound cooked steak

Sprinkle with flour and sauté in oil the onions, olives, celery, parsley, garlic and seasonings for 5 minutes.

Add tomato sauce and stock and bring to a boil, then simmer for another 5 minutes. Arrange a layer of rice on the bottom of a well-greased casserole. Cover with thin slices of steak. Pour over this the cacciatore sauce. Warm in a 300 degree oven for 10 minutes.

Sometimes, I've discovered, creating a recipe is considerably easier than naming it. Luckily a friend of mine who delights in poking fun at my frugality with leftovers was on hand the night I decided to do something with the night before's extra green beans, which I'd saved.

"You get too carried away with those leftovers," I was told. The result was simple—and very tasty . . . my Carried-Away Beans.

CARRIED-AWAY BEANS

For 2

½ pound green beans (cooked)
¼ cup sour cream
½ teaspoon lemon juice

¼ teaspoon caraway seeds, pulverized
salt and pepper to taste

Combine everything in the top of a double boiler and warm thoroughly 15 to 20 minutes over moderate heat.

Creativity with leftovers often means coming up with new solutions for old problems. Egg yolks, for example. Every time you use egg whites, you've created another problem: what to do with the yolks? You can always keep them around for the next time you're scrambling eggs and throw them in. But if you're trying to cut down on your egg intake, maybe some more enterprising solutions are in order.

For me, leftover egg yolks stored in a refrigerator jar means I'm halfway home on two of my favorite recipes, Florentine Casserole and Welsh Toast.

FLORENTINE CASSEROLE

For 2 or 3

½ pound wide noodles
2 tablespoons butter
2 tablespoons flour
1 teaspoon salt
1 teaspoon pepper
2 cloves garlic, minced
¼ teaspoon ground
   nutmeg

1 teaspoon dry mustard
3 cups milk
3 leftover egg yolks
10 ounces spinach
1½ pounds ripe to-
   matoes
½ pound cooked ham,
   cubed

Boil the noodles in heavily salted water until almost tender. Drain and cover with cold water. In a large saucepan start the sauce by melting the butter and stirring in the flour. When it bubbles, add the salt, pepper, garlic, nutmeg and mustard. Boil 2 cups of the milk and stir into the roux; simmer until it begins to thicken. Beat the egg yolks with 1 cup of milk, and add slowly to the white sauce. Continue stirring until it has thickened.

Layer the bottom of a well-buttered casserole with noodles. Lay on half of the spinach. Then layer with half of the tomatoes. Run this under the broiler for 10 minutes. Remove and spoon on half the sauce and the ham. Then layer on the rest of the noodles, the spinach, and the tomatoes. Cover with the remaining sauce. Bake in a 325 degree oven for 30 minutes.

WELSH TOAST

For 2

2 cups milk
1 tablespoon butter
1 tablespoon flour
½ teaspoon salt
½ teaspoon pepper
2 leftover egg yolks

½ pound cheddar
cheese, grated
4 tablespoons horse-
radish
4 slices bread

Bring 1 cup of the milk to a boil. Meanwhile, melt the butter in a separate enamel saucepan, and stir in the flour. Simmer this mixture—the roux—until it bubbles. Slowly add the roux to the milk, stirring until it thickens and bubbles, usually about 5 minutes. Add salt and pepper.

Beat the egg yolks and the other cup of milk together in the top of a double boiler. Stir in the white sauce (above), grated cheese and horseradish. Cook slowly for 30 minutes, stirring from time to time—the use of a double boiler will keep your stirring time to a minimum. Serve on toast, topping with a strip of bacon if you like.

NOTE: If you're using a double boiler, you should be able to keep the sauce warm indefinitely . . . great for preparing ahead and serving "short order"!

Cooking with leftovers is one thing: using food, or rather parts of foods that would be discarded by some the first time around, is another field in which I like to work. Earlier in this book I gave my recipe for Green Peas Perfection, which called for the use of pods (in cooking liquid) as well as the peas themselves.

While the tops of broccoli—the florets—are considered the most edible portion of the vegetable, I know that the stems are equally nutritious. One day I decided to see if the stems, which some people are quick to toss into the garbage pail, couldn't be turned into a tasty, tender dish. Here's what I came up with:

BROCCOLI STEMS

1 or 2 servings

1 tablespoon pine nuts, minced	2 cups broccoli stems (cooked)
½ teaspoon lemon juice	½ teaspoon salt
⅛ teaspoon pepper	1 tablespoon olive oil

Sauté ingredients over high heat for 2 or 3 minutes.

It would be very misleading to give you the impression that every time I set out to create something in my kitchen, I meet with success. On a recent trip to the market, I studied the prices of the various prepackaged stuffing mixes, the kind that have been introduced in the past year or two by several firms. The basic idea—enjoying stuffing without having to cook something that needs to be stuffed—is a good one, but whatever convenience the packaged foods offered seemed, to my way of thinking, negated by the high prices.

I set out to make a personalized version of a stove-top stuffing, and I was confident that the result would be successful. In any case, the first time around I ended up not with stuffing, but with something that could only be called "dentist's delight." My colleagues in dental medicine could be sure that anyone who made the mistake of trying to eat this dish would be in their offices in record time, with broken teeth!

More stock, I decided was the answer. Unfortunately, too much stock was the ingredient I used, and mush was the result. I then managed to solve the texture problem, but the taste wasn't quite what I thought it could be. Still, several attempts later yielded just the result I was looking for—a pan stuffing that is tasty, simple and much more economical than the prepackaged varieties. Try it. Work out your own herbs and vegetables.

PAN STUFFING

3 or 4 servings

5 cups mixed vegetables (onion, leek, cabbage, green pepper, celery, etc.)
1¾ teaspoons salt
3 tablespoons herb potpourri (thyme, sage, tarragon, oregano, etc.)

5 tablespoons bacon drippings
¾ cup flour
3 teaspoons baking powder
½ teaspoon pepper
1½ cups cornmeal
2 eggs
1¼ cups stock, chicken or vegetable

Sauté the vegetables, 1¼ teaspoons of the salt, and all the other seasonings in 4 tablespoons of the bacon drippings for 20 minutes. Sift flour, baking powder, pepper and the remaining ½ teaspoon salt. Stir in the cornmeal. Beat the eggs and stock together. Stir this into the flour mixture.

Grease an enamel pot with the remainder of the bacon drippings. Pour in the flour-and-liquid mixture (above), cover tightly, and cook slowly for 10 minutes. Stir in half the sautéed vegetables and cook for 5 minutes more. Then add the rest of the vegetables and continue cooking for another 5 minutes. Serve good and hot.

Stuffing is a safe recipe, and the result is one that almost all of us like. But with cooking, as with any form of creative endeavor, we must remember that responses are subjective. The artist, amateur or professional, who paints must be satisfied with his work, and must face the reality that not everyone else in the world has an appreciation for his talent.

The same holds true for cooking. What may be a masterpiece in your opinion (and to your taste buds) may not suit the taste of a loved one or friend. Often I've created a recipe that I thought was excellent, only to find that someone I shared it with couldn't stand it. At one time, I found this response painful. Even now, if one of my creations gets a less than enthusiastic response, I'll try to be objective and see if the recipe can stand improvement. But one of my kitchen credos is short, simple and particularly pertinent to creative cookery: Sign It Before You Ruin It!

Like an artist who wants to add yet another subtle touch of color to a canvas, the cook can be tempted to add yet another taste, a subtle refinement of texture. If too many cooks can ruin the broth, then too many flavors can ruin a good dish. Knowing when to stop "improving" is important, and this kind of knowledge comes only with experience.

Experience is the only teacher also for the subtle art of substitution, but I can offer a few tips from my own years in the kitchen. The important thing is not to be intimidated by the recipe; if your jar of oregano is empty, substituting the same amount of that marjoram you never use will not spell disaster. Or when bread crumbs are called for, and you're fresh out of stale bread to run through the blender—use blendered crackers instead. Two parts scallions to one part garlic —both minced finely—can serve as replacement for shallots. And when heavy cream is required for any purpose except whipping, you can always "make your own" by blending milk with melted butter.

Better still, use your own judgment. Once you begin using your kitchen creatively, you'll be surprised at how cleverly you can outwit recipe authors—myself included. Just be certain you don't outwit yourself. Since it's virtually impossible to come up with a recipe that will please everyone, accept it as a fact of life and concentrate on what will please *you*. But give yourself a break and allow yourself to be reasonably, if not easily, pleased.

Too many dishes—I repeat—have been ruined by trying to add just one more ingredient, or another step toward that elusive perfection.

This lesson, obviously, applies not only to cooking, but to our basic approach to life. Very few situations turn out just as we would like them to: something could always be better. It's important, in purely practical terms as well as for our peace of mind, to know when to quit—namely, when you're ahead.

As you cook, you'll be further ahead if you add a measure of creativity to your kitchen. Perhaps, like me, leftovers will be your specialty. Or perhaps you'll find that pastries or some type of international cuisine attracts you. Pursue it, and you'll find that as your expertise increases, your enjoyment does too.

And for my "concluding remarks," may I offer you a sampling of my more successful creations? Please enjoy them.

CHRISTMAS FRUITCAKE PUDDING

2 pounds fruitcake	a sixpence (or a dime)
½ cup whiskey or brandy	

Crumble a fruitcake and stir in the liquor. Form into a large ball. Stick in a sixpence. Wrap in an old linen napkin or handkerchief. Steam in a colander until hot all the way through.

Fruitcake is a Christmas tradition that everyone seems to like but no one wants to eat. Making it is a project I remember my mother and aunts setting aside several full days for. They had to shop for the candied fruits and nuts they wanted, cut them up and then bake the cakes—at least a dozen, to be mailed to friends and relatives far from home. Even the uncles had a hand in the preparation. Only at fruitcake time was any alcoholic beverage permitted in the house: a half pint of bourbon for all that batter. For many years after I left home, a large cake arrived as certain as the first week of December. I could never give it all away. That's how this pudding came about which should be eaten with Hard Sauce, for which a recipe follows. The sixpence is for luck.

HARD SAUCE

A true indulgence. You should be selective about the times you have it, but in early January with Christmas Fruitcake Pudding it's a must.

> 1 cup confectioner's sugar
> ⅓ cup butter
>
> 1 to 2 teaspoons your favorite flavor extract
> 1 pinch salt

Sift the sugar and slowly cream into the butter. Stir in the flavoring and salt. Chill (in a mold). Learn the glory of hard sauce: try it with a hot apple dumpling.

APPLE DUMPLING

4 to 6 servings

A childhood favorite. Why it was fondly referred to as a "cat" I cannot tell you.

1½ pounds dried apples
4 cups water
1 cup brown sugar

1 teaspoon allspice
pie pastry, enough for
two crusts

Soak the dried apples overnight in the water. Boil slowly with the sugar and allspice for an hour, or until most of the liquid has been absorbed. Mash.

Roll out the pie pastry into a rectangle ¼-inch thick. Place the apples in the center. Fold over the sides and the ends of the pie pastry and seal. Center it in cheesecloth that has been soaked in cold water. Gather the ends of the cloth together and tie. Submerge the package in cold water and boil slowly for an hour. Serve hot, with cold hard sauce.

FRICASSEE OF VEAL AND LETTUCE WITH DILL SAUCE

2 or more servings

I never thought much about Greek food until my friend Niko cooked for me. But this dish was a new experience and one I cannot forget.

4 bunches scallions,
   whole
¼ cup oil
2 pounds boned veal
   shoulder
4 heads lettuce

½ to ⅔ cup chopped
   fresh dill
⅓ cup butter
⅓ cup flour
3 eggs
¼ cup lemon juice

Chop the scallions and sauté them in the oil in a deep enamel pot with a cover. When soft, remove with a slotted spoon and reserve. Cut the meat into moderately thick slices, so that 2 or 3 pieces will make a nice serving. Brown the meat in the pot, then cover with water and simmer, with the lid on. At the end of about an hour, quarter the heads of lettuce and put on top of the meat. Put the sautéed scallions on top of that and simmer covered for 15 minutes. Then sprinkle on the chopped dill, cover and simmer for 10 minutes more.

Make a white roux with the butter and flour. When it has bubbled, drain the liquid from the veal and lettuce and slowly stir it into the roux. Simmer until it has thickened. Cool. Beat the eggs and add the lemon juice to them. Then slowly whisk the eggs into the white sauce and heat until it again thickens.

Put the veal and lettuce on a large platter. Stir any residual juice or some milk into the sauce if it seems too thick. Then spoon the sauce over the veal and lettuce.

BEEF ROLL

3 or 4 servings

At last! Something really different to do with beef. We might as well eat it while we can still afford it.

½ cup chopped onions	1 teaspoon rosemary
½ cup chopped green peppers	2 cloves of garlic, smashed
½ cup chopped celery	1 cup cream cheese
1 teaspoon salt	1 pound flank steak
½ teaspoon pepper	(sliced in half on the
1 teaspoon ground thyme	bias and each thin half divided to make 4 thin
1 teaspoon oregano	slices)
1 teaspoon meat sauce (see page 52)	2 tablespoons oil
	1 teaspoon lemon juice

Cream the chopped vegetables, lemon juice, and spices with cheese until soft. Spread the mixture into the slices of the steak and roll and peg together with toothpicks.

Brown by rolling in hot oil for 5 to 10 minutes, then place in a covered dish and bake at 300 degrees for 15 minutes.

BUTT BEAN STEW

Feeds 4 or more

Being creative doesn't always mean using exotic seasonings or hard-to-get ingredients. Sometimes the simplest dishes lend themselves best to a free hand and an open mind.

3 cups dried beans (your favorite or a combination)	3 cups chopped onions
	1 teaspoon cloves
	3 cups chopped celery
3 pounds smoked ham butt	7 cups stock

Cover beans with boiling water and let sit for one hour. Drain. Remove net (if there is one) from butt, cut out fat, then cube. Combine it with the beans and the rest of the ingredients and boil slowly for 1 hour, or until the beans are done.

FISH SOUFFLÉ

4 to 6 servings

If you're a novice at soufflés, this is a good one to start with. It needn't rise so high or be so light as most soufflés, so your chances for success are greater than usual.

4 tablespoons butter
3 tablespoons flour
1 cup cooked fish
1 teaspoon salt
½ teaspoon pepper
1 teaspoon dill
1 tablespoon cornstarch
6 eggs
½ cup fish stock or clam juice
1 tablespoon lemon juice
Parmesan cheese
½ cup milk
1 teaspoon cream of tartar

Preheat oven to 400 degrees. Melt butter with flour, in medium-sized enamel pot. Bubble and blend for 1 minute. Put aside. Puree fish, stock, lemon juice, salt, pepper, dill and cornstarch. Put aside.

Separate the eggs, reserving 3 yolks. Butter the soufflé dish well and coat with dry grated Parmesan cheese; don't forget the sides. Scald the milk for 2 minutes. Put aside. Beat the egg whites with a pinch of salt and a teaspoon of cream of tartar until almost stiff. Hold in the refrigerator. Add the yolks slowly to the fish puree and stir. Put aside.

Finish beating the egg whites; stir ⅙ into the fish mixture; then *gently* fold the rest into the sauce. Spoon lightly into a soufflé dish. Put into the oven. Set heat at 375 degrees for luck. Bake for 45 minutes.

SAUSAGE AND PEPPER CASSEROLE

2 or more servings

½ pound smoked sausage
2 cups water
4 cups sliced peppers
1½ cups sliced onions
2 cloves of garlic, smashed
½ cup oil
2½ teaspoons salt
1¼ teaspoons pepper
5 cups diced potatoes
1 cup grated cheese
paprika for garnish

Cut the sausage up into half slices. Simmer in 2 cups water until it evaporates. Add the peppers, onions, garlic, 1 teaspoon salt and ½ teaspoon pepper; sauté over moderate heat for 15 minutes. Remove with a slotted spoon to a paper towel. When well drained, put into casserole dish.

Over moderately high heat, heat oil, 1½ teaspoons salt, and ¾ teaspoon pepper. Add the potatoes with a slotted spoon and cook for 5 minutes. Do not let stick to the pan. Remove potatoes with the slotted spoon and drain on a paper towel. Then spread them on top of peppers and sausage. Cover with grated cheese. Sprinkle with paprika. Bake at 375 degrees for 45 minutes.

FRIDAY NIGHT

To me Friday night is the best night of the week. It's the end of another round of workdays, and the beginning of the weekend. I frequently celebrate it with an orgy of cooking and eating, or trying to create Lucullan dishes from prime bits of leftovers. This "successful accident" is so good that I find myself buying the ingredients to start from scratch.

4 tablespoons butter
½ pound leftover Brie cheese
⅓ cup cooked sweetbreads
½ teaspoon chopped tarragon
¼ teaspoon coarse salt
½ teaspoon coarse pepper
½ pound linguine

Melt the butter. Put one half into the top of a double boiler, and add Brie, sweetbreads, and seasonings. keep warm.

Cook the linguine in salted water to desired texture. Drain. Add the rest of the melted butter and toss over a very low flame. Then add the cheese mixture, stir well, and serve.

Subject Index

Recipe Index

THE FAMOUS BESTSELLER ABOUT THE PHENOMENON THAT'S SWEEPING THE COUNTRY

60 hours that transform your life ™

est

erhard seminars training
by Adelaide Bry

"Adelaide Bry did a great job. The book is readable, accurate and gives a balanced view of *est*. Adelaide has demonstrated her integrity as a writer by extensive research, verifying the quotes she uses, checking and rechecking her facts; and by stating her opinion as opinion rather than as fact. I support the author."

Werner Erhard
founder of *est*

Selected by Modern Psychology Book Club

AVON 29652/$1.95

est 8-76

**36 WEEKS ON
NATIONAL BESTSELLER LISTS**

**SELECTED BY THREE MAJOR
BOOK CLUBS**

SYLVIA PORTER'S MONEY BOOK

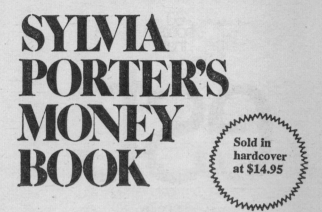

Sold in
hardcover
at $14.95

**How to Earn It,
Spend It, Save It,
Invest It, Borrow It—
And Use It to Better Your Life!**

*"The definitive guide to every phase of personal money
management,* **THE MONEY BOOK** *may become the
standard reference on personal finance."*

San Francisco Chronicle

"SYLVIA PORTER'S MONEY BOOK *should be on
every family's bookshelf along with the Bible and the dic-
tionary."* **Betty Furness, NBC Today Show**

The nationwide #1 bestseller—now available in
paperback in a deluxe, large format (5¼"x8")
edition. 28603/$5.95   SPM 8-76

the Relaxation Response

by Herbert Benson, M.D.

with Miriam Z. Klipper

Nationwide
#1
Bestseller

It could be the most important book of your life!

A simple meditative technique that has helped millions to cope with fatigue, anxiety and stress. Featured in *Family Circle, House and Garden, Good Housekeeping* and scores of magazines and newspapers across the country.

"In transcendental meditation you pay $125 and you get your mantra. You may do as well by reading *The Relaxation Response*."

Money